T0039320

OUT OF THE BLUE

My History of Freefall, Ethanol, and Skyfall

RANDY LIPPINCOTT

Order this book online at www.trafford.com
or email orders@trafford.com

Most Trafford titles are also available at major online book retailers.

Print information available on the last page.

ISBN: 978-1-4907-7963-8 (sc)
ISBN: 978-1-4907-7965-2 (hc)
ISBN: 978-1-4907-7964-5 (e)

Library of Congress Control Number: 2016920775

Trafford rev. 01/06/2017

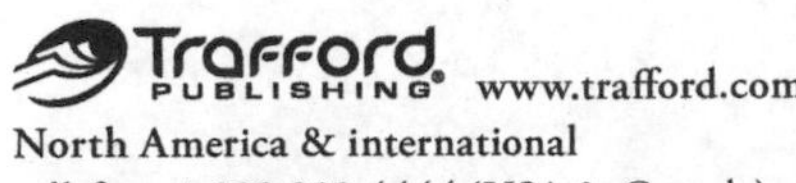
www.trafford.com
North America & international
toll-free: 1 888 232 4444 (USA & Canada)
fax: 812 355 4082

CONTENTS

DEDICATION

I dedicate this book to my parents, Dick and Rosalie Lippincott for my early introduction to aviation and permission to start skydiving. And to Shorty Janousek who instructed me in skydiving and taught me "why the birds sing."

My gracious wife, Joyce Berk-Lippincott, has made all that I do in retirement possible. Thank you for standing by me and putting up with my work on this book. I could have never done it without your support.

Edited by Carla Bruce. Also, Terry Ryan has given me perspective, editing, and organizational assistance in the preparation of this book.

ACKNOWLEDGEMENTS

In appreciation to the following for their influence, support, and cooperation in writing this account of my exposure to and experience with the ultimate liberation of freefall. The list is in chronological order.

Jim Chumley was the wrestling coach during my senior year in high school. Coach Chumley served in the Navy and knew how to instill a sense of dedication, drive, sacrifice, and competitiveness in his team. This springboard not only vastly helped me in my military service in Special Forces but has also inspired me throughout the rest of my life. "When the going gets tough, the tough get going." Jim was a model of "a manly man" for all the team members. He was the epitome of using sports to bring out good qualities in young people and develop strong lifelong characteristics. The wrestlers returned the favor by challenging him to quit smoking, to which Jim obliged. He still enjoys the freedom from tobacco to this day.

Leota (Mike) Janousek B-1748, C-6067, who showed her love of the sport, knowledge of the early years, maintained a library of club and personal history, and altruistically allocated "The Short Man" to the club for all those years. Mike, you are the unsung hero of the Lincoln Sport Parachute Club (LSPC). We all thank you for being the faithful servant during the early days of skydiving, of sharing your home, your life, and supporting the LSPC.

Command Sergeant Major David L. Clark D-259 made my professional skydiving career possible. Without his strategic phone call to First Sergeant Don Strickland in June 1971, I would never have had an opportunity to train and jump with the elite 7th Army Parachute Team. Command Sergeant Major Clark's involvement was pivotal in my jumping métier. I looked up to and tried to emulate this exceptional man in the distinctive Green Berets.

First Sergeant Donald (Diamond Don) Strickland D-909, my first sergeant when I was assigned to the 7th APT in 1971. Don was responsible for offering me a position on the 7th Army Parachute

Team, and I will always be in his debt. Don was a real class act, and was later called, "Diamond Don," referring to the award for his first 2,000 freefalls. His Diamond Wing number is 15, and his Gold Wing number is 113. He was a Cardinal Supreme and signed me off for my Cardinal the first month I was on the team in West Germany.

Command Sergeant Major Harold B. (Stan) Stanley D-2319, my first sergeant on the 7th Army Parachute Team. He was like a good-natured father and a big brother combined. Kind, soft spoken, and gentle; he was the most unpretentious person that I had ever met. He saved my bacon on more occasions than I care to recount and I am eternally grateful to him. He was a distinguished member of Special Forces with multiple tours in Vietnam. He was "salt of the Earth." I love Stan as did all of the team members, and we would follow him anywhere. He was the consummate soldier, leader, and a tremendous person.

Judy Wasley Kraft, Mike Wasley's widow and my hostess while I was in West Germany, unassuming, and a good friend during my time on the team. Judy is still the kind of woman that any man only dreams about; kind, gentle, accommodating, and ultimately giving of herself. Yes, a genuine domestic goddess! Judy was grace incarnate. I loved Mike and Judy, and believe that they loved me.

David Layne D-3102 was a fellow teammate on the 7th Army Parachute Team. Born in the United Kingdom, he moved to America in 1966 when he started jumping in August at the Greene County Sports Parachute Center. Later he was drafted into the Army in December 1967. David served with the Golden Knights, rotated through Vietnam, and eventually was assigned to the 7th Army Parachute Team in West Germany. He was our liaison with the British Red Devils because they shared a common language.

Sam Alston D-3176, a 7th Army Parachute Team member and my roommate during most of my stay on the team. Like me, Sam loved to jump, was immature, and fun loving. He was a little bit of a loose cannon—and like I said: "A LOT" like me. I loved to travel with Sam, enjoyed his story telling, and warm and animated friendship.

Terry Ryan was an early "guinea pig" for my jumpmaster skills, having first jumped under my guidance on my dad's farm in 1974. We continued to skydive together in Lincoln. He is a fellow Cornhusker, graduate from the University of Nebraska, and served in the Army as a Division intelligence analyst in West Germany. Roommates during my time in Lincoln, Nebraska, we recently reconnected after 40 years. We were practically neighbors in Scottsdale, Arizona, for the last 20 years. Unwittingly, we both lived in Alaska during the 1980s.

Terry "Lobo" Loboschefsky was my best friend in Utah. We made many memorable jumps and trips together. Lobo and I ultimately left skydiving, "ironically because of drugs," to learn technical rock climbing. We thought that we could scare ourselves for longer periods of time than the two or three minutes that it took for a jump. Lobo loved all things airborne. Later on, he learned to fly ultralights and then built his own Christian Eagle in his basement that he flies to this day. Retired, now he is an accomplished aerobatic pilot, airport manager, and restores vintage aircraft.

Larry K. (Bags) Bagley D-4522 joined the Utah National Guard 19th Special Forces during his senior year in high school and later graduated from the Utah Military Academy as a second lieutenant. He served as a helicopter pilot in Vietnam and later as an air traffic controller when we were skydiving together in the 70s. His first jump at Fort Benning, Georgia, was in 1963, Larry started skydiving in 1965 and logged over 5,000 jumps. Subsequently, he became national director of the USPA where he served for 20 years – eight as president. He was awarded the prestigious USPA Lifetime Achievement Award in 2013. Before retiring from the National Guard in 1990 as a Major, he logged almost 4,000 hours in helicopters and fixed-wing aircraft.

FOREWORD

Randy Lippincott has written an intriguing book of general interest. Since many readers will not be parachutists, let's start with a brief history found on the "Commencement" paneling engraved in granite at the Hall of Fame of Parachuting in Falicity, California.

Parachute concepts are traced back to antiquity, particularly in China. Leonardo da Vinci drew a design in 1483 but lacked aerial transport for a test. The first parachute jump, from a balloon, was successfully made in Paris, France in 1797 by Andre-Jacques Garnerin.

From the 1903 birth of the airplane to the mid-1950s, the then dangerous parachutes were used mainly for saving lives and for war. The round parachute oscillated and drifted with the wind; hence, a precise landing location could hardly be selected by the parachutist.

Through the mid-20th century, parachutes were made of silk or porous nylon to lessen the considerable (opening) shock. Unfortunately, this also hastened the rate of descent. The design, which remained standard after World War II, frequently caused harmful landings to the airman who left damaged aircraft, and to thousands of airborne soldiers.

In early days, the few who volunteered to jump, usually at fairs, were called barnstormers and suffered a high rate of injuries or fatalities. Thus, a social gap based on means and different appraisal of risks separated pilots and civilian parachutists. Pilots who reasonably equated parachuting with catastrophe viewed voluntary parachuting as near insanity!

The public lumped all airman together in an exotic and high-risk category. The United States Army strictly forbade freefall parachuting that it associated with civilian fatalities. Air Force doctrine stated, as late as 1957, that stability in freefall was impossible. Such was the situation in 1956 when the concept of parachuting as a sport was proposed to a reluctant public.

The Hall of Fame of Parachuting honors the many aspects of the use of the parachute. These panels include individuals and organizations whose innovations and accomplishments with the parachute provide humanity with dignity and respect and celebrates the versatile parachute whose functions include the saving of lives, exploration, military missions, firefighting, aerial delivery, and sport.

It is significant that Randy Lippincott took part with much success and personal valor in more than one aspect of parachuting: Military Missions, Sport, and Competition. He was among the Pioneers of Sport Parachuting, and, throughout his life, has been deservedly and highly respected by fellow parachutists. You're in for a treat as you read this captivating book.

—Jacques-Andre Istel, I–1, D-2,
Chairman, Hall of Fame of Parachuting

The Eagle Has Landed

Unobstructed lies the abyss below,

What awaits no one may know.

Gravity is the only law to obey,

The air parts endlessly to make way.

Narrowly the ground interrupts my flight,

It all takes place from an awesome height.

—Randy Lippincott 2014

PREFACE

I was basking in the glow of the release of my autobiography, *Three Days of The Condor or Fifty Shades of Dry,* about my 36 years of technical rock climbing. As it turned out, my first book was a springboard, when it changed my life's focus. It is the first volume of my autobiographical trilogy. In all the excitement, I realized that I should write about my first truly passionate love—skydiving. Yes, it just came to me, *Out Of The Blue.* Sure, it had been nearly 40 years and would take both effort and research. It had, in fact, been a long time and my dusty logbooks were a faded diary and a reference source. I would have to rekindle old friendships and interview veteran jumpers. Skydiving had been my golden period of adventure, my age of discovery, and the focus of my youth. It is a skill that I have often thought of renewing, but it has always been a hard choice between dividing my time and resources with so many of my other recreational and professional activities. Nevertheless, to refresh my perspective, I started skydiving again. Incredibly, it had been 13,852 days between jumps, and it was just like coming home. I was walking on air, oh how I do love the freefall!

The third book in my autobiographical trilogy is about my half century of aviation. *Fifty Years Fly By, or My Brush with Aviation* will be a collection of adventures from a half century and nearly 8,000 hours of flight time ranging from the Alaskan bush to my humble beginnings in Central City, Nebraska, starting on a grass field in 1966. It concluded with the presentation of the prestigious Wright Brothers Master Pilot Award on my Fiftieth Anniversary of flight June 14, 2016.

A BRIEF HISTORY OF THE PARACHUTE

Leonardo Da Vinci (1452-1519) formalized the design of the parachute, but recognition for its invention goes to Sebastien Lenormand (1757-1837). Frenchman Andre J. Garnerin (1769-1823) is credited with being the first to use the parachute successfully on a regular basis.

In 1912, Captain Albert Berry of St. Louis, Missouri, was the first to jump from a moving airplane. During the First World War, parachutes were issued to balloonists but not to American aviators. The common-held belief was that if someone jumped from a moving plane, a person would not have control of their arms to pull the ripcord in freefall.

Tiny Broadwick was the first woman to make a jump from an aircraft on June 21, 1913. In 1914, Broadwick gave the first demonstration parachute jumps to the United States government. On her fifth jump that day, she was the first person ever to make a premeditated freefall when she was able to open her canopy in midair.[1]

On April 28, 1919, American Leslie Irvin, who later founded the Caterpillar Club, made a freefall from a De Havilland biplane from 1,500 feet. By 1922, the seat pack-type parachute was adopted by the military. At the beginning of World War II, the European and the American armies trained and deployed airborne troops. Emergency parachutes were issued to aviators to use when it was necessary to bail out of a disabled aircraft.[2]

---

1 http://www.parachutehistory.com/women/broadwickt.html.

2 World War II - Prisoners of War - Stalag Luft I, web site. http://www.merkki.com/caterpillarclub.htm.

SKYDIVING ALTITUDE RECORDS

Many pioneering efforts have been instrumental to the evolution of what skydiving is today. The following five events are examples of the deep roots of skydiving held in American history that reflect both military and civilian contributions. I have been inspired by the following men and their extraordinary events, starting with Captain Joseph Kittinger who piqued my interest early in my life.

Joe Kittinger 102,800 feet in 1960

On August 16, 1960, Joseph W. Kittinger made the "granddaddy" jump of them all from 102,800 feet, well into the stratosphere. Unparalleled at the time, the Air Force captain launched from Tularosa, New Mexico, wearing a spacesuit, in a gondola towed by a giant helium balloon to the incredible altitude. He experienced several glitches in the four and a half minutes of total freefall. The pressure suit on his right hand failed and caused severe swelling. His helmet gave him a choking feeling around his neck during freefall, and he landed on his instrument box, which failed to release from his harness. His overall time for the "Highest Step in the World" took 13 minutes and 45 seconds. His top speed was an incredible 625.2 mph!

Kittinger made over 50 jumps with my First Sergeant Harold B. Stanley in High Altitude Low Opening (HALO) training for the official occasion. Stanley told me that Joe never did master the art of freefall, and all of that reinforced the use of the drogue chute that was released 16 seconds after leaving the gondola.[3] I would have given anything to have been the one to make that jump into the history books.

---

3 *Joseph W. Kittinger and the Highest Step in the World* by Gregory Kennedy http://stratocat.com.ar/artics/excelsior-e.htm.

Johnny Carson 12,500 feet in 1968

I heard about Johnny Carson's jump in 1968 at the time that it occurred. The TV icon and unpretentious late-night talk show host made an almost unheard of perfect first jump in freefall. It was truly sensational! I had no idea then, but it was what we called Harness Hold (which later morphed into Accelerated Freefall [AFF]), and it was very progressive at the time. He didn't use a static line, and he didn't make a tandem jump; it was honest freefall with an instructor jumping at his side from 12,500 feet. It was from the same altitude needed to make a 60-second delay, and Johnny pulled his own ripcord.

Johnny's jump was shot for TV and documented him training for the jump and then even practicing parachute landing falls (PLFs). The film revealed that Carson had great composure and style, and that the skydive came off without a flaw. But, most of all, it showed him having fun. I wanted to be just like Johnny! And, like Johnny Carson, I, too, actually packed the rig that I used on my first jump. His skydive took place in Elsinore, California, in 1968.[4] My first jump would have to wait for one more very long year.

Felix Baumgartner 127,852 feet in 2013

After 53 unremarkable years, over the New Mexico desert in a balloon with a gondola, Felix Baumgartner broke four of the five records that Kittinger set. This time, on October 14th, Joe Kittinger was the voice at the Ground Control Center for the entire operation of the Red Bull Stratos Project.[5]

Felix obtained a speed of Mach 1.25 or 843.5 mph. He also set records for the greatest vertical freefall without a drogue and highest

---

4 Johnny Carson http://articles.orlandosentinel.com/2009-10-06/news/0910040056_1_platt-water-oak-lady-lake.

5 *Touching Space: The Story of Project Manhigh* by Gregory P. Kennedy released by Schiffer Publishing Company of Atglen, Pennsylvania (www.schifferbooks.com).

absolute altitude.[6] During training, he suffered claustrophobia in his spacesuit and was treated by a sports psychologist.[7] This seemed more than a little odd for the daredevil who also held a record for the lowest base jump of 95 feet from the hand of the Christ The Redeemer statue in Rio de Janeiro![8]

Alan Eustace 135,890 feet in 2014

This time, from Roswell, New Mexico, Alan Eustace also used a helium balloon but no gondola and was all done in a clandestine manner. He was attached to the balloon in his spacesuit and positioned in a semi-horizontal attitude ready for freefall. On October 24, 2014, Eustace broke the altitude record that had only stood for two years. His privately designed suit was very high-tech to protect him from the elements in the stratosphere. Alan used multiple GoPro cameras and an off-the-shelf radio for ground control communication.

Mr. Eustace cut himself loose from the balloon with the aid of a small explosive device. He plummeted toward the Earth at speeds of 822 mph, which even set off a small sonic boom heard by people on the ground![9] His project was planned over a three-year period in total secrecy.

The record was exciting, and I still want to be a supersonic man, jumping from even greater heights. Faster than a speeding bullet. Just how high do you have to go to lose gravitational pull from the Earth or drift into orbit?

---

6 "Alan Eustace, D-7426, Bests High-Altitude World Record." U.S. Parachute Association. October 24, 2014.

7 Tierney, John (14 October 2012). "Daredevil Jumps, and Lands on His Feet". *The New York Times.*

8 Dittrich, Luke (14 July 2010). "The Man Who Would Fall to Earth". *Esquire,* p. 4.

9 http://www.nytimes.com/2014/10/25/science/alan-eustace-jumps-from-stratosphere-breaking-felix-baumgartners-world-record.html? r=0

Luke Aikin 25,000 feet with no parachute in 2016

Aikin jumped from 25,000 feet on July 30 over Simi Valley, California, in a televised event called *Heaven Sent.* He trained for two years to make the jump into a 100 X 100-foot net. Luke used GPS and lights on the ground for guidance to his target. The 42-year-old wore oxygen until 15,000 feet and was accompanied by three other skydivers most of the way. Just before impact, he rolled onto his back as planned.[10]

Luke is a third generation skydiver and has been a jumper since age 16 with over 18,000 freefalls. In addition to movie stunts to his credit, he instructs Special Forces troops in the art of skydiving. Aikin was a Red Bull team member and was the stand-in for Felix Baumgartner 127,852 foot jump in 2013 if something had happened to Felix.

I wanted to personally log this one-of-a-kind chute-less jump into a forgiving net.

10 http://www.nytimes.com/2016/07/31/us/skydiver-luke-aikins-without-parachute.html? r=0

PROLOGUE

Grateful for my early exposure to skydiving, I am thankful that I gained the basis for my discipline from the Lincoln Sport Parachute Club (LSPC) under the direction of the late Shorty Janousek. I also appreciate that I had the opportunity to jump, to skydive professionally, and to have served with the prestigious 7th Army Parachute Team. For a guy from a small farm in Nebraska, it meant the opportunities for travel, and international competition. I was also mentored by some great men who loved to skydive and honestly cared about me as though we were cut from the same cloth.

My father signed the waiver for me to start jumping and later facilitated my skydiving by personally flying for me. It became a family affair when my brother and friends joined in.

To tell the skydiving history is also to impart my intense love story. It is about deep passion, heartache, depression, astounding tales, grueling work, faith against all odds, and thrilling excitement. My story is one of aeronautical exposure from paper planes and hanky parachutes to earning the highest license in aviation and skydiving, the Airline Transport Pilot (ATP) rating and the D-License respectively.

CHAPTER 1
The Formative Years

My essential need for speed, that incredible sensation of blurred motion, was nurtured early in life.

My father's shoestring relation by marriage, Carl Sisskind, along with my grandfather, Harvey Lippincott, landed a Cessna 172 unannounced on State Highway 14 in front of our house one warm, sunny Sunday in February 1955. They taxied into our yard and before Carl left he had convinced my parents to let a five-year-old boy and his seven-year-old brother Jerry make a 70-mile return flight to Kearney, Nebraska. Carefully hoisted into the backseat, my brother Jerry and I were buckled in. Carl did his run-up in the driveway and then taxied toward the highway as my parents watched from the yard. When he was sure that the road was clear of traffic, he rolled onto the two-lane blacktop, and we took off to the north, away from the power lines.

We accelerated at a fantastic rate and when it seemed we could go no faster, we began to float in the air. My heart raced with the increase in altitude; it was fantastic! I couldn't take in everything at first in the three-dimensional adventure. The view from above was so unusual that I wanted more. From a bird's-eye view, I recognized most of the neighboring countryside. I had just "slipped the surly bonds of earth," for the very first time! This adventure remains one of my most memorable and life altering to this day.

The big blue Midwestern sky was clear of clouds, and the wind was calm. My nose was riveted to the plexiglass window on the left side in the back seat behind the pilot-in-command. It was truly exciting to see how small the cars on the highway appeared and that the farmhouses and barns all seemed miniaturized but still very real. The topography was laid out in an organized fashion and the roads stretched like guitar strings to the horizon. The rolling incredible vast expanse of farmland patchwork was the very essence of the Midwest. From my seat, I believed that I could see the "whole world" as never before. It looked more like a giant sized 3-D map of infinite dimensions.

At that moment the seed of flight was planted in me. I knew that someday I would take flight as the sole pilot at the controls. In less than the one hour that the trip took, I was captivated by the idea of aviation and all things related. The fact that my older brother was throwing up in the seat next to me did nothing to dampen my experience.

I remember my grandfather turning around in his seat, smiling with satisfaction and patting my knee with his huge warm but soft hand. Then our cross-country flight came to an abrupt halt when we started our descent to the airport. The airplane seemed to stand still when at altitude, but closer to the ground, I could tell that we were moving very fast. Then I saw the runway approaching as a blur; seconds later, I heard the sound of the tires chirping as they first touched the concrete. The ride was over but, my brain was still cataloging all the new information: The view, the machine, the pilot's effortless actions, the sensations of acceleration, flotation, and seemingly motionless, just sitting in the air. Wow, that was a lot to take in for a five-year-old.

After we had landed in Kearney, Harvey and Carl drove us to the Greyhound Bus Depot in the back of a red 1950 Studebaker pickup truck. We were deposited there after lunch to wait for the next bus that would take us back to Central City. Alone and unsupervised, we were still in a state of overwhelming amazement and giddy excitement. To experience my first airplane and a bus ride at age five wasn't bad for a Sunday in Nebraska! That was truly exciting stuff and the genesis of my unending desire for exploration and adventure—a voyage that has lasted a lifetime.

In October 1957, I stood in my pitch-dark yard looking up at the night sky and got my first glimpse of the Russian satellite, Sputnik, as it crossed the Milky Way slightly to the south from West to East. It was awe-inspiring! I will never forget the way my realization of a man-made 23-inch sphere in orbit made me feel and the fact that we could hear it beeping on our radio. How could a gadget launched from Earth look like a star and stay in the sky night after night? Although Sputnik only continued to circle the earth for the next three months, it crossed the night sky every 93 minutes and was traveling at a colossal rate of

18,000 mph. This was the beginning of the space age, and it was like nothing man had previously embraced. It was thrilling, and I wanted to be part of it. I started hyperextending my neck as a kid, looking up at fluffy clouds, airplanes, contrails, and nighttime satellites. I was, as many had been before me, fascinated with flight.

America responded to the launch of the infamous Russian satellite. Werner Von Braun, the Father of Rocket Science, was employed by the United States Government to help us gain an edge in our ballistic missile design. Tasked by President Kennedy, we fully embraced the Space Race and were right in the middle of the Cold War.[11]

> On May 25, 1961, President John F. Kennedy stood before Congress and proclaimed that "this nation should commit itself to achieving the goal, before the decade is out, of landing a man on the moon and returning him safely to the Earth."[12]

My personal parachuting journey actively started at a very tender age on the top tier of my father's windmill, just below the large galvanized weathervane. I fabricated small parachutes for various qualified feline candidates, climbed the imposing metal structure to the top, deployed my little unauthorized experiments, and watched them oscillate safely to the ground. It was great fun, and *most* of them opened nicely. Occasionally there was a water landing in the horse tank if the wind was particularly squirrelly or the "volunteer" did not cooperate fully. I would repeat the effort with different sizes, weights, and shapes of parachutes, each time making a careful note of the particular performance. These efforts occupied many hours of my youth, and I learned basic aeronautical principles by trial and error.

---

11 http://blog.al.com/huntsville-times-business/2012/03/wernher_von_braun_and_jfk_were.html.

12 Howard E. McCurdy, et. al., "Helpful Lessons from the Space Race." Issues in Science & Technology 27.4 (2011): 19-22. Academic Search Premier. Web. 23 Oct. 2013.

Others I learned by accident, such as being thrown from a speeding three-wheeler into a wet reed-filled ditch on the way to school when I was in the second grade. My older brother was driving and accidentally flipped the scooter on the gravel road near our one-room country schoolhouse. This happened immediately following my climbing around Jerry (while underway) from the unauthorized "jump-seat" position, over the steering wheel, and into the front cargo box. It was the first time that I was ejected through the air for any distance.

Some principles were learned from observation. At school, the older student Aaron Petersen constructed a fantastic hand-made kite and left it tied to a fence post at recess. When school was dismissed, it was still hovering patiently in the sky. Kites definitely had a place in my quiver of activities. Aaron also demonstrated the fantastic whirling nature of a short wooden lath launched through the air and its unusual buzzing sound. All of these cumulative exposures laid the groundwork for my propensity toward freefall.

At age 13 I tried "distance jumping" on my red bike in our long gravel driveway at home. With each effort, I tried to improve my airborne distance and speed. Halfway up the narrow but stout plank, I ran off the side and smashed directly into the massive unmovable stump the board was resting on. The front wheel was crushed all the way into the hub. Spokes were bent and broken, and the wheel rendered useless. The result was additional freefall time but, that adventure ended in a very painful displaced right wrist fracture as well as a mangled bike. I was given a general anesthetic to set the fracture, but it took several days to pick the embedded rocks out of the skin on my back. And no, I had not been wearing a shirt! The old plaster cast sure dampened any fun I would have had at summer camp that season. Over the years, I have used that injury, in addition to both fractured collar bones, as an excuse for my poor cursive penmanship.

During my youth, I became fascinated with building and flying balsa model airplanes that I made from scratch. They were both glider and gas-powered with the Cox .049, the standard size gas engine that fit my budget. It was wonderfully intense, made for meticulous work, and instilled a sense of mechanical and aeronautical aptitude in me.

When not on a mission, these treasures hung from the ceiling in my bedroom as incentives and constant reminders of what lay ahead for me. And yes, I watched and was inspired by the old black and white TV shows of both *Sky King* and *Ripcord*. The dreamer in me believed that one day, I would pilot a real plane and jump with a parachute…a long way off but how thrilling that would be!

I always sought adventure and thrills on the farm even if it was pretend. In my enthusiasm for all things aeronautical, I constructed a full-sized rolling plywood cockpit simulator in the barn. I equipped it with various discarded dials, gauges, and control levers that made up the instrument panel and throttle quadrant for my "realistic" simulator. The single ejection seat was an interchangeable inverted empty five gallon can; no seatbelt or shoulder harness was required. No need for power, fuel, flight manual, or a windscreen as my imagination took care of all of that for me. Yes, it was the first F-22 Raptor—way ahead of its time. The simulator was so realistic that, years later, my little brother told me he believed that it was no kidding "fully operational."

My first combined solo flight and freefall occurred in 1964 when I was 15. A harrowing experience of being violently dislodged off my Honda 150 motorcycle put me in freefall, near "terminal" velocity. A massive Chrysler New Yorker slammed into me at 65 mph. It would have maimed or killed a "normal" person, but God intervened in this truly supernatural event! This "jump" has gone unlogged for well over 50 years and like Luke Aikin, no parachute was required. Neither was it my first nor last closed-head injury; some were due to excessive speed, some to inattention, and some to contact sports.

At 16, I was a licensed student pilot of my father's airplane that could easily exceed 120 mph. At 18, I continued to push the envelope when test driving a Norton motorcycle that easily did an honest 140 mph on the local blacktop. Fortunately, my parents did not recognize the blur when I unexpectedly passed them in the opposite direction on the two-lane highway in broad daylight! I was only testing the water as my father had done at my age.

My earliest truly exciting organized adventure was an actual unimpeded (intentional this time) freefall at age 19. The jump was a coup d'état for me! Later, I realized that this experience was my first genuine love—perhaps even an obsession. Candidly, I didn't care about anything else. Most likely this was because it was my first quantitatively predictable exposure to the natural drug—adrenalin. I could live, eat, and breathe skydiving! Freefall was my genuine passion. I remember my brother Jerry being frequently perturbed with me because all I ever talked about was skydiving! I had expectations of standup landings, my first valid benchmark of 100 total jumps, opening a private drop zone (DZ), and holding multiple skydiving records. For example, the number of jumps in a 24-hour period (which currently is an unbelievable 640 held by Jay Stokes), the highest altitude, and any other esoteric concoction that I could fathom. Any hard earned money spent on skydiving was summarily justified. All I wanted to do was to hurl my body, from some form of an airship, at most any altitude, toward the ground.

> There's no way to defy gravity. Falling or climbing - it's always the pull that makes the activity worthwhile. To me, gravity provides contrast to the most important task, finding the levity to remain happy while you're scared, to remain smart when there's danger and remain excited when faced with so many unknown factors. To exercise a very tiny amount of control while being aware that full control is totally beyond your capability and purpose—that's when I feel the lightest! Gravity will just keep pulling on me, but I think that's just a reminder to let something within me float….
>
> —Abbey Leroux and Bill Voelker

I had an innate desire to jump and loved freefall—the more, the better; the higher, the better; the faster, the better. My father gave his permission for me to start jumping, and his enthusiastic support of skydiving and facilitation through his piloting our very own jump aircraft, runway, and DZ acted as my springboard. The summer of 1969 was truly my time of exploration.

In those early years, I made mistakes and had some close calls but survived my clumsy efforts. Completely unlicensed and unsupervised, I even jumpmastered my 15-year-old brother for his first static line jump with my father's consent. After all, Dad was flying the airplane, so it had to be alright! These were the pioneering years of the sport. However, it was a different story when my mother discovered our little illicit *soirée.* Of course, I have always lived by the adage that it is easier to "ask for forgiveness than it is to ask for permission." We were family and always tried to stay within the law, have a splendid time, and even entertained some neighbors along the way.

Fear Is My Friend

Skydiving is primarily a mental activity with the laws of gravity thrown in for good measure while fear and panic are close brothers. The first must be controlled to contain the second. Fear in skydiving is essential, and it can be a real motivator. Without apprehension, you don't develop a healthy respect for the sport and, therefore, longevity in the activity. Fear keeps you safe. The dread of serious real consequences helps focus the mind on the details. Specific principles, that when left unattended, can and have led to injury and death. Trepidation will prompt you to read fatality reports, because the same mistakes are committed over and over, only the players change. To err, after all, is part of the human condition. Ironically, panic has absolutely no room in parachuting and specifically in freefall. Conversely, you must never become complacent but rather walk a fine line between the two. Like scuba diving, you must plan the dive and dive the plan! The inner persona of skydiving transcends the fear of falling or potential injury. It is not necessarily a macho thing.

To understand and conquer fear, you must first acknowledge that you have it. You need to accept it not only as reality but also as a natural emotion, but one that is controllable. Since I had already experienced a prior worst-case-scenario with my motorcycle and was willing to improve on that, I was prepared to give my full measure. I had no problem moving on with absolute confidence and without distraction. I believed that I was potentially just as capable as anyone else! If others could perform the specialized task, then so could I!

Starting with small experiences (like indoor skydiving for example), you can build on that and increase self-confidence. My initial static line jumps and those that followed helped my confidence grow. They aided in the transition from the "normal" world to the transient interruption of gravity during freefall. Then, with repetition, I developed muscle memory, so if an emergency occurred, my automatic reaction would be pure reflex. Ground school and mock-up practice make for both mental and muscle memory, helping you safely work through any anxious moments.

Anxiety is much like the anticipation of fear, only not as intense; it is often manifested as "butterflies in your stomach." One may find comfort in activities of repetition, and overcome apprehension, but first, you must "get your mind right." President Franklin D. Roosevelt addressed the subject of fear in his first inaugural address:

> So, first of all, let me assert my firm belief that the only thing we have to fear is…fear itself—nameless, unreasoning, unjustified terror which paralyzes needed efforts to convert retreat into advance.

The study of fear in humans has shown that it can be overcome with proper training and desire.[13] Learned fear can be reversed by repeating a positive result over and over, thus overwriting the bad memory.[14] It is easier to overcome a fear of falling when you learn and accept skydiving at a young age. I didn't know any better, and that comfort level and attitude never wore off.

Recently; I had an unexpected "fearful" experience at home in Scottsdale, Arizona, while walking back from the community

---

13 Dr. Gregory J. Quirk, http://www.md.rcm.upr.edu/anatomyneurobiology/gregory_quirk.php

Quirk GJ, Garcia R, and Gonzalez-Lima F. (2006) Prefrontal mechanisms in extinction of conditioned fear. Biological Psychiatry 60: 337-347.

14 Ibid

swimming pool. I was in my swimsuit with only a towel over my shoulder when I heard an ominous rapidly approaching buzzing noise. A massive, unprovoked swarm of bees was headed right for me. Somehow I remembered what a beekeeper had told me only a month earlier. He said that bees sense fear (the natural chemical release of adrenalin) and aggressively respond to it. As long as I was not afraid of the imminent onslaught, and above all did not run, I would not be stung. I slowed to a stop, stood still, shut my mouth, closed my eyes, kept my arms at my side, and slowly started to exhale and relax. I was instantly enveloped by the massive swarm. In mere seconds, though it seemed much longer, the swarm of stingers "the black wind" cleared me, and the sound faded as quickly as it had appeared. With swim trunks as my only attire, I controlled my fear and was rewarded. After "swimming" in a sea of bees, I was not stung once!

My personal fear has been one of adaptation. I feared rejection, failure, and not fitting in. Unfortunately, in elementary school, I was teased because of my buck teeth and small stature. I had real confidence problems and a genuine inferiority complex. I felt isolated from my classmates, indeed in a one-room school, and even though my older brother was present. I was a bona fide social pariah. My life seemed insignificant and hopeless. I was my own best friend, worst rival, and constant critic.

In spite of parents who loved me and provided a safe and comfortable home, my entire childhood was lonely. I felt isolated and often depressed. I felt hated, ostracized by my peers, and even bullied at home by my older brother. I was so insecure that I was unable to raise my hand in school to be excused to visit the outhouse and held my bladder as long as physically possible. While sitting at my desk, I remember watching the little yellow telltale stream inch away from me on the contrasting oak floor. The dreadful rivulet led right back to me and unimaginable embarrassment and disgrace. It was an absolutely horrible feeling and painful memory.

District 33, 1958, photographer unknown. Back Row, Left to Right - Doug Nitzel, Anne Grafe, Kathy Gregg, Jeanne Gregg, Mrs. Belitz, Jerry Lippincott; Front Row, Left to Right - Mary Randall, Gail Gregg, Randy Lippincott, Dwayne Randall, Polly Petersen.

Early on, my philosophy was that I came into this world by myself and would unquestionably die by myself. Therefore, it wasn't much of a stretch that I also lived life all by myself. Fear's grip on me was diluted by all my other negative emotions; and to a lesser extent, I did not value my own life that highly.

When I studied Native American history, I came to appreciate and respect the lifestyle, resourcefulness, and ingenuity that the Plains Indians practiced. It was often nomadic with a minimalistic ideology coupled with a "hunter-gatherer" lifestyle. I yearned for that kind of knowledge and independence. I had many things to learn from Native Americans to be able to live off the land and in harmony with nature. I wanted to learn cunning, be courageous enough to go to battle, and count coup.

> There is a battle of two wolves inside us all. One is evil. It is anger, jealousy, greed, resentment, lies, inferiority, and ego. The other is good. It is joy, peace, love, hope, humility, kindness, empathy, and truth. The wolf that wins? The one you feed.
>
> —Cherokee Proverb

I felt that if I could ever become accomplished at something extraordinary, that it might make me more acceptable—if to no one else then, at least, to myself. Like Bruce Lee, I felt that I was not wired to live much past the ripe old age of 30. I believed that those were the cards that I had been dealt. Therefore, I had better get busy and accomplish or experience everything that I wanted to at an accelerated pace, no matter how irresponsible the activity.

This "attitude of Providence" caused me to have a relaxed outlook toward death. Not that I had a death wish, but I was not concerned about coming close to death. I grew up in a Christian family and had a good relationship with God. My risk taking may have seemed unbridled to an ordinary person. But from this posture, I had an open mind; and no difficulty with the unnatural acts of skydiving, piloting small aircraft, rock climbing, scuba diving, or racing motorcycles.

While I had the chance, I needed my light to burn brightly. Maybe this had evolved demonstrably from my early brush with death on my horse, an accidental shotgun discharge near my face, and, later on, my serious motorcycle accident. I had peered into the abyss more than once and had come back to complete my earthly walk.

Like my father, I accepted the patriotic call from my country and volunteered for duty in Southeast Asia. I willingly pursued the training in Special Forces and accepted that my return trip, like many Army veterans, would surely be in a box covered by the American flag. I would be proud to die in battle.

> A greater love has no one than this. That he lay down his life for his friends.
>
> —John 15:13

I knew God's grace, had embraced death, and I was not afraid. If I died in service to my country, it would be an honorable demise doing what pleased me. Not many people have the luxury of consciously and decisively making that kind of choice. Somehow it was instilled in me, by example, during the first 20 years of my life. My father and all of the adult males in the rural community where I grew up were World War II combat veterans. They had volunteered when their country called. Every one of those men had signed over their lives and the future of their families to Uncle Sam and the homeland that needed them to take up arms against the "Axis of Evil." I understood that freedom was not free and must be earned by each successive generation. My neighbors never spoke of the great war. Those heroes, disguised as ordinary hard working farmers, never bragged about it, never wore their dog tags or displayed their tattoos or battle scars. Some took advantage of the GI Bill and went to college. With tremendous family support and loving young wives, these men just came home and resumed living productive lives as "The Greatest Generation." That was how I wanted to live and die. I wanted a legacy of helping to preserve freedom and the American way, one generation at a time.

Uncle Sam Wants You!

Like most boys growing up in rural America, I had my first firearm at age ten on the family farm and became very comfortable with weapons early in my life. In 1968, the movie *The Green Berets* planted the desire for adventure in me. Later, when I joined the Army, I learned that John Wayne and Special Forces (SF) were my keys to the realm of "Black Ops" and real-world adventure. I pledged my life to Uncle Sam, and my training focused on honing the killing machine in me. What I received in return was travel, skill, and knowledge along with the opportunity to exercise all three in a foreign land. James Bond's Skyfall was not just a remote, austere country estate but a state of mind for me. It was true grit, ingenuity, stealth, lifelong hard training, and above all, self-discipline. I was developing a mental resilience along with situational awareness. Could the metronome in me be switched on or did I even have "The Right Stuff?" I wanted to be worthy of the top secret clearance that came with earning the Green Beret.

> The same Green Beret that was authorized for Special Forces by President Kennedy October 12th, 1961. The President further showed his unfailing support for Special Forces in publishing an official White House Memorandum to the US Army dated April 11, 1962, which stated in part that "The Green Beret is again becoming a symbol of excellence, a badge of courage, a mark of distinction in the fight for freedom."
>
> —John F. Kennedy

I regarded myself as a patriot as well as someone who naturally heeded the call to duty. I categorically signed my life away and trained with the Special Forces to serve in the Southeast Asian theater of combat. However, the military had other plans, and I was stationed in Germany like my father before me. The journey provided an exceptional adventure and many unexpected twists and turns. With my new assignment, Europe was transformed into my playground. I jumped with the British Red Devils, and I traveled to Great Britain to jump for Prince Philip and Miss Great Britain. James Bond 007 was indeed my inspiration. He was a brand-new exciting and romantic figure in 1962 with the movie *Dr. No.* I wanted to be just like him; confident, deadly, and very skilled in the art of survival!

> Goldfinger could not have known that high tension was Bond's natural way of life and that pressure and danger relaxed him."
>
> —Ian Fleming, *Goldfinger*

Bond's English tradition, as well as that of Military Intelligence Section Five (MI-5), and the proverbial stiff upper lip are accurately illuminated by Tennyson:

Tho' much is taken, much abides; and though
We are not now that strength which in old days
Moved earth and heaven; that which we are, we are;
One equal temper of heroic hearts,
Made weak by time and fate, but strong in will,
To strive, to seek, to find, and not to yield.
—Lord Tennyson

The military is a giant indifferent machine. However, I did take advantage of the opportunity to increase my jumping exposure as the Army condoned skydiving activities near military bases. Freefall is a normal progression for the airborne trooper and was encouraged. Individuals are not necessarily celebrated, but I drew a long straw for once. By training in Special Forces, I met and associated with SF veterans steeped in tradition and long on real world experience. These were worldly combat veterans and an incredible source of knowledge and camaraderie. I had found another family, only larger; men coming together, doing manly things in a team environment just felt right. I was the "young buck," introduced into the tribe and was trained and tested for battle. Command Sergeant Major David Clark was the key player in securing my position and First Sergeant Don Strickland on accepting the recommendation that I was assigned to the very elite and distinctive 7th Army Parachute Team (APT) in Europe. I just happened to be in the right place at the right time or, as my older brother once expressed, "it was the Forrest Gump in me." I jumped headlong into the excrement and came out smelling like a rose. The 7th APT is where I started to focus on my first love affair…skydiving, every day, and almost every waking hour. It was the very dawn of my "Golden Age." I was going to have to put away my honorable Praetorian plans.

A Man's Heart Plans His Way

The following quote helps emphasize the sense of limitless freedom and excitement stirred in a young man's heart all made possible through skydiving, i.e., the birth and sanctioning of an adrenalin junkie:

> As children we allow our imaginations to run wild, taking us to incredible places, letting us become anyone and do anything. There's no limit to the adventures we create or the excitement we share. We explore faraway lands, bag giant monsters, fly to the moon, and journey to new worlds of wonder. The magic of *freefall* [author's substitution] brings the possibilities of man to life.
>
> —Morgan Freeman
> Universal Studios 100 year celebration

To me, this quote describes the kinds of emotions born in the imagination through the introduction and art of skydiving; it is individual, beautiful, and awe-inspiring. Recently, after a hiatus of 38 years, my exhilaration for the sport has been renewed; it was a long time to wait to get my knees back in the breeze.

Freefall is the singular event that cannot be duplicated or accurately explained without actually having had the experience. Jumping is the communion between the individual skydiver and the invisible cradle of air that he surfs upon that becomes the essence of the experience. Freefall is a very direct, physical, and personal connection with a fundamentally pure element that is quintessentially unadulterated nature. In every practical sense, it is the glorious but temporary suspension of gravity.

The expert skydiver uses this inconspicuous medium to exercise his art form. It is like nothing else, seemingly endless, unlimited, and inexhaustible, truly the elixir of human life itself at the cellular level. To play in it on a global scale, ironically brings the game full circle. Once you have jumped, the only trace of your journey may be photographic, in the recesses of your mind, or a logbook entry. In the realm of the unexposed, there is no comparison to draw from unless you are an accomplished three-dimensional surfer in a 120 mph (yet to be devised) life-sized vitual reality game.

Since we live in a primarily three-dimensional world, at a walking/running pace or driving on the freeway at 75 mph, our brains are not wired for the raw 120 mph sphere of pure freefall. The celestial world of skydiving is not just down; it is every which way but up. Much practice is required to develop awareness and assimilation of this high-speed "four-dimensional" travel. The brain is not naturally receptive or programmed to process this vast amount of dazzling Euclidean-based information. It takes some time to download the software to your brain, which is the ultimate supercomputer. We categorically are not used to "swimming" at 120 mph. Time is needed to adjust and learn new reactions and responses.

For example, there has been a similar recent revelation in baseball. The top professional baseball hitters have routinely been bested by female fast-pitch softball players. When the size and delivery of a baseball are exchanged for a softball, the visual cues and behavior of the ball change dramatically for the batter. This change is enough that the professional hitter is unable to compensate adequately and hit the different sized ball.[15] A definitive learning curve is needed to make adjustments.

Over time, the jumper makes a similar mental adjustment, unlearning what he has experienced as standard physics and survival throughout his life. Skydiving is not a marathon; it is an exceptionally fast sprint. The fast twitch muscles come into play for a definite reason as everything can happen quickly. Mental agility is just as connected. Simply put, man is not at home falling at terminal velocity. Freefall is, in fact, an unnatural act. It is counterintuitive and must be mastered and practiced over time and with intention.

Some of this explains why skydiving, my first real love, was a foreign and forbidden fruit for me. As my initial exposure to skydiving, it was an emotionally passionate and open relationship with an unbridled element of nature. I could completely throw myself into this mind-expanding event. I recall it fondly, but I do recognize that the past is just a story we tell ourselves.

---

15 http://www.realclearscience.com/blog/2013/11/why-barry-bonds-strikes-out-to-jennie-finch.html

Recently, when I completed my recurrency training after nearly 40 years of inactivity, I fell in love all over again. Skydiving felt so amazingly comfortable, and I believe for all the same reasons. Every jump has the same consequence as that first one, and even after 1,315 jumps there is a bit of the first time every time I make the leap, although now each skydive is individually savored. I can easily swallow my ego to learn from each and every jump. All the programming had already taken place years ago. All I needed was a "software update," and a reboot of the old system—my brain!

CHAPTER 2
The Spring of '69, Masters of the Sky

Thirty-three degrees below zero can complicate a wintery day even in Nebraska. I once made the mistake of washing my car on a beautiful sunny Sunday afternoon in the winter. That night, the temperature fell dramatically, and I was sealed out of my Vega for more than 24 hours. My key would not penetrate the lock, and the doors were frozen shut even if I could have inserted the key. There was no way to get it warmed up enough to melt the ice without setting my car on fire or bringing it indoors. I would have to wait for the ice to melt.

Thankfully, all weather changes. In early February, I was outside between freshman classes at Nebraska Wesleyan in Lincoln when a flyer on a billboard caught my eye. It was one of those busy bulletin boards with the notes stuck on découpage-style. The flyer read, "Free Introduction to Skydiving by Marv Helman at Love Library on the University of Nebraska Campus." I thought, free is good, and it sounds intriguing. What do I have to lose? After all, it was aviation-related! Although I had never seen anyone jump, I thought I knew about skydiving. When I had learned about the Joe Kittinger jump from 102,800 feet in 1960, that had sparked my fascination in the sport, and it had been smoldering this entire time. I just knew that the act of skydiving had to be a remarkable thing to experience.

That Saturday night, I was in a gathering with a dozen other people listening to Marv's "spiel," and watching a short movie, *Masters of the Sky*, by Carl Boenish. When Marv demonstrated his personal gear, I was spellbound. His equipment looked so professional, beautiful, clean, and utterly enticing.

I listened intently as Marv described the components of the reserve along with the primary container and harness. He talked to the group about his helmet and goggles, special imported pneumatic French jump boots, and his professional looking full-length zippered Pioneer jumpsuit. I could already visualize myself dressed in skydiving gear. Then he held up the primary parachute container to point out the bungees, the flap that protected the cones and grommets with exposed pins attached to the polished steel cable, the ripcord, the harness, and the chest and leg straps. Next came the actual shiny ripcord handle. It was curved but shaped like a D-ring, and it invited the grasp of a hand. Like a functional work of art, it was bright chrome and something to be appreciated and admired. I watched Marv caress it as he slipped it from the molded elastic pouch. I could see the handle was attached to a small but stiff steel cable contained in a flexible metallic housing. This allowed a fair amount of play so that it could be held well away from the body before final activation. Marv's movements throughout this demonstration were fluid and without resistance; he made it all seem perfectly natural.

Then, he gave a casual but swift tug on the ripcord handle, and a spring-loaded brightly colored pilot chute SHOT OUT—no longer restrained in its gray nylon container. It was almost instantaneous in its delivery. He had intentionally pointed it directly at the audience. The spring activation, along with the pilot chute fabric popping the air, was akin to striking a down comforter with a tennis racket—whack! The bridle line pulled on the sleeve-encased main canopy, and it plopped out onto the stage floor. I thought, so that's how it works! Now he had 100 percent of my attention! I wanted to learn all the secrets of the parachute. This was a long way from my early days of experimentation on the windmill.

Next, Marv showed us the suspension lines (550 paracord), which were neatly stowed in heavy-duty rubber bands at the base of the flat sleeve in an orderly S-folded manner. As Marv pulled on them to demonstrate the next phase of the opening sequence, he stretched out the container and harness to one side of the theater and then pulled the solid blue cotton sleeve off the brightly colored nylon taffeta canopy. The Para Commander (PC) seemed very complicated yet simple, very matter of fact, and oh so seductive! Yes, I was definitely hooked! Skydiving was something I had to do. The multicolored canopy was the Ferrari model that I wanted to test drive one day. It all looked so beautifully mechanical and romantic at the same time. I was totally mesmerized! I was ready to pursue a singular monastic path to obtain a similar device and exercise it as many times as I could justify or afford.

"Mad Dog" Marv went on to describe how the PC was highly maneuverable, and could even penetrate a moderate wind. He pointed out the control toggles and the risers; then he demonstrated how to "cut away" the main parachute in case of an emergency. These were called "single shot" Capewells and were very advanced. The Capewell is a mechanical (used in early military parachutes) quick-release device used to attach the parachute to the harness.

I was captivated by the insight I was gaining. All the new terms started to make sense, and I wanted them permanently cemented into my lexicon. There was absolutely no question I could do all of this! It was exciting and seemed potentially limitless. I knew that this was something I could excel at—OH, BABY! I loved all things aviation-related, had nearly mastered piloting an aircraft, and this looked both exciting and doable. Yes, I willingly drank the Marv Helman "potion" of nylon and cadmium plated steel. Bring it!

My next mission was to proselytize my father. Even though he was a pilot and should understand these things, I had to convince him that this was a good idea. After all, he was the one person who had to agree that it was advisable for me to jump out of a "perfectly good airplane." I tried to think through my argument or even the possibility of having to use double reverse psychology before making the long distance phone call home. As it turned out, I didn't need to browbeat him at all. He was perfectly willing to drive long-distance to watch the presentation and be enlightened. All I had to do was give him the time and the place. This was real progress!

The following weekend, my father attended the same Introduction to Skydiving along with me. After Marv's performance and detailed safety report, I convinced Dad to sign the waiver to begin my Skydiving Orientation. He too drank the "Kool-Aid." Little did he know that later that summer he would be recruited to fly for my friends, Steve Steckmyer and Dan Hord, and me. Shortly thereafter, I would even jumpmaster other first-time static line students from my dad's plane—namely my brother, Loren, and my roommate, Terry Ryan.

The static line deploys the parachute without any input from the jumper. There is no ripcord or hackie to pull. The student jumper falls away from the aircraft with the top of the canopy tied to the airplane via the static line and an 80-pound break cord. The tether is to ensure that it is elongated before the apex is ultimately released. Once the jumper falls far enough, and the parachute is fully drawn out in a precise order, the break cord snaps and the canopy inflates. The static line stays with the airplane, leaving it for the jumpmaster to retrieve and safely stow out of the way. It can be reused hundreds of times because of its durability.

As I recall, my lofty goals were a standup landing in the beginning and then a big granddaddy goal of making 100 total jumps—a legitimate indicator that could take years to gain that level of expertise. My quest for experience was a soaring ambition and almost beyond comprehension! Nevertheless, I knew even then that I would become an accomplished jumper. Although it seemed so far off, it was an honorable and seemingly attainable goal. I was ready to start the adventure. Did I mention that I had never actually seen anyone skydive up to that point?

I did know that Charles Lindberg had done it right here in Lincoln. He made his first three jumps while working on his pilot's license just like me. If he deemed it necessary and prudent then so did I.

Charles Lindberg on Parachute Jumping

> I watched him strap on his harness and helmet, climb into the cockpit and, minutes later, a black dot falls off the wing 2,000 feet above our field. At almost the same instant, a white streak behind him flowered out into the delicate wavering muslin of a parachute—a few gossamer yards grasping onto air and suspending below them, with invisible threads, a human life, and man who by stitches, cloth, and cord, had made himself a god of the sky for those immortal moments.

A day or two later, when I decided that I too must pass through the experience of a parachute jump, life rose to a higher level, to a sort of exhilarated calmness. The thought of crawling out onto the struts and wires hundreds of feet above the Earth, and then giving up even that tenuous hold of safety and of substance, left me a feeling of anticipation mixed with dread, of confidence restrained by caution, of courage salted through with fear. How tightly should one hold onto life? How loosely give it rein? What gain was there for such a risk? I would have to pay in money for hurling my body into space. There would be no audience to watch and applaud my landing. Nor was there any scientific objective to be gained. No, there was deeper reason for wanting to jump, a desire I could not explain. It was that quality that led me into aviation in the first place—it was a love of the air and sky and flying, the lure of adventure, the appreciation of beauty. It lay beyond the descriptive words of man—where immortality is touched through danger, where life meets death on equal plane; where man is more than man, and existence both supreme and valueless at the same instant."[16]

—Charles Lindberg,
the first person to fly non-stop solo
from New York to Paris.

[16] GW Galloway re: Charles Lindberg on Parachute Jumping. Wed, 21 Jan 1998 23:21:27 -0500 Precision Aerodynamics, Inc.

CHAPTER 3

Ken-Get Shorty

Ken and Shorty were pioneers at the onset of the Golden Age, the dawn of sports parachuting and skydiving. Their journey of discovery started in 1958. George Kenton (Ken) Sisler had worked as a rugged smoke jumper fighting forest fires. Named after the famous Simon Kenton, a frontiersman and soldier who had saved the life of his friend, Daniel Boone, Ken had volunteered in the military. The Kenton name was bigger than life and quite a legacy to live up to, even after all that time.

Released from the service in July of 1959, Shorty Janousek had cut his teeth on the silk in the All-American 82nd Airborne. Ken and Shorty met through mutual friends, and both were determined to return to the sky as frequently as possible.

They founded the Lincoln Sport Parachute Club (LSPC) in 1958; the club became formalized in February of 1959 but not incorporated until December 22, 1961. Ken was the organizer and was instrumental in writing the club bylaws. Shorty was focused on all of the technical aspects; he acquired his rigger's license, pilot's license, and eventually his ultralight and balloon pilot's license. Janousek was also an accomplished scuba diver during that same period.

Their first endeavors were remedial at best. In the beginning, they scrounged a shared unmodified parachute and took turns making solo jumps out of a two person aircraft with the other person, of course, being the pilot. Between jumps, they had to return the canopy to the Lincoln Air Base to be inspected and repacked. These steps added to the incredibly convoluted process, for there were many hurdles to overcome.

It was a juggling act to procure a parachute, schedule an airplane, arrange for a pilot to fly it, and then wait for the weather to cooperate. However, these problems were conquered sequentially and evolved in subtle ways. Any single missing item could block the entire process. Over time, out-of-date surplus canopies were modified as Shorty became adept at rigging. Eventually, as the club expanded, they located and purchased a four-seat aircraft. The loft was the remodeled private garage belonging to Shorty and Leota (Mike) Janousek. In 1964, Shorty added on to the garage to make it a legitimate parachute loft for student training and parachute repairs. It was just one big happy family at 929 Furnas Avenue in Lincoln, Nebraska!

When I asked how Shorty's wife, Leota, acquired the nickname "Mike," I was told the following story: Leota's family had just moved to a small town in Nebraska where a neighbor girl became her best friend, and they always walked to school together. Their paths crossed in front of a man's house who relentlessly teased them and always called them Mike and Ike for the traditional candy by Just Born. Leota did not want to be named Ike since that was General Eisenhower and an old man's name. "Mike" just seemed to be more fitting for a girl, and it stuck. Her friend was forever Ike!

Ken was in the Air Force stationed at the Lincoln Air Base during the time that the club was formed. Later, he earned a Bachelor of Science degree and as the consummate volunteer he enlisted in the Army. Working as an Intelligence Officer, Sisler was assigned to the 5th Special Forces Group. Ken suffered fatal wounds when his platoon was ambushed while on a mission deep in enemy territory in Vietnam. During that action on Februrary 7, 1967, he earned the nation's highest award for his heroic actions. First Lieutenant Sisler's official Medal of Honor citation reads as follows:

> For conspicuous gallantry and intrepidity at the risk of his life above and beyond the call of duty. 1st Lt. Sisler was the platoon leader/adviser to a Special United States/Vietnam exploitation force. While on patrol deep within enemy dominated territory, 1st Lt. Sisler platoon was attacked from three sides by a company-sized enemy force. 1st Lt. Sisler quickly rallied his men, deployed them to a better defensive position, called for air strikes, and moved among his men to encourage and direct their efforts. Learning that two men had been wounded and were unable to pull back to the

> perimeter, 1st Lt. Sisler charged from his position through intense enemy fire to assist them. He reached the men and began carrying one of them back to the perimeter, when he was taken under more intensive weapons fire by the enemy. Laying down his wounded comrade, he killed three onrushing enemy soldiers by firing his rifle and silenced the enemy machine-gun with a grenade. As he returned the wounded man to the perimeter, the left flank of the position came under extremely heavy attack by the superior enemy force and several additional men of his platoon were quickly wounded. Realizing the need for instant action to prevent his position from being overrun, 1st Lt. Sisler picked up some grenades and charged single-handedly into the enemy onslaught, firing his weapon and throwing grenades. This singularly heroic action broke up the vicious assault and forced the enemy to begin withdrawing. Despite the continuing enemy fire, 1st Lt. Sisler was moving about the battlefield directing air strikes when he fell mortally wounded. His extraordinary leadership, infinite courage, and selfless concern for his men saved the lives of a number of his comrades. His actions reflect great credit upon himself and uphold the highest traditions of the military service.[17]

In 1969, the Ken Sisler Memorial award, trophy, and Ken's portrait were predominantly displayed on the west wall above the packing table at the parachute loft. That memorial kindled a fire in me to join the Green Berets. Ken was a posthumous role model for me, and I wanted to be just like him. Somehow 1st Lt. Sisler reached across time, and spoke to me about duty, honor, and country.

The motto for Special Forces is *De Oppresso Liber*, or roughly translated, "liberate the oppressed." I did not fully understand until

---

17 http://en.wikipedia.org/wiki/George_K._Sisler.

much later that he made significant contributions to the club at the grassroots level and to the nation on a personal level. Ken had more than earned his place of prominence in the skydiving and military arenas. I grew up in a military family, and Ken's example helped foster my patriotism and love of the skydiving sport.

Even though Ken and Shorty are both gone, their legacy lives on with the Lincoln Sport Parachute Club. It might be the longest continuously operating non-commercial parachute club in America, and most likely in the world. Currently, it is located in Weeping Water, which is east of Lincoln, Nebraska. They reached a milestone in 2013 when they became landowners of the area including the club building and runway. They paid off the mortgage and celebrated with a record three-day weekend of jumping from a Twin Otter on loan from Skydive Chicago.

During most of my career, the military and civilian skydiving histories overlapped and continued to have much in common. Both disciplines have separate vocabularies, and to the non-military person and non-skydiver, some of the terms and abbreviations may be confusing. I have endeavored to explain the significance of words when appropriate and tried to use a minimum of technical terms when possible. Your reading experience will be more enjoyable if you embrace them with an open mind. Skim the ones that you do not find intriguing and "let the story flow." Please feel free to dog-ear the glossary as all of these terms are defined at the end of the book.

CHAPTER 4

Now You Know Why Birds Sing

I attended jump instruction at 929 Furnas Avenue at the Lincoln Sport Parachute Club (LSPC) loft two nights per week for three consecutive weeks. I wished that they had an accelerated program because I didn't want to wait that long to jump! Without hesitation, during that period, I purchased all my gear before seeing anyone make a live jump. Shorty Janousek had the conventional student equipment in stock once I explained my budget. The complete military surplus, sport modified 28 foot 7TU, sleeved canopy in a surplus B-4 container (standard military nomenclature for this parachute unit) was $40. The TU modification described the configuration of the drive slots in the back of the parachute that gave it forward motion and the capability to turn. I purchased my complete World War II surplus 24-foot twill reserve, which had been recently packed, for a whopping $20! I paid the full amount in cash—with small bills of course. Then, to complete my skydiving getup, I collected my motorcycle helmet and goggles, my farm coveralls and work boots. I was ready to go!

I learned to pack my personal parachute in class. That skill is an advantage to the skydiver. The more proficient I became at packing, the more opportunities I had to jump. I carefully practiced folding it in the second story hallway outside my dorm room at Burt Hall on the Nebraska Wesleyan Campus. The standard packing table is 36 inches wide and 49 feet 6 inches long. Other than asking someone to step over my shroud lines, I don't think anyone gave me a second glance as I worked at folding the canopy and stowing the lines perfectly with the stout little rubber bands. I loved to feel the ripstop nylon fabric respond to the circular pumping motion, also known as flaking, that I made with my arms to neatly separate and organize the individual panels. When each pie-shaped section was properly separated, I placed the respective cords in the aluminum line guide that I had purchased and used religiously. All of this was in preparation for completing the packing process of the individual panels and pulling the sleeve down over the canopy.

Next, I diligently stowed the lines neatly at the base of the sleeve, laid the risers smartly on their respective sides in the container, and neatly s-folded the now encased canopy into its compartment. Once the mass of fabric was in place, I would compress it by kneeling on the sleeve in preparation to close the opposing flaps of the container. With a little practice, I could draw the sides of the pack together, place the first locking cone quickly through the first grommet, and then secure it with the appropriate ripcord pin. Next, the pilot chute was centered over the apex of the canopy, the large stout spring was compressed, and the remaining cones were secured in a similar manner. The protective cover over the exposed ripcord pins was snapped closed to complete the pack job. Bungees were fastened in their respective positions, and the ripcord handle secured in its elastic pocket. This routine was mechanically performed in the reverse process of the very systematic opening sequence. The B-4 parachute container was serviceable and ubiquitous to the early sport of skydiving in the United States.

The deployment progression started when the ripcord was pulled, and the pins cleared the cones; the container popped open, the spring-loaded pilot chute was launched into the slipstream and pulled the bag or sleeved canopy out in an elongated fashion. The suspension lines came unstowed from their rubber bands; the sleeve or bag was dragged off the canopy, which allowed it to inflate. The process took one and a half to two seconds and generated about five Gs or five times your body weight of force when executed at terminal velocity (120 mph).

Classes focused on parachute nomenclature and the basics of safety. Protecting the ripcord handles while moving about in the aircraft was critical. An inadvertent deployment inside the cabin with an open door could pull the jumper through the side of the plane. DO NOT PASS GO! DO NOT COLLECT $200! Not only would this gravely damage the airplane, but also likely cause your death; and you would also fall into disfavor with the other jumpers inside the plane. Students were shown photos of the resulting devastation. Yes, it was a real potential life-threatening danger. Departing the aircraft was emphasized to help position the student for a controlled stable exit, the first freefall, and actual autonomous ripcord activation.

The first five jumps were mandatory static lines so the jumpmaster could critique the exit, stability, and the student's presence of mind to pull a "dummy" ripcord handle. I also was trained in canopy control and avoidance of obstacles upon landing. Typical hazards included tall trees, power lines, buildings, water, and the jumpmaster's car. Each danger had a unique procedure or body position to assume, thus minimizing potential injury to the jumper. Power lines were my greatest fear. Of course, the fundamental principle was to avoid putting yourself in a dangerous position in the first place. Because I was already a pilot, the principles of steering the canopy and the landing flare were intuitive concepts for me.

Emergency procedures were stressed and performance-based. The cutaway (mechanically separating you from the main chute whether in the air or being dragged on the ground—it had nothing to do with using a knife) was practiced on a static display setup in the parachute loft. A stationary pair of risers hung from the ceiling simulated being under a canopy. The student wore a harness equipped with standard Capewells, which is the quick-release device used to attach the parachute to the harness. These could easily be attached or disconnected. I had to learn and practice activating the mechanical devices simultaneously by feel and without hesitation. It was mandatory to know and understand how to use the exact type installed on the rig I was going to jump.

We learned the different kinds of malfunctions, how to recognize them, and the appropriate response to each category of emergency. The cutaway was the principle task to be mastered if one expected any longevity in the sport. The purpose of the cutaway was to separate yourself from a malfunctioned main canopy, go back into freefall, and once clear of the "bad parachute," deploy the reserve canopy. This sequence was to avoid a main/reserve entanglement rendering both canopies useless. Today's version of the Capewell is called the Three-Ring Release. It is lighter, nearly foolproof, has no mechanical parts to fail, and is simple to use with one hand.

Spotting was taught in theory but was a skill that had to be mastered over time. The idea was to fly over the known target at 2,000 feet (the altitude that you were supposed to be under an open canopy, which, in 2014, changed to 2,500 feet) and throw a wind drift indicator (WDI) out of the aircraft. A WDI is a colored, usually bright yellow ribbon of weighted crepe paper 10 inches wide by 20 feet long. The WDI should take two minutes to reach the ground from 2,000 feet. The vertical velocity is the same rate at which a person under an open canopy typically descends.

The jumpmaster makes a notation of the distance and vector from the target where the WDI comes to rest. Then he draws an imaginary line the same distance upwind from the target (in the opposite direction). That area is the "spot," or the opening area.

If the jumper did nothing, he would drift downwind and land very close to the target area. The jumpmaster uses common landmarks to describe the spot to other jumpers. With a steerable canopy, the jumper can be somewhat off the wind line and still land in the target area; this region is referred to as the "wind cone." All spotting is predicated on being able to tell exactly when you are over the spot, and being able to identify straight down when sticking your head out the airplane door.

Finally, we learned and practiced parachute landing falls (PLFs) off of Shorty's picnic table in the backyard. The idea was to keep the feet together, knees slightly bent, and distribute the impact laterally along the entire body. This military technique minimized ankle and leg injuries for the student. Visually anticipating contact with the ground is normal for a person. Prior earthly experience has been one of acceleration during a jump from any height. Under the influence of gravity, it is customary to anticipate contact with the ground and flex the knees or draw the feet up to absorb the shock.

In a harness under a parachute canopy, the rate of descent is relatively constant, although it can be slowed momentarily through canopy manipulation. Therefore, to expect ground contact and draw your feet up, you would have already taken out all the shock absorbing capacity of your legs. The landing then would be feet, butt, and the back of your head! To distribute the impact of landing evenly, the PLF used the full-length side of the body (rocking chair fashion). You also were instructed to keep your feet and legs together so as not to try to brace for your impact with a single foot, leading to a possible fracture.

Those early sessions gave me the laid-back confidence to pack my parachute for my very first jump—and every skydive afterward. Packing proficiency meant being ready for the next load to take off and more logbook entries. I didn't know if I was a "test pilot" or "test dummy." At first, I used a surplus modified T-U 28-foot canopy; later, as an instructor for a student rig, I used a 35-foot steerable T-10. Following that, I used a "high performance" sports parachute, the Para Commander (PC). My last parachute in 1973 was the Cloud, which was a third generation ram-air canopy.

Not until I had 1,219 freefalls did I experience my first malfunction with the problematic reefing system on that black and red Cloud. However, at that point, I was confident, careful, and calculating. The malfunction was, in fact, a non-event. When I looked up and saw the hopeless condition of my primary canopy spinning wildly above me, I naturally cut away and activated my reserve just as I had learned so many years earlier. The only note in my logbook was that I had to walk to recover my main canopy.

March 16th, 1969. The day finally arrived for my very first actual parachute jump out of an airplane. My date with "Providence" over Agnew, Nebraska, the classic wide spot in the road. A cloudless blue sky stretched overhead, and there was no wind as the sun strained to melt three inches of new snow on the frozen late winter ground. I was filled with anticipation as I drove northwest of Lincoln with my equipment in the back seat of the car, including the parachute that I had packed the night before—unsupervised—in the dorm hallway on the floor. My head was spinning with possibilities, and I was both excited and anxious about the upcoming events.

Upon arriving at Agnew, I parked my car at the so-called "Polack International" runway and headed to where my instructor, George Vlasak, C-4806, was waiting. He checked all my gear, particularly that my reserve had an unbroken seal and that the date on the packing card was current. He verified that it had been inspected and packed by a Federal Aviation Administration (FAA) certified rigger within the last 120 days. Most likely it had been Shorty. Next, he set up my rig for the static line jump I was about to make. As the other jumpers organized for the load, I finished donning my gear. Then, with my new B-4 surplus rig securely in place, I waddled toward the aircraft with helmet in hand. Since I was the student, I would be the first out at 2,800 feet and the last to board the jump plane. The bottom edge of the door was neatly covered with duct tape to protect against any sharp metallic edges. Of course, any skydiver worth his salt wouldn't call it duct tape; after all, it was "hundred mile an hour tape" for obvious reasons!

The jumpmaster was a fellow skydiver; he was typically a senior jumper or instructor-rated individual, who coordinated boarding, the exit order, jump flight procedures, spotting, and finally emergency operations with the pilot. He was also responsible for the student jumper's safety and individually inspected the student's gear and supervised the jump. He was also responsible for operating the door (if there was one), ensuring that the aircraft was at the proper altitude and airspeed for a safe exit. He coordinated the spot and exit timing with the pilot who obtained clearance from Air Traffic Control (ATC or Center). In those early days, a blanket "Notice To All Airmen" (NOTAM) was filed, and no jump aircraft had a transponder.

The pilot was already in the left front, and only seat on the plane. George had me stand next to the door while he secured my static line to a D-ring on the floor of the aircraft. It shared part of the same connection to the floor as the pilot's seatbelt. None of the other jumpers had seat belts available to them or cared about it. Once I boarded, I sat on the floor with my back to the instrument panel. The right front seat, control column, and the door had been completely removed.

We taxied out and took off to the north. The unrestricted view from the right-hand side of the plane brought back memories of my first flight as a five-year-old. I vividly recalled the same profound sensation of rising above the ground. Soon, my left leg was chilled to the bone in the cold wind blast of the open door, and I started to shiver. Yes, of course, I was shaking from the cold. Why else would I be trembling involuntarily?

I was reminded to guard my reserve ripcord handle very carefully because of the grave consequences of an inadvertent opening inside the cabin of the plane! If this occurred, the jumper would be violently pulled through the side of the aircraft in a most unceremonious fashion. Yes, it bore repeating! A few minutes later, George was on his knees as we turned onto the "jump run," at 2,800 feet above ground level (AGL). He gave a couple of corrections to get us lined up and then yelled "cut" to the pilot. George's order was the signal to slow the plane to make it easier for me to get out into the crisp slipstream.

Communication was difficult because of the noise of the wind blast in the open door, the airplane engine, the propeller, and my helmet; but my mind was clear regarding my singular purpose. At last, George yelled, "Get out!" I knew that my path to freedom and glory was through that door. With little hesitation, I swung my legs to the left and leaned out into the stiff wind far enough to grab the strut with both hands. I thought I had total awareness of my actions but initially catching my breath was slightly distracting. I stood with my left foot on the rigid step and my right foot on the aircraft tire (the pilot dutifully applied the brake so the wheel would not spin out from under me). It was all as I had rehearsed and everything seemed normal.

Once I was in position, I turned to look back at George for further instructions. In an instant, he slapped me on the left thigh and yelled a resounding "GO!" For a split second I thought, does he mean me? Then, as I was sure that the time-space continuum had a warp in it, what was to happen next had no association with my prior connection with reality and the visible world. I do believe, in retrospect, that it was a time dilation event for me. It was barely noticeable and easily dismissed because that was my first intentional exposure to time distortion as described by Einstein. I learned through repeated exposure that the mind accommodates the event in a seamless fashion. Today, I no longer give it any notice.

However, on that day, time was considerably slowed in a most unnatural manner. I knew where I was and what my mission was, but I had never experienced this amount of gravitational "flux." I did not see any intrinsic logic in connecting the proverbial dots. Was my brain unnecessarily racing, or was I only riding the clutch? It was classic mind lock! I was unable to think fast enough to assimilate the information from all of my senses so the gray matter naturally shut down and the screen froze awaiting a reset. The real world was blurred along with a figment of my overloaded imagination.

Only about 25 percent of my physical world was registering. Where was the rest of it? Was it in fact missing or was it cloaked? Space below my feet seemed boundless, stretching as far as the eye could see. It was like nothing I had ever experienced! Maybe like nothing else on Earth! There was no lingering to savor the view, the sensation, the moment, the icy wind on my face, or the faint transient smell of oil and exhaust as I stepped from the aircraft. Already past the point of no return, I could never go back to what I had been before I exited that door. Forty-seven years later, the impression is still indelible and forever burned in my memory.

The time was 11:15 a.m. I flexed my knees slightly and hopped backward. My arms and legs were spread, back arched, head up, and spread-eagled for aerodynamic stability. I had practiced the same movements many times on the ground. My forward velocity through the air was nearly the same as the speed of the airplane, but the 80 mph headwind quickly pushed me clear of the landing gear. I threw my arms out and extended my neck to make a controlled exit. At least, that's what I thought I was doing! As I looked down with an unobstructed view of the Earth, I knew at that instant; I was the sun, the moon, and the stars. The world was literally at my feet. I might as well have been a real astronaut for that one moment as it was such an unvarnished disconnect with reality. My sensory bombardment was analogous to taking a drink of cold water from a fire hose. I knew what I wanted, but I could not anticipate the results. I had just plunged into a sea of air.

I felt the canopy being peeled off my back as the container relaxed. In an instant, seemingly just as the parachute was opening, I experienced a gentle but firm deceleration as if I were in a very comfortable and secure giant swing. There was no sensation of falling; it was only an acceleration and deceleration with nothing more than a firm cushion of air holding me up like a monumental wave building but not quite ready to break. The kinetic energy was palpable, with feelings of being both placid and comforting. I felt surrealistically calm and safe—like I was coming home. It was exhilarating and sublime, and any anxiety I had turned to elation. Time had become translucent. Then, suddenly, it was quickly catching up with me. As I looked up to check my canopy, the fabric was still flexing and waiting to complete the final spasms of the opening sequence. The process was all according to the strict laws of physics and in perfect accordance with what I had been taught. See, I knew it was going to work all along!

This was it! This was the beginning and the ending. This was the alpha and the omega. It was the zig and the zag. This was my very own yin and yang. The sudden hush after canopy opening was awe-inspiring and intoxicating. It was ultimate liberation, unlike anything I had ever experienced. Stillness and tranquility overcame me, something that I have never forgotten to this day. As if in suspended animation, it was indeed freedom unknown to the average person. Floating under the canopy was like flying my personal wily, wind-powered aircraft, so wonderfully alone and exquisitely noiseless. I was suspended in space. Yes, the absolute silence was golden! If this was a preview of independent flight, then freefall must be virtually spiritual. I was freakishly encompassed by nothing but air and totally by myself. It was utterly sensational! The parachute and harness seemed incidental to the act. The aircraft had already vanished from my view and conscious thoughts. At that point, I knew that I was truly in God's hands, surrounded by His works, and only through His grace could I repeat this extraordinary act.

I now believe that no matter how many total jumps one may make, each jump is a complete experience; and that precious, unique event comes full circle only when you have safely landed. It starts when you pack your parachute and step into your gear. You risk your life once you exit the aircraft and enter a complex series of aerodynamic maneuvers with others or by yourself. The experience evolves with the opening sequence of your parachute and then the piloting of the canopy to your planned landing area, also known as the DZ.

The event concludes with the landing flare and touchdown. All of this can be interrupted by the wind, another canopy in the air, a fellow skydiver in freefall, a lost contact, or a broken steering line. At that point, the skydiver must rely on his training and spontaneously start the problem-solving process. What an awesome and exhilarating experience!

Back to reality. There was no room for indecision. First; I made a wind check, then I exercised my toggles and tried some turns to establish positional awareness. I needed to become oriented and instantly started a turn toward the assembly area of the DZ. I was facing east by southeast and headed downwind. There were no worrisome obstacles in my path that required me to negotiate them or be concerned. There were no power lines. The jump had already been a seminal event for me.

Man small.
Why fall?
Skies call.
That's all.
—Andy Keech 1974

My vector to the DZ did not change as the wind was dead calm. I thought that a PLF did not apply to me and that I would attempt a standup landing to celebrate my initial experience. It was a mental set up for the classic first mistake. My vertical descent was an estimated 16 feet-per-second as I fixed my gaze at the white ground and retracted my feet just before impact. My legs flew out in front of me on the wet snow. I landed feet, butt, and then the back of my head on the slightly muddy unforgiving surface just under the virgin snow. My instructor had advised against looking down and had predicted what had just happened to me. I guess some lessons must be learned the hard way! The most important thing was, did anyone see me? I was about 250 yards west of the staging area so I quickly "shook it off" and picked myself up with a slightly damaged pride. I was feeling exhilarated with my fantastic introductory aerial voyage as I brushed the mud off my somewhat sore butt and bruised ego. I s-folded the suspension lines and canopy in my now grateful arms, careful to keep the pilot chute off the ground, I plodded back through the snow to the packing area. The jump was the most fantastic day of my life! Looking up at the sky was never going to be the same for me! Skydiving was like a magnet.

Once exposed to its pull, I was naturally programmed to return to it time and time again. Polarized, I was never able to get too far away if I was to maintain any harmony in my life.

It was following my first parachute jump that I remembered Shorty's words, "Now you know why birds sing." I felt the joy of becoming a member of the "skydiving brotherhood." The experience of flight was a similar feeling but, skydiving was unencumbered freedom. Yes, it too, made me want to sing out, to rejoice in my newfound adventure.

CHAPTER 5
The Accidental Skydiver

My first parachute jump was surely a turning point in my life, but it was not my first freefall. This "accidental" skydiver was first exposed to freefall from the seat of a motorcycle at age 15. No, it was not an Evel Knievel trick, and I know it sounds odd. I flashed back to my childhood of helping my dad move irrigation tubes at two in the morning, and suffering in silence through the muggy midday heat loading 60-pound green bales of dusty hay on the farm. I remember the summer heat that could scorch the pursed lips and tongue if you sucked in for any period. Dirty, grimy, and sweaty, they were my growing years, and I worked hard, but my dad paid me for my efforts.

I wanted to use the 75 cents an hour that I earned to purchase a real motorcycle. My dad's wish when he was growing up was to have a bike, but it was denied him. I assumed his vision and made it mine. With a motorcycle, I would have unfettered freedom. Gasoline was never an expense because of the 300-gallon, self-serve fuel barrel we had on the farm. First, I saved $25, then $100, and at last, I had the $460 to buy a brand-new white 1964 Honda 150 Dream motorcycle. I had grown up alongside the highway and knew the rules of the road but had not yet exercised them. I had operated a D-4 Caterpillar in the field, driven a three-wheeler and the family car on the country gravel roads. However, with no experience of driving on the highway, I made a nearly fatal mistake.

My motorcycle was less than two weeks old, and I gave the visiting friends of the family, the Gangwish kids, a joyride. I took them one at a time to the river bridge one mile north of the house on the edge of our farm. On each of the initial trips, I had crossed the Prairie Creek bridge and turned around in a meadow before approaching the highway to check for traffic. In late September of 1964 on an overcast, windy Sunday afternoon on my last trip, I made an impulsive U-turn in the middle of the two-lane bridge on State Highway 14. I was by myself.

As it turned out, it was directly into the path of a late model large black Chrysler New Yorker passing me at the legal speed limit of 65 mph. While heading north into the wind, the nut on my rearview mirror vibrated loose, and I was unable to secure it with one hand. I was positive that I had checked and saw there was no traffic behind me. In retrospect, I guess enough time had elapsed for the rapidly approaching car to catch up with me as I slowed for my U-turn. When I crossed the white center line, my physical existence passed into a separate dimension. I looked up as the massive car came into focus and our destinies crossed.

In ultra-slow motion, my mind raced to debate and explain the out-of-place supernatural vision I was witnessing. What was happening? I truly thought it was a cruel joke. It was, in fact, bizarre! It was absolute denial on my part; the circumstances were impossible and could not be happening to me; I could clearly see a car unavoidably approaching me at a very high rate of closure. I was suspended in time waiting to be T-boned. It was an extremely vulnerable position. At that point, I knew that I was a goner! No one could survive what was about to happen.

There was simply no escaping the inevitable. The tires screeched on the dry pavement for a fraction of a second, and then the sound abruptly turned off as a blinding white light enveloped me. My story could very well have ended there, and most likely should have. Unconscious and airborne, my body was ejected 35 yards upriver off the highway bridge. Like a rag doll, or, better yet, a lawn dart, I landed on the bank of Prairie Creek far below the overpass. The back of my head was lacerated on impact when the trajectory of my flight was abruptly interrupted by a lone piece of concrete on the otherwise sandy riverbank.

My only protection was the foam Pioneer Seed Corn baseball cap that I was wearing. The little bump and scar on the left top of my head would become a lifelong reminder. I could have drowned in the creek if the arc of my flight had been slightly different; I could have been unconscious, face down in the icy water. It would have taken the driver of the car, an older gentleman, ten to fifteen minutes to extract himself from the car, negotiate the steep embankment to the water's edge, discover the body downriver, and facilitate any recovery—all long after I had expired.

I didn't actually "come to" until I was oddly standing directly over my still running bike. What had just happened? A real part of the puzzle was woefully missing. I turned to see the car 55 yards down the highway twisted nearly 180-degrees counterclockwise still pointing at me. The left front fender was crushed into the wheel, and the vehicle was completely disabled. As I looked in the other direction, I could clearly see the short pair of fresh skid marks on the road disappearing like a mirage from where I stood.

The elderly motorist walked over to escort me back to his car. I can only imagine what was going through his mind, "How can this kid still be alive, I just hit him with my car?" He asked if I was okay and I told him that I was. The driver had plenty of time to focus on me, but I had been stunned by the sudden appearance of the full-sized car! Next, he held his arm up at a perfect 45-degree angle to indicate my witnessed flight path off of the motorcycle. Mathematically, my apogee was some 15 feet higher than the bridge but a total of 35 feet or three and a half stories above my point of impact on the riverbank.

The two elderly female passengers in the car were shaken up. The lady in the back seat had smashed her knees into the front seat because seatbelts weren't standard equipment at the time. I felt bad for them, but there were no apparent serious injuries. Thank goodness no one's head had hit the windshield. In retrospect, I am thankful that the car didn't roll over and eject the occupants or worse. I would have been the one at fault!

The retired banker behind the wheel ushered me into the backseat of his car, sheltering me from the wind while we waited for help. For some reason, I didn't attempt to move the motorcycle off to the side of the road; it was like "preserving a crime scene." I think everyone was still in a state of shock. The vehicles were offset, blocking both lanes of traffic. As we waited, I instinctively removed my baseball cap and placed my left hand on the back of my neck. I felt an unusually sticky dampness on my fingers and could see the bright red blood on my hand. Requiring firsthand information, I carefully teased a two-inch flap of the scalp with my left index finger to feel an intact skull and periosteum (the tough membrane that covers the bone). I was thankful not to see any gray matter or feel any bone fragments. It was as if I was blindly examining someone else's head wound. It didn't hurt, and luckily I didn't even have a headache, but I could tell that the full thickness skin flap was going to require a visit to the Emergency Room.

The driver handed me a wad of Kleenex to mop up the blood. In a few minutes, a good Samaritan stopped, and I asked him to notify my parents. All I could think about was that my dad was going to kill me when he found out that I had just wrecked my brand new bike! Shortly after that, Mother picked me up and drove me directly to town to have an x-ray of my head and my scalp sutured. I felt all right at the time and was only remorseful about the new motorcycle. Meanwhile, Dad came down to the bridge and hauled my crushed bike to the barn. I can't imagine what was going through his mind as he struggled with the mangled mass of twisted steel.

My parents consoled and cared for me in my time of need and took care of my laceration and bruises without the threat of criticism. Later, I learned in my Special Forces training, "What doesn't kill you makes you stronger." However, my father was furious when he learned from my mother that Dr. Brown's Sunday afternoon exam and skull x-ray had only been cursory since I appeared to be okay. Father was acutely sensitive to potentially fatal, unrealized injuries in the family. His brother had died of an undiagnosed ruptured spleen from a football injury at my exact age. Dad immediately contacted the doctor and insisted on a house-call and a thorough neurological and abdominal examination in his presence.

Dr. Brown was at the house within the hour. He found no signs of an urgent intracranial or active internal organ bleeding. I don't believe that he did a fundoscopic exam (small light and lens, used to look through the pupil into the back of the eye) to check for optic nerve bulging as an indicator of brain swelling. My folks were told to check back with him if they noticed any changes in my mental status. I slept in the basement on the opposite end of the house, and I could have easily succumbed during the night. No one would have found me until the following day if, in fact, I was suffering from an epidural hemorrhage (arterial bleeding on the brain).

Although I was able to walk away from the crash, when I woke up the next morning my body was literally paralyzed with pain. Every muscle screamed in protest; it was like nothing I had ever experienced! Each major muscle group had been insulted beyond its design limits. Micro-muscle fiber tears bled and oozed overnight leading to irritable, inflamed, and extremely painful swollen muscles and joints. It was like a lactic acid build up from doing 10,000 push-ups, 10,000 sit-ups, and 10,000 pull-ups! Blinking my eyes was the only movement that wasn't excruciatingly painful! I was unable to move from my bed under my own power. Yes, it felt like I had been hit by a Mack truck! It was the closest thing to rigor mortis that any living person could experience. I hoped to be excused from school because there was no way to attend class on a stretcher! Time was the only thing that was going to heal my injuries. My small frame had been wounded by the forceful and traumatic acceleration from zero to 65 mph in 0.4 nanoseconds. Ejected from the bridge, I had somehow miraculously ricocheted off of my motorcycle and survived. I had just experienced my first freefall, even if I couldn't remember it.

Unfortunately, this was not my first concussion. Years earlier, at age seven, while galloping on my horse through a grove of trees on our farm, I accidentally struck a branch, or maybe it was a tree; I don't know which because I never saw it. Unconscious in the saddle, I stayed on the horse for the quarter mile to the corral and barnyard. When I came to, I was flat on my back in the manure, looking straight up at the blue sky. Silver, the horse, was standing next to me, patiently waiting for my next command. When I came into the house, my mother described my state of mind as "confused." I believe that after that equine encounter I was assigned a full-time "Angel." She was probably thinking, what will happen to this kid if he operates a machine with more than one horsepower?

Some 16 years after the bridge mishap, I stopped at the family farm in Nebraska on my way from New York to Salt Lake City. For old time's sake, I casually returned to the Prairie Creek bridge and the scene of the accident. Although the highway had been resurfaced,

I could still identify the impact zone on the railing. That day, as I retraced my path and thought back on the details of the "thrill ride," I unexpectedly experienced *déjà vu.* I had just recovered my mental "black box" from the accident scene and, after all those years, it was a bit rusty and scarred. Yes, I had an epiphany; it just came to me like it was there all along but repressed. It was like I just found an old black and white VHS tape on a dusty top shelf and was playing it for the very first time! What follows is the account of that accident just as it was replayed for me:

I had a mental image of the car bearing down on me, the ever-so-brief instant of screaming tires on the blacktop, the complete absence of impact, the brilliant white light that enveloped and, I believe, protected me and my limbs. After that, I "saw" myself getting up from the sandy riverbank, zombie-like, and crawling up the steep, dry weed-covered embankment to the blacktop on my hands and knees. At the top of the rough slope, I struggled to stand up and instinctively walked toward the sound of the motorcycle that was still running.

This scene from my past, like the horrific opening scenes in *Saving Private Ryan*, continued to play out: I had been stunned by the concussion but, little by little, I started to become aware of my surroundings. Gradually my senses, one at a time, were coming back to me as I recovered from the profound impact. I was looking down at the Honda and could visually focus on it; next, I gradually recognized the sound of the wind blowing and the sick chugging engine. Following that, I started to become aware of my surroundings and the situation that must have led up to that. It looked like a "giant" had crushed my new motorcycle with devastating force. The smashed bike was on its right side and was still dutifully chugging along in first gear. The back tire no longer in contact with the pavement seemed to be symbolically in the throes of dying. Reflexively, I knelt down, grabbed the mashed key on the right-hand side of the headlight, and switched off the engine.

The bike was positioned in the exact spot where I had been traumatically separated from it, pointing in the same direction; as if I had just laid it over. The car did a "perfect" pirouette around my last known position on the asphalt as if I had been protected by an invisible force field. The car's left bumper struck the concrete banister at the same instant that the right end of the bumper impacted my bike just behind my left leg. Physics caused the enormous car to rotate counterclockwise, and it skidded backward down the highway.

Yes, my first unwitting freefall was without a parachute! I'm not a cat with nine lives, but I remember my dad always told me it's better to be lucky than good! Much later in life, I realized that I did have a full time "Angel" watching over me, and I've always been thankful for her.

Now, I had two jumps under my belt. The first was without a parachute from the seat of my motorcycle in 1964, and the second was a static line done in 1969 with a military surplus parachute. It would be another anxious week before my second static line with the Lincoln Sport Parachute Club. On my third jump, I was more confident of my exit and even met my first goal, which was a stand-up landing!

The summer of 1969 was busy for me, and I tried to take advantage of the opportunity to jump every weekend. My first trip away from the home DZ was at Benton, Kansas, which is where the movie *The Gypsy Moths* with Burt Lancaster, Gene Hackman, and Deborah Kerr was filmed. It was a cutting edge but dated, film about romance and the love of skydiving with the mystical and dreaded batwing. Similar to moths being attracted by a single light, they were drawn to the flame of risk. It could make you feel invincible like you did not need to use your parachute— that you could, in fact, actually fly! Today, technology has made it much closer to the truth, but back then, it was more like science fiction!

The jump at Benton was my first competition, and no one had explained that I was to jumpmaster myself. Oh well, I had ten jumps so what more could I possibly need to know?

I knew and understood the principles of spotting, and now it was time to apply and practice it. The first two jumps were all right, and I made it reasonably close to the target, but the third blew my chances of winning the novice division. I knew I could get the hang of this if I were just given time to practice. It was my 11th, 12th, and 13th jumps after all! I understood the physics, but the execution needed more work.

My next four jumps were back in Lincoln with the club before school was out for the summer and I headed to the farm and my family—with all of my gear in the trunk.

I convinced my dad to take me up in the Cessna 172 twice during that first weekend home. He removed the right control column (steering wheel) and seat but, in no uncertain terms, he said that the right-hand door was not coming off for the jump. Dad believed the aircraft would become difficult and unpredictable to control. I thought that I would let him work through his inhibitions over time. The fear of not being able to control the aircraft was a stronger emotion than reason could overcome at that point. These were my 18th and 19th jumps. Those early skydives were usually from 3,500 feet. Simply put, they were "hop and pops." It was an exit followed by a brief freefall of three to five seconds and then pulling the ripcord handle without tumbling out of control. I was still learning to crawl proficiently before being able to walk upright!

My dad initially didn't like to fly very high, and for whatever reason, he felt more comfortable closer to the ground. Many of our neighbors could testify to that. Dad had spent his entire life working the land and loved to monitor the soil and crops at a low level. Often, while doing so, he would spot an unsuspecting neighbor in the field on his tractor diligently tilling his crops. Dad would maneuver around behind the target a few feet off the deck at 120 mph. The result was predictable and always given and received in good temperament. It would scare the bejeezus out of any regular person in the otherwise tranquil and focused environment. My father was a lifelong safe pilot but liked to have fun, and skydiving seemed to fall squarely into that category.

Later, back in Lincoln, I quickly earned my A license as a student. Parachuting licenses were A through D with add-ons such as instructor, jumpmaster, instructor/examiner, etc. Each license has a minimum number of total jumps and other specific requirements of progressive difficulty starting with the basic A license. The letter indicates the increasing level of mastery, and the following number indicates the order in which it was issued. My highest license was awarded in June 1971 and is D-2973. In other words, there were 2,972 total D-licenses assigned before mine. Presently they are closing in on number D-36,000 for the expert license.

When I was working on my B license, I experienced my first "Delta" or tracking with legs extended, arms by my side for horizontal movement in freefall. I also made my first attempt at relative work (RW or aerial maneuvers by two or more freefalling skydivers with each other usually to organize geometric formations) on my 24th jump. It was exciting, but I knew that progress was going to be slow since I was instructing myself. My total freefall time to that date was just over five minutes. Typical jumps were from 7,500 and 9,500 feet and were 30 and 45-second delays respectively.

During the following weeks, my jumping was divided between the club in Lincoln and at home on the farm. Over time, I was able to coax Dad into additional altitude for a longer freefall with each jump. He seemed to be gradually getting more comfortable with greater heights through repetition as well as my urging. My spotting practice was improving somewhat in the interim. When my friend Steve Steckmyer and I jumped together, I would get out first and hang in the slipstream from the bottom of the door with both hands. Steve held the door slightly ajar—just enough to keep it off my fingers.

To facilitate spotting, I would cock my head left or right for corrections that Steve passed on to my dad. When we were over the spot for release, I would give Steve one big nod. That was his signal to push the door wide open and leap out head first. I had to synchronize my release before the door slammed shut on my fingers. A temporary loss of attention and ill-timing allowed it to happen only once but with no permanent disability. I was a quick study after that painful episode!

The notation in my logbook on drop number 33 states that B.J., Stu, and I took off from Lincoln Aviation and jumped over Agnew from 3,500 feet. I spent that first year assuming that B.J. was just some genuinely reserved "guy" but I had no idea that "he" was a "she!" To help reinforce my memory, recently I received the following related email about B.J. in remembering the passing of fellow LSPC skydiver John Peters:

My most vivid memory of John was one-night drinking beer at the Loft, prior to Shorty putting on the addition— which had the restroom.

First let me preface this for those who did not have the privilege to ever meet B.J. Holden—this person always wore a t-shirt, one or two flannel shirts, depending on the OAT (aeronautical abbreviation for outside air temperature), a blue jean jacket with '101' on the buttons, and had a haircut that was short—very 60-ish. B.J. was an electrical engineering student working on a doctorate.

Holden stepped outside to take care of some physiological needs and then John very quietly slipped outside going around the other direction. In a minute or two John came back inside shouting 'She squats, she squats!' and B.J. followed John back into the Loft where she proceeded to start swinging violently at him. We finally got B.J. settled down by buying her another beer, but she never stopped swearing at John the rest of the evening.

Later I learned that B.J. was short for Barbara Jean—after obtaining her degree, she went to work for the Navy in China Lake California...."

Regards,
Larry Bartlett D-2876[18]

By 1969, I was in Central City and between jumps 36 and 37. At that time many monumental aviation hallmarks were being made every day. Apollo 11 landed on the moon July 20th, 1969, with 25 seconds of fuel remaining. After 20 minutes on the Sea of Tranquility, Neil

---

[18] Reprinted with permission of Larry Bartlett.

Armstrong exited, stepped down with his left foot and declared, "That's one small step for man, one giant leap for mankind." His words struck home for me; they embodied the very essence of what it meant to be an American aviator. It sure made me feel proud! That was over 47 years ago, and it still sparks pure American exceptionalism in me to this day!

That summer, I made plenty of other memories. In August, the LSPC flew out to Hemingford in Western Nebraska to jump at the Box Butte County Fair. They featured an exciting Demolition Derby with a dozen or more cars as part of the entertainment. We were dropped by a Douglas DC-3 twice on both days of the fair. I stayed at Dan Hord's Aunt Gerdy Heath's ranch. It was the first time I had ever seen a king-sized bed, and as I recall, Steve, Dan, and I all slept in it together.

Following that adventure, we talked Steve's dad, Jean Steckmyer, into taking us up in his Piper Tri-Pacer. The challenge was that we sat in the back seat and had to get around the standard rear door to hang from the strut while we waited to acquire the exact position to leave the aircraft. My second jump from the Tri-Pacer was at the Riverside Dance Hall outside of Central City, Nebraska. I was headed to my job as a ticket taker for the Saturday night event and thought the entrance might be novel. As it turned out, my landing that time was on a beautiful soft sandbar near the riverbank. It was my 50th jump and the first jumps from a Piper PA22 Tri-Pacer. I repeated this performance several times that year, landing mostly on the golf course near the park entrance where I was positioned to sell tickets to the dances.

Other jumps also bordered on the gymnastic. Not only was getting out of the back door of the Tri-Pacer while airborne a tricky and strenuous effort but at one point I had to re-enter the aircraft after I jumpmastered Steve. I exited by myself on the next pass. Thinking about it now, Jean must have been near a stall and at full power with both of us in the wind. However, this allowed me the agility to open and maneuver around the door, then to hang on the strut, and finally to return to the back seat. It was not the only contortion that I performed to skydive from all types of airplanes.

At the club, the jump aircraft either did not have a door or had an in-flight door that when open was held up under the wing, out of the way, by the wind. At home Dad did not want to take the door off, so with the door on we had to push it open against the wind. On jump number 54 out of my dad's plane, I made a door on exit while my little brother was occupying the front seat. I don't even see how it was possible to get past that seat with someone in it, push the door open, and exit while wearing all of my gear. I even had to think small. Of course, my rig consisted of both a primary parachute and a bulky chest mounted reserve chute securely in place. I had to push the door open against the wind to dive out, while protecting my ripcord handle, in a paranoid fashion, against accidental premature deployment in the very tight environment.

My mother, Rosalie, had earned her pilot's license when she turned 40. We were all proud of her accomplishment, but she rarely exercised her skill independently. Over time, I asked her to fly for me to jump but she refused my repeated requests. Although she could see my father's enthusiasm for the sport, the confidence was not transferrable. I don't believe that she felt comfortable enough with all the variables of taking the front seat out and having the door open in flight. These unnatural acts were foreign to her. She never feared for me while I was jumping, but she did not have the confidence to be the pilot-in-command. In her later years when piloting was no longer a possibility, she expressed regret that she had not taken advantage of that opportunity. It would have been a unique and exceptional experience to have had her share this with me and have her signature in my logbook. Mom was always supportive but did not want to risk her involvement in a lethal outcome; she absolutely could not bear the possibility of being instrumental in her son's death. As a spectator, however, she never doubted the success of my jumps.

Dad not only loved to fly but he also loved sharing aviation with others. Many of his passengers had never flown in an airplane. Some of those very lucky passengers got to view my skydiving up close from our Cessna during their adventure. Now and then when I return to my old stomping grounds, I have conversations with some of the locals, and they remind me of their graphically vivid memories of watching me skydive first hand from their seat in my dad's four-place airplane. They all tell me that they couldn't believe how fast I fell away from the airplane and that I looked right at them and waved with a great big smile on my face! Just this year it was Ron McGuire that related his fascinating version of the same story.

September of 1969 turned out to be a hectic month from a skydiving standpoint. Steve Steckmyer and Dan Hord were from Central City, and both had gone to the same club in Lincoln that I had. Like me, they purchased used gear and were frequent flyers at the Skydive Lippincott DZ. The Nebraska State Meet was held in David City, and I took First Place in the Novice Division. At the time, I had a grand total of 60 jumps. Of course, I jumpmastered myself and made my first real competitive jump in high wind conditions with my military surplus parachute. Thinking back on it, I felt more like a kamikaze or that I was reenacting my "lawn dart" performance by trying to "throw" myself at the target. It was my first state meet, and I was determined to beat a much more experienced Mike Janousek B-1748—my instructor's wife.

Nebraska State Parachute Meet 1969.
First Place Novice, Central City Republican Nonpareil photo.

Leading up to that weekend, Dad and I had an opportunity for a quick practice jump on the Central City Airfield. We always filed the appropriate Notice To All Airmen (NOTAM) by phone at least one hour before the drop in accordance with the Federal Aviation Regulations (FARs). The skydive was from 5,000 feet slightly east of but still landing on the airport. It all seemed routine until I deployed my canopy and was sitting in the harness at the prescribed 2,500 feet. I was facing north when the Frontier Airlines commuter passed within 200 yards in front of me at my exact altitude at a very high rate of speed. It was on its descent and approach into the Grand Island Airport 20 miles to the west. If that had happened in today's aviation world, it would be considered a reportable near miss. Yes, my luck was holding! My "Angel" was on duty!

I guess it didn't matter who had the right-of-way as long as we had no direct contact with each other. Dad was on the radio with Minneapolis Center and had informed them when it was one minute prior to the jump. I can only guess that Minneapolis was busy or simply dropped the ball. After all, it wasn't exactly congested airspace on the Nebraska prairie! There was nothing to do except enjoy the novel view of a nearby passing airliner. I wonder what the people looking out the left side windows were thinking. Were any of them Rod Sterling fans? Incidentally, it had not been close enough for me to crawl onto the left wing like one episode of the futuristic TV program! Yes, the "Father of the *Twilight Zone*" had also been an Army paratrooper during the Second World War!

That same summer, I begged, and finally persuaded, my hometown doctor and pilot to fly for Steve Steckmyer and me in his low wing Piper Cherokee 180. It is not the typical aircraft used for skydiving, but we wanted the novelty of it in our logbooks. The Cessna 182 is a high wing airplane and was typically flown without the door to make egress easy for the skydiver. Nevertheless, I convinced Dr. E. T. Zikmund that we, in fact, could open the right passenger door in flight and then be able to close it securely once both of us were outside. I assured him that we could actually stand or huddle on the right wing in a 100 mph wind (there was a handle beside the door and a broad abrasive non-skid strip on the wing). I also said that I could spot and give him hand signals for corrections so that we didn't have to walk that far, or hit the tail when we jumped—and do it all from over 7,000 feet in the air!

Of course, this was only my personal closely-held theory because we had never tried it before. Score! Everything turned out as advertised, but we did have to walk a bit. Looking over the leading edge of the wing was an entirely different perspective than I was used to. It was my first time, so cut me some slack. However, I was still losing credibility with Steckmyer since he had to walk too! In researching this book, I contacted the doctor's son, Steve Zikmund, who informed me that his 96-year-old father still talks about taking us up for that jump. The doctor said he had to give a maximal amount of left aileron to keep the plane level with us out on the wing; however, once we departed he almost rolled the airplane due to over correction. I love that the story has a life of its own!

We saw these types of stunts on the cover of the *Para-Gear* catalog and were sure that if they could do it, we sure could too! We didn't realize it then, but we wanted to be on the original Red Bull Team. After all, if we looked up to James Bond, we had to start acting like James Bond and cut through all the red tape.

The Central City Airport Opening Extravaganza was September 14th, 1969, and some of the club members from Lincoln had come down to participate. The wind was a very borderline 15 mph for the first jump. By our third drop, the wind was gusting up to 30 mph out of the southwest. In retrospect, I'm not sure why we felt compelled to perform in those adverse and extreme conditions, but it did not stop us from putting on a show or taking advantage of the free jump opportunities. Steve's dad climbed to 4,400 feet. It took us almost 25 minutes in the little airplane to gain the altitude due to the stiff winds on jump run. The spot was as far away as I had ever calculated. The zephyr on the ground was high, but at altitude, it was the jet-stream.

The jump aircraft was a Piper/PA22 Tri-Pacer. Steve and I were in the back seat with the only exit on the left side. Somehow, I managed to open the door, circumvent it enough to stand on the tire, and hang out on the strut in the wind. Of course, I went first and waited for a very protracted time to make it far enough upwind for the release spot.

At last, we had covered enough distance, and I signaled to Steve that it was time to go. Fifteen seconds of freefall wasn't sufficient time for us to make a two-man hookup. Honestly, I was more concerned about landing in front of the gathering that day. Unfortunately, the "in front of" was on the upwind side of the audience and posed the real danger of being dragged into the throng. In retrospect, they could have easily collapsed the parachute for me.

I focused on keeping the distance far enough away but ended up precariously close and covering the ground very rapidly. At that point, it looked like I was going to land in the crowd, so I had to turn quickly and run with the wind at the last possible second. My focus was on the spectator's safety, and I forgot all about the real possibility of having to cut away my canopy to keep from getting pulled across the ground. That last miscalculation caused me to land downwind at a very high ground speed and rate of descent. My inexperience was showing. This was the worst of all undesirable combinations—the classic "crash and burn." I hit hard enough for my face to impact the metal instrument panel on my chest reserve. I was dazed, and my chin was filleted open and bled profusely.

The 28-foot canopy did not have a chance to deflate in the strong wind; rather, it instantly dragged me head first violently across the rough terrain at about 25 mph. I didn't have enough wits about me in my stunned condition to naturally "dump" a Capewell (to cut away half of the canopy and allow it to deflate) as I had been taught to do in this classic scenario. Rolling, tumbling, fighting, straining to gain control of a single riser after well over 75 yards of battle, my canopy finally came to rest on an electric line pole along the west side of the airport road.

By the time I was able to stand, I could hear my parachute starting to rip. Each gust of wind added to the extensive tear along the single distressed panel. That sickening sound seemed hopeless but instantly motivated me. At last, I was able to remove my helmet, reserve, and harness. I knew what I had to do next. In my grass stained and bloodied jumpsuit, I climbed the power pole and struggled to pull the shredded canopy free from a six inch long bolt close to the active and deadly power lines at the top. The adrenalin must have been working because I don't recall previously climbing a wooden power pole—and I did it without any major splinters or hesitation! The real saving grace was that I was not electrocuted!

Robotically, I field packed the heme-soiled, torn, pathetic orange and white ripstop canopy. My dad was there and, of course, he was worried about my bleeding facial wound. All I could think about was my poor parachute. As the onlookers thinned, I walked over toward my reserve and helmet where I had left them lying on the ground. At that moment, Arvid Strandberg, a spectator who wanted only to help me, picked up the reserve by the ripcord handle. And just like that, the pilot chute was ejected, and the white twill fabric fell onto the ground. I saw red, felt the pain, noted the blood on my face, parachute, jumpsuit, and impulsively acted in anger. That was the last straw! I could no longer contain my frustration with the situation. Strong profanity spewed from my mouth directed at the "Good Samaritan." I admit that it was an impetuous act and was unintended; unfortunately, it is one that I can never take back. Arvid never fully understood what he had done and that the reserve had to be repacked by a rigger in Lincoln. He has since passed away, and I regret that I spoke harshly to him in that instant of exasperation when he was just trying to help me. I have forgotten any discomfort that I had with the physical trauma, and my facial scar is nearly invisible, but I still wrestle with the memory of my rude behavior. Now, many years later, I am unable to retract it.

Then, not only did I have to send the parachute to Lincoln to see if it could be repaired, but I also had to have my reserve repacked at the LSPC Loft (for a total of $3.75). My father took me to the doctor's office to have my chin laceration sutured. Aeolus, the Ancient Greek Ruler of the wind apparently had not been pleased with me on this occasion in which the lesson was painful and expensive but was burned deeply into my memory.

By the end of that summer, Steve and I had already volunteered for the Army. We took the bus to Omaha where we passed our physicals and raised our right hands for the Oath of Enlistment on September 29, 1969. My father had flown a total of 18 times for me and others to jump. The recreation was short but sweet that summer and I recall it with great fondness and innocence.

In 1970, after I had left the club for the military, an LSPC high altitude jump was organized. It consisted of three skydivers and Shorty as the pilot. Straws were drawn, and the first guy got out over Agnew, Nebraska at 15,000 feet. It was like dumping ballast with each person's exit to lighten the load for the continued ascent. The remaining three people, which included the pilot, started using oxygen. When the 18,000-foot guy got out, the remaining jumper put down his mask to close the in-flight door and reportedly said that he noticed the symptoms of hypoxia, a pathological condition in which the brain lacks adequate oxygen in that short time. Shorty and Larry Bartlett continued until the stock 182 (carburetor only, no turbo or supercharger) ran out of power and lift at 21,000 feet. Larry removed his mask and then exited into the thin air. He told me that he got pretty hypoxic and lightheaded for the first 4,000 feet of freefall but was having fun at about 10,000 feet when his ear developed a painful blockage. Larry said he could stand the suffering no longer and opened at 5,000 feet. He had just wasted nearly 20 seconds of freefall time. No, he didn't recall any onboard transponder or clearance into the strictly controlled airspace as it just wasn't an issue in those early days of jumping.

CHAPTER 6
Twin Sons from Different Mothers

In the spring of 1969, my friend Steve Steckmeyer graduated high school in Central City, and I completed my first year of College at Nebraska Wesleyan in Lincoln. During the summer, I helped Dad on the farm and also worked as a carpenter for Johnny Sanderson. I encouraged Steve to skydive with me, and Dad facilitated our consuming passion. That summer, Steve had accumulated almost 30 jumps, and I had a total of 71 skydives. One day, during a hiatus waiting for the airplane, Steve mentioned that we should enlist in the Army together on the "Buddy System." It sounded like a good idea to me. Our families were patriotic; the country needed us, and I had not declared a major in college after my first year. It seemed logical that we volunteer for airborne duty in spite of my draft number being 350. The draft selection was randomly assigned according to date of birth, and 349 out of 366 birthdays (the draft included February 29) were picked before mine. Out of all the eligible males, 99 percent would have been taken before me. In other words, I would never have been drafted for the Vietnam era two-year obligation. Instead, I volunteered to serve for three years. I guess it's what you call fuzzy logic, but I was able to pick a military school or specialty. In my naïveté, I foolishly choose Airborne….

Perhaps it was the words of JFK that echoed through my subconscious:

> My fellow Americans, ask not what your country can do for you, ask what you can do for your country.
>
> —John F. Kennedy, January 20, 1961

My father was silently concerned, and my mother knew the cost of war all too well. My older brother Jerry was already serving in Vietnam and stationed with the crew of an LCM-6 (Landing Craft) based at Nha Be. Jerry was assigned an 81mm direct fire mortar on the bow of the medium sized boat. He would be the first target in the enemy's sights. I knew it was unusually hard on Mom to have half of her children (my older brother and me) serving overseas at the same time.

Steve Steckmyer and Randy Lippincott, waiting for the bus, to be inducted into the Army. Photo by Rosalie Lippincott.

Steve's parents and mine saw us off from the Greyhound Bus stop in Central City for the one-way trip to Omaha and our induction into the Vietnam-era Army. We had endorsed the "check" for Uncle Sam to cash any way he saw fit. Yes, that even included the possible return journey home in a body bag. That night, Steve and I went to the movie, *The Heart Is A Lonely Hunter* in which Alan Arkin played a deaf mute. Although the film was a desperate tragedy, I hoped that the Army wasn't going to be so bad.

The flight to Fort Polk, Louisiana, was my first commercial jet airplane ride; however, it did not have the feeling of a festive social outing. I felt conflicted about leaving home.

Upon deplaning at a remote part of the airfield, we fell into a sloppy nocturnal formation with the drill sergeants yelling at us at the top of their lungs. It was 2:00 a.m. local time. In the dreary light, the condensation from their breath when they shouted seemed to make the scene more like a "B" movie. The extemporaneous early morning instruction was no way to start a vacation! Where was the love? We were directed to "police" the parking lot—pick up any cigarette butts and trash. And with that, our military training had begun! In the faint light, I dutifully reached for an indistinct white object that I thought was a shredded cigarette butt. However, it turned out to be a well-organized chunk of phlegm (what we later called "lurkers"). Maybe the Army wasn't going to be as much fun as I thought if this was any indication of the level of abuse.

Later that morning we received our buzz cuts, better known as whitewalls. We were issued I.D. cards, dog tags, two pairs of combat boots, an issue of fatigues and our summer and winter dress class "A" uniforms. All of our worldly possessions fit into a single olive drab (OD) duffle bag. This same routine had been repeated millions of times by G.I.s (G.I. stood for Government Issue, but since World War I it also referred to the foot soldier). We mechanically boxed up our civilian possessions and addressed them to be sent home. That cardboard box seemed like the final tangible strand of the umbilical cord. It was the last goodbye, and I was well past the point of no return.

At the Reception Station, Steve and I spotted the Special Forces (SF) Recruiting Office, which was a solitary small white building set off by itself. We knocked on the plain white door and entered. The first thing we noticed was the 12-foot long well-nourished boa constrictor in a large wire cage on the floor at the end of the desk. My thoughts in chronological order were: I wonder when that snake ate last? It looks most impressive. I want one just like him! The sergeant behind the desk explained the program and then administered a timed aptitude/psychiatric test to both of us. He explained that we would have to volunteer for Airborne Duty following Basic Training and Advanced Individual Training (AIT). That was not going to be an issue for us. We would also undergo background checks to qualify for a top-secret clearance, which was mandatory for any Special Forces training.

Steve and I rationalized that since we were going to Vietnam, it should be with the most highly trained soldiers possible. Special Forces seemed to meet all the qualities and would offer us expert training in communications, medicine, engineering, operations and intelligence (O&I), and on all types of weapons, both foreign and domestic. Everyone had a specialty Military Occupational Service (MOS) and, as time permitted, we would even be cross-trained in a secondary MOS after we had our unit assignments. We were also promised the opportunity for additional training in high altitude low opening freefall jumps (HALO), scuba diving (learning to breathe and operate underwater), as well as sniper, ranger, and jungle schools. It was a plethora of incredible opportunities to acquire new skills, travel to foreign countries, and meet new and exotic people—and ultimately kill them. At that time, there was no foreign language prerequisite. We would do all of our "talking" with hot lead or cold steel, which were the universal communicators. Enlightened by the movie *The Green Berets,* starring John Wayne, there was no turning back.

Basic training was a shock to both of us! Steve and I did not end up in the same platoon or even the same barracks. He made friends in the "S" part of the alphabet easier than I did in the "L" section. I remember that he seemed to have a remarkable ability to acquire a Butterfingers candy bar wherever he was. I also vividly recall the way I felt that first depressing Saturday night at Fort Polk, Louisiana. I was very lonely, felt hopeless, and unsure of myself being away from home and family. I'm sure Steve had some of those same emotions, but I felt as isolated as I could be. It seemed that the buddy system was not working for me.

Army life got even rougher when my company drill sergeant died in a head-on car accident in his new Ford Torino coming back from a three-day weekend in Texas. His replacement, Sergeant Collins, was a son-of-a-bitch. He was the devil incarnate, and we all hated him with a vengeance. He was very cruel, truly sadistic in his training, and loved to abuse his position of power. If any of us had gone to Southeast Asia with him, he would have been the very first to be "fragged," a commonly utilized method in Vietnam of selectively killing someone with a grenade that you hated. It was, "anonymous friendly fire."

I completed basic training on schedule at Fort Polk even though I had been hospitalized three days for bacterial pneumonia. My infirm break was precipitated by a triple dose of vaccinations given on a single day followed by a forced march and bivouac in the freezing rain. My immune system had been overwhelmed.

Steckmyer and I had just started Advanced Individual Training (AIT) at Fort Gordon, Georgia when we came home on Christmas leave 1970. It was a long bus ride from Augusta, Georgia, to Central City but we were both happy to be back in Nebraska, in uniform, and with our families. I think Steve spent more time with my folks that year than he did with his own!

By then my father had perfected the art of flying for skydivers in the Program for Impromptu Master Pilots or "PIMPs"—something like, "would you be my PIMP?" We had finally convinced him that the aircraft could safely fly with the door off and the right seat out just like all the other jump planes. Dad was having a lot of fun and was as anxious to have us jump as we were to make a skydive. He loved our adventures together. It was "our thing" and helped strengthen our bond.

The weather cooperated that December, and we had been skydiving at the farm. The light was fading fast following the winter solstice. We had learned early on not to let a perfectly good airplane take off without us, and that day was no exception. That Christmas Eve, Steve complained that my spotting was unacceptable because he missed the DZ on a couple of occasions; he said that he could do a better job on his own. I gave him that opportunity on the "fly away" back into town. He would spot himself over the Valley View Golf Course. Dad climbed to 5,300 feet (nearly a 20-second delay) by the time we were lined up over the Valley View Golf Course south of town. Steve gave a couple of corrections to my dad for the optimal spot. The agreed upon target was the first hole in front of the clubhouse.

I had never been on the first green—let alone on the golf course, but I was confident that I would land closer to the target than Steve. On our jump run, Steve emitted an odor in anticipation of his upcoming freefall. It was not gas. It was not a belch. It was a primordial release of spirits in the "olfactory" realm. His involuntary response was an ancient reflex of releasing a scent, warning one's enemies and marking one's territory; it was akin to adrenaline, the fight or flight hormone. This scent was transient, spontaneous, and unique to Steve. My father was the first to point this out to me, saying that Steve emitted it just before every jump that he had ever made.

After Steve's final correction, he told Dad to cut the engine and said that he was ready to exit. Without hesitation, he shoved the door open and disappeared into the darkness. Dad banked the airplane to the right, and I was concentrating on Steve because I wanted to verify that his canopy opened. He never turned around and waved at me because he was too focused on the target. By then, the sun was at least three degrees below the horizon; official twilight was upon us. Steve's main surplus canopy was entirely OD dark green, a color used for camouflage and impossible to distinguish from the background clutter even if he had opened immediately upon exit. Steve's muted form vanished in seconds. There was no way for me to identify his dark figure in the pale light and I hoped he was not having any difficulties. After all, I had supervised the packing of his chute following the last jump on the farm and felt responsible. There was a brief but very real, fleeting thought of potential tragedy, but I instantly dismissed any negative feelings as I focused on my upcoming task.

Due to the rapidly fading light at the time of Steve's jump, the horizon had fused to a point directly below him, and he was unable to differentiate it from any other. Time had blurred reality. His involuntary sense of ground proximity was triggered, but only at the last possible instant. The canopy was still inflating when his right leg impacted the cold hard ground. Steve didn't just break his leg; he broke his fall *with* his leg instead of a fully deployed canopy! He didn't have a chance. He had literally been flying blind!

For perspective, terminal velocity is usually achieved after approximately 12 seconds of freefall. The body accelerates at 36 feet per second squared until it reaches 176 feet per second or 122 mph in the "face to earth" stable position. Once the ripcord is activated, the opening procedure takes roughly two seconds or around 350 feet with the old style parachutes. The opening process is intentionally sequenced or drawn out to make the opening shock more palatable. The resultant force is about five Gs or five times the strength of gravity on the individual. It is a reassuring jolt for the young skydiver. If needed, the opening shock of the emergency parachute takes about half a second and generates about 12 Gs at terminal velocity. In other words, 12 times the force of gravity on a person and it intentionally takes considerably less distance to fully deploy.

Under an open canopy, an average-sized man descends at about 1,000 feet per minute, or about 32 feet in two seconds. In other words, the 382 total feet above the ground that Steve must have deployed his canopy would have taken slightly more than two meteoric seconds to cover in freefall. Any hesitation in the perfectly optimal opening process of the old military surplus parachute would have ended in an unplanned fatal impact at or near terminal velocity. In retrospect, this jump could not have been any closer to a lethal event.

However, completely unaware of what had just transpired with Steve, it was my turn to prove my jumpmaster acumen. After a wide orbit at the same altitude, Dad again dutifully lined up on the "clubhouse jump-run." I gave a couple of corrections in the darkness, a "cut," shoved the door open, and entered the void. By this time, nearly ten minutes later, the sun was a full six degrees below the horizon, and it was an official "night jump." I had already said goodbye to my sister Ronda in the backseat, and I launched into the imposing blackness. Unlike Steve, I limited my freefall purposely to about 15 seconds to afford myself an adequate margin of safety. I wanted to have a little wiggle room in case I had any difficulty in the foreign night sky.

My primary focus was on the mercury light in the parking lot at the clubhouse. It was my only visual reference other than the stars, and they were nowhere near there! The night jump was not an environment for the average novice jumper! After the reassuring shock of my parachute opening in the ethereal expanse, I looked up at a perfect orb of darkness punctuated by 10,000 points of light. I felt like I was in fact part of the heavens looking down on a silent earth! It was refreshingly chilly and pristine, a mesmerizing distraction that was hard to give up in the consuming quiet. The glowing yellow yard light beckoned from below, and my pride hung in the balance. My goal was to beat Steve in the spotting competition, but where was the target? The canopy responded nicely in the cold, dense air, and reacted positively to my limited input. I easily made my first night standup landing in that modest and confined gravel parking lot.

By the time I had field-packed my rig, I thought that Steve should be rounding the corner, grinning ear to ear as the victor. Eventually, I figured he might need help so I left my gear and walked past the clubhouse and out toward where I thought the first green must surely be. I called out to Steve, but there was no answer from the murkiness. By this time, my eyes had nearly adjusted to the darkness, and after several hundred yards I heard a painful and worrisome moan. I rushed toward the sound and found Steve flat on his back in the rough, still in his harness, and grasping his right thigh with both hands. He told me that his femur was broken. I tried to comfort him by saying that his leg did not appear to be grossly deformed. Then for warmth in the bone-chilling darkness on the damp grass, I covered Steve, with the parachute that had failed him. I decided not to ask him if I could "play through," and he never thought to ask me how close I had landed to the first green. The competition was over. Sadly, we both lost!

I got up and frantically raced through the darkness back to the clubhouse and then about another quarter of a mile to the greens keeper's home to call for an ambulance. It arrived almost at the same time my dad and sister showed up after putting the airplane away. Steve was taken to the Grand Island VA Hospital for stabilization, and I rode home with Dad to tend to a severe earache, that up until then, I had been able to ignore. Although I felt some minimal ear pain during the day while jumping, that night the pain was the focus of my being. I was miserable! Ronda told me that I had physically pounded on my ear during the ride home. I found it a total distraction, and I simply didn't know enough to take a decongestant for it. Today, something like Afrin would relieve this sort of distress in minutes. The pain then was terrible and, in retrospect, in some way may have been sympathetic for all of Steve's agony from his femur fracture. I felt terrible and thought that somehow I was to blame for his injury. Our strong competitive drive often pushed us to try and outdo the other.

After several days, a military flight stopped to pick up my buddy in a specially modified Air Force Boeing 707. The entire left side of the fuselage opened like a clamshell, and Steve, the bed, traction apparatus and all, was loaded in the horizontal position with a forklift in the frigid air. They flew Steve to Fitzsimons Army Hospital in Denver where a rod was placed in his femur. After a prolonged rehabilitation, he returned to active duty and earned a position on the Army Rifle Team where he served for the remainder of his tour of duty. Following his discharge from the military, Steve only jumped a few times with me after that ill-fated night.

During initial jump training with the LSPC, Steve had a close call nearly colliding with a corncrib at the edge of the DZ. His depth perception, or his outright vision, had failed him on more than one occasion while skydiving; additional serious crashs in his paraglider helped support this theory. In more recent years, a misjudged landing in his experimental homebuilt airplane bent the landing gear. On one occasion, in Nepal, his paragliding sent him to the hospital with a severely fractured pelvis. When I asked Steve about these events, he explained them away as freak downdrafts or some other odd meteorological events. But I wondered if it could be pilot error or a problem with visual acuity. Later, among his skiing buddies, Steve earned the nickname "Woody." Apparently, on more than one occasion, he misjudged his environment. One time he even impaled a tree while skiing and ended up looking like Woody Woodpecker. Affectionately and in good humor, like the person, the name stuck. Without Steve's bad luck, he wouldn't have had any luck at all!

That winter, I returned to Fort Gordon without Steve. Then it was on to Jump School and the Special Forces Qualification Course (Q-Course) followed by medical training at Fort Bragg, North Carolina. Again, I was by myself and lonely. Ultimately, I was stationed in Europe and was assigned to the 7th Army Parachute Team where I made 800 freefalls in 17 months. The Demonstration Team consisted of 16 enlisted men and one officer stationed in Bad

Kreuznach, West Germany. We wintered in Aviano, Italy, to facilitate jumping year round. During my second season on the team, I competed on the international circuit.

Over the years, Steve and I visited each other. In 1975, I drove to Bend, Oregon, where Steve was active in motocross and working at a bike shop. His need for speed was now satisfied by racing bikes. It had not been dampened by his last ride in his mother's cherry red GTO when he wrapped it around a light pole on Main Street in Central City. Yes, there was a chance that alcohol may have been an influencing factor, but that possibility somehow evaded detection. Steve put down roots in Bend and developed lifelong relationships. On that trip, we both rode motorcycles to tour Crater Lake, and the nearby lava flows in perfect fall weather. During that time, I had no idea that Steve was preparing for a prestigious engineering job with the Boeing Aircraft Company.

Steckmyer had a continuing need for the thrill of adventure. Although he lived a quiet professional life, his personal experiences were far from "quiet." The rock and ice climbing, the skydiving, sailing, paragliding, backcountry skiing, building and flying a kit plane, motorcycles, shooting, all shouted for a voyage of discovery and adventure. Pushing the envelope just a little, he never quit or backed down from any challenge. He never spoke poorly of others or took advantage of his friends. He was a sincerely mild-mannered gentleman to the very end.

Following his various accidents, Steve had shoulder surgery in 2010; however, they were unable to repair his rotator cuff. By the end of his rehabilitation that autumn, he was anxious to return to paragliding. On the first strenuous hike back up the local hill with Ray Kehl, Steve complained of not feeling well and sat down to regain his strength. Ray told him not to worry that he would set up the gear while Steve rested. When Ray turned back to Steve, he found him slumped over, dead of a massive heart attack. Just like that, my friend was gone.

At Steve's memorial service, I discovered how incredibly low Steckmyer had opened that fateful night on the golf course 40 years previously. Steve had shared the detailed story of that dubious jump with his nephew, who retold it at the memorial. Steckmyer had explained to his nephew that he experienced a type of euphoria on that skydive and didn't want the jump to end. Steve was enjoying the unique and overwhelming freefall experience and consciously chose to prolong his jump, even as he penetrated the devastating darkness. He had become mesmerized by the combination of soothing muted light, cold dense air, and a fixation on his target. At the last possible second, he sensed the earth approaching and forced himself to pull the ripcord. Fortunately, the chute deployed in an expeditious fashion. Steve related that he counted one-one thousand, two-one thousand in the night, then without warning, the frozen turf violently surged up out of the pitch darkness! He felt the searing pain in his thigh, heard the audible pop of his femur, and knew that he had fractured his leg. He had narrowly escaped with his life. His parachute had not fully opened at the time of impact. Steve had nearly fallen off the razor's edge. "He who hesitates will inherit the Earth," is an old skydiver saying.

Later, I pondered what Steve's nephew had shared at the memorial service. His story led me to think about all that would have been changed for me if Steve had died that disastrous night.

If Steve's jump had been fatal, that would have changed many relationships. My father certainly would never have flown for me again or given his consent for me to continue skydiving; or, for that matter, to follow my dream of being a pilot. I'm sure that he would have sold or permanently parked the airplane and felt personally responsible for Steve's passing. We would have never known the actual cause of his demise, certainly not in his words; only that he failed to pull his ripcord in time and that his equipment was not found to be defective in any way. Our two families would have never had the same relationship again.

I carried the "what might have been" even further: Most likely, I would have fallen into a deep depression, unable to forgive myself for such foolish behavior. My SF training would have never taken place, and I would have been sent straight to Vietnam. I might have assumed a "Rambo" mentality and died as I volunteered for point man on all of my first missions against the Viet Cong (VC — a communist military organization). A "death by enemy" wish may have overtaken me because if Steve were unable to come home, then I didn't want to return either. That's how I thought the Buddy System was going to work for me.

Steckmyer may have resided in the Northwest, but he lived by the Midwest adage, "Live your life to make your family proud." Steve was very family oriented; he loved my folks and always made time to visit them when he was in Nebraska. Dick and Rosalie, my dad and mom, had adopted Steve emotionally, similar to the way Jean and Joyce Steckmyer accepted me over the years and always made me feel exceptional. Mom explained that Steve was like another son to both she and my Father. I know Dad felt Steve was an special person and loved him as a son. They would sit and talk and talk and kid and laugh together. How I miss that now! When Steve died, Mom wrote his parents that she thought the "Dick and Steve Comedy Hour" had begun in Heaven. They seemed to have the same sense of down-home humor!

I am thankful that Steve survived that tragic jump but even more so that I never witnessed or was first on the scene of any skydiving fatality. Years later, my dad told me that if he had ever seen my canopy malfunction and no reserve deployment, he would have flown the plane into the ground. Dad's story was not bravado; he just said it matter-of-factly, as though he had thought about it and knowingly rehearsed the final actions in his mind. His younger brother had died before him, and he did not plan to be around to bury his son prematurely. My heart immediately went into my throat as I was nearly unable to fathom the depths of emotion behind my father's words. I would never have knowingly placed a friend in that position, but I had done so with my dad. Not only was I risking my life when I jumped, but also I had been gambling with two lives all along—both Dad's and mine.

Steve, I miss you, my friend. You have always taken the road less traveled, and I am a better man for having known you!

> Yet knowing how way leads to way,
> I doubted if I should ever come back.

I shall be telling this with a sigh
Somewhere ages and ages hence:
Two roads diverged in a wood, and I—
I took the one less traveled by,
And that has made all the difference.

—Robert Frost 1920

CHAPTER 7
Airborne School March 1970

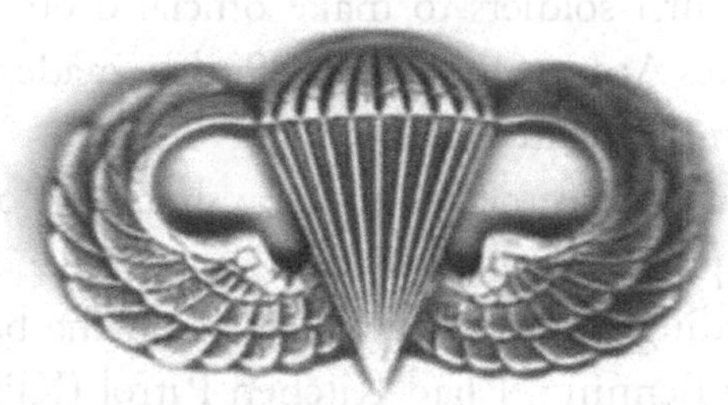

I had just completed AIT for the infantry soldier at Fort Gorgon in Augusta, Georgia, and was shipped directly to Airborne School at Fort Benning. Jump School was not for the meek or indecisive. Fort Benning, Georgia, was like all the other Army posts in the South. Built in the 1930s and 1940s, they used coal heat and the bases were neatly organized and painted. The troop barracks had no insulation or furnace; any warmth came from two GI wool blankets and a hot shower. Often the water in the "butt cans," also known as ashtrays, which were red number ten, tin cans, froze solid during the night.

In 1940, the War Department approved the formation of a test platoon of Airborne Infantry. The platoon moved into tents near Lawson Field, and obtained an abandoned hangar for training and parachute packing.[19] Temporarily, they traveled to the Safe Parachute Company at Hightstown, New Jersey, and trained using the 250-foot free parachute towers from the 1939 New York World's Fair. Drops from the tower added realism otherwise impossible to duplicate outside of an airborne descent, and proved to the troops that their parachutes would function safely. Impressed, the Army purchased two and erected

---

19 The Airborne School has US Army Black Hat cadre and additional instructors from the USN, USMC, and USAF to train students in the use of the static line deployed parachutes.

them on what is now Eubanks Field at Fort Benning. Two more were added, and today three of the original four towers are still in use.[20]

Less than 45 days after it was formed, members of the Test Platoon made their first jump from a Douglas B-18 over Lawson Field on August 16, 1940. Lieutenant Ryder and Private William N. (Red) King became the first soldiers to make official drops as paratroopers in the United States Army. On August 29, they made the first platoon mass jump held in the United States.[21]

Somehow, I always seemed to get the short end of the stick, and this was no exception. Upon arrival, I was privileged to spend my waking hours feeding the rest of the troops on the base. During my first week at Fort Benning, I had Kitchen Patrol (KP) Duty, and my specialty was pots and pans. The kitchen work gave me time to get oriented to Fort Benning, and to observe some of the testosterone-filled Special Ops guys who were there to prove themelves. The SEALs were enrolled to earn their jump wings and to propagate their reputation. I believe their pass rate was 100 percent, and some would have even jumped without a parachute if instructed to do so. They shaved their heads, stood out, and were always itching for a fight. It was partially psychological warfare (Psyops), and their behavior was marginal, at best. When I started Ground Week, I was designated as 0555, and it was displayed in large numbers on the front of my helmet. All the instructors seemed to like the way it sounded when they yelled, "triple nickel." They enjoyed telling me to get down and give them 25 (pushups)! During orientation, they spelled out their expectations in no uncertain terms: I was required to be physically fit!

20 Ibid.

21 Ibid.

Randy Lippincott (Triple Nickel), graduated Jump School March 27, 1970, photo Courtesy U.S. Army.

If I wasn't running, then I was doing pushups. We all ran everywhere anytime we were outside. If we weren't in line or performing a task, we were running. No student walked anywhere. It was intense, and we were pushed intentionally to weed out the "legs" (non-airborne material) and those who apparently did not want it bad enough. These were the troops who didn't have the discipline, mental stamina, or physical ability to take a "little" punishment. Calisthenics, which even included more running in combat boots, was a prelude for advancement and completion of the program. Course graduation meant earning the coveted Silver Jump Wings, which was also an absolute prerequisite to advance to the Special Forces Q-Course and the prestigious Green Beret brotherhood.

Tower Week came next. This was more of the same with the addition of exiting the mockup aircraft door. I had to master the mass exit procedures from the 34-foot tower, hold my exit position, and count out loud. Once I cleared the door, my risers were attached to a pulley on a cable that allowed me to bob a little and slide down to the landing area where I had to execute a military PLF. Some people quit; others were terminated if they could not follow instructions, or if their performance was not up to standards. No one got a free pass.

An enormous mobile fan was used to drag us along the ground under an inflated parachute. It could generate hurricane-force winds so that we could practice emergency canopy deflation. I was familiar with that unnatural horizontal position from the Central City Airport opening and the traumatic, windy mishap. This exercise was designed for us to practice cutting away one riser and instantly collapse the parachute. I had already learned this lesson the hard way and had the seven-month-old scar on my face to prove it. The real test was the 250-foot tower where we were purposefully suspended under an open canopy as it was hoisted to the top and released. We would drift down under the open parachute, "slipping" away (pulling down on a pair of risers causing the canopy to spill air from one side thus pushing it the opposite direction) from the tower, if necessary, and then demonstrate a mandatory good PLF. No more stand up landings for me!

Jump Week was just that. It was a lot of preparation, equipment checks, and sitting around waiting to load the aircraft. Colonel Welsh gave the motivational orientation for our first jump. Once we boarded and climbed to altitude, which was a measly 1,250 feet, we were given the standard commands on jump-run: "Stand-up…hook-up…check equipment…sound-off-for-equipment check!" Once you had checked your gear and the back of the guy ahead of you, it was time to wait for the soldier behind you to shout his number and "okay," and slap you on the back. Next, you would do the same, and right on down the line until the last guy in front of the jumpmaster or the beginning of the "stick" gave the final "okay!"

Much of this time, the jumpmaster had been down on his belly looking out the door and noting our position on the jump run. If the timing was off, we would not hit the DZ. The next command was "stand IN the door." The first jumper in the stick had better have his mind right, because if he hesitated that screwed up everyone. Once the green light came on, and the jumpmaster was satisfied with our position, he yelled: "GO!" All he wanted to see was butts and nuts! We were supposed to be like "white on rice" to the guy in front of us. Each moment of separation out the door was 100 yards on the ground. The last students in the stick might not only miss the DZ but be separated from the unit, particularly if it was a night jump.

Even though I had some skydiving experience, I wasn't bored by the process. I knew that I had to learn the military way of doing things. Before I ever arrived at Fort Benning, I was told not to mention that I had skydiving experience. There was no individual exceptionalism in airborne training. The Army didn't care what your prior experience was, and the instruction was only given one way. Everyone was treated equally, and it was all performance-based. Everything that I did was to fit in, and I followed directions. I would have liked to do some personal skydiving on the weekends, but this was not going to happen until I finished the SF Q-Course at Fort Bragg that spring.

We made the mandatory five jumps over an eleven day period. The delays were all weather-related. My first military jump was from a C-130 Hercules, right door. I wrote in my logbook: Made a good PLF, watched two "Mae West" malfunctions, beautiful day. This type of malfunction comes from a suspension line over the middle of the canopy, forming two smaller "balloons" that look like a brassiere—a "Mae West."

The second leap was an equipment jump that took a little more skill to manage the bulky gear, and the landing technique was the most critical. Before the PLF, I was instructed to lower the heavy equipment bundle on a fifteen-foot lanyard attached to my harness. The line effectively decreased my total weight at the moment of impact, and it worked pretty well. That drop was from the Lockheed C-141 Starlifter. My logbook read: First jump from a jet, "beautiful," walked out on "Cloud 9," good opening, left door exit. I vividly remember the stout metal perforated deflector in front of the large door, the feel of the ephemeral hot air on my face, and the smell of kerosene from the jet engine blast.

All the rest of the school drops were from the C-130. However, I jumped the incredibly super loud Fairchild C-123 Provider at Camp Mackall and the vintage Fairchild C-119 Flying Boxcar on the Sainte-Mère-Église Drop Zone at Fort Bragg, North Carolina. My fourth logbook entry read: Left door exit, the first drop in seven days of waiting, one malfunction on my stick. I always wondered if the guys with failures earned full credit for that jump or if they had to do it over for pay. Not all of them were actual malfunctions. Sometimes guys just got excited and pulled the reserve ripcord handle causing it to deploy alongside their already-open main canopy. It was obvious what they had done. They landed with two fully functioning parachutes, one green, and one white; both were slightly askew. Upon Jump School graduation, I was awarded the distinguished Silver Wings to wear on my uniform. It was a great start to my military adventure, and I was so very proud!

> Show me a man who will jump out of an airplane,
> and I'll show you a man who'll fight."
> —Lt. Gen. James M. Gavin

The Jump School airport was Lawson Army Airfield at Fort Benning, Georgia, but the Fryar Drop Zone was across the river in Alabama. We used the standard T-10 and, later in Special Forces, used the MC-1 steerable T-10. I graduated on March 27, 1970, which was Good Friday. While on jump status, I earned an extra $55 per month. That was big at the time; my monthly pay, when I was discharged was $366 not including the "hazard pay." It meant that I was required to make a "pay jump" every 90 days for proficiency. I could do that standing on my head!

CHAPTER 8

Special Forces Training

The Special Forces Patch indicates that the owner is Airborne-qualified. The arrowhead symbolizes Native American ingenuity and resourcefulness. The teal blue background - US Army Branch Assigned. The V-42 Fighting Knife was uniquely designed by Case Knives for the First Special Service Force (also known as the Devil's Brigade). The dagger refers to the cloak and dagger tactics used during Black Ops, the unconventional nature of Special Forces Operations. The three bolts of lightning indicate the ability to strike rapidly by Land, Sea, and Air.

The United States Army Special Forces also known as the Green Berets because of their distinctive service headgear, are a Special Operations Force tasked with five primary missions in today's Army: Unconventional Warfare (the original and most important mission of Special Forces), Foreign Internal Defense, Special Reconnaissance,

Direct Action, and Counterterrorism. The first two emphasize language, cultural, and training skills in working with foreign troops. Other duties include combat search and rescue (CSAR), counternarcotics, counterproliferation, hostage rescue, humanitarian assistance, humanitarian demining, information operations, peacekeeping, psychological operations (Psyops), security assistance, and manhunt exercises under the direction of the United States Special Operations Command (USSOCOM).[22]

Special Forces traces its roots as the Army's premier proponent of unconventional warfare from the Office of Strategic Services (OSS) which, in 1947, became the Central Intelligence Agency (CIA).[23] The OSS was formed in World War II to gather intelligence and conduct operations behind enemy lines in support of resistance groups in Europe and Burma. In June 1952, the 10th Special Forces Group (Airborne) was established under Colonel Aaron Bank. Concurrently with this was the establishment of the Psychological Warfare School, which has become today's John F. Kennedy Special Warfare Center and School. The 10th Special Forces Group (Airborne) deployed to Bad Tölz, West Germany in September 1953. The remaining cadre at Fort Bragg formed the 77th Special Forces Group, which, in May 1960, became today's 7th Special Forces Group.[24]

I was proud to train with SF. The modern day Special Forces can trace their lineage through more than 200 years of unconventional warfare history back to the American Revolutionary War. The legendary Francis Marion was one of the fathers of guerrilla fighting and covert war, and he had great success against the British as the "Swamp Fox."

My SF training started immediately following Jump School graduation. I passed the timed written qualification exam, received my Top Secret Clearance, and was on my way to Camp Mackall;

---

22 Joint Chiefs of Staff (17 December 2003). "Joint Publication 3-05: Doctrine for Joint Special Operations."

23 "U.S. Army Special Forces Command (Airborne) History." U S ARMY SPECIAL OPERATIONS COMMAND.

24 Ibid.

where it is still the setting of primary training to become a member of U.S. Army Special Forces. For me, it was the Qualification Course (Q-Course). At the time, it was a month long field exercise but now has been subdivided into the Q-Course and Special Forces Assessment and Selection (SFAS), advanced boot camp and Airborne School on steroids. Currently, an additional course is the punishing Survival, Evasion, Resistance, and Escape (SERE) training.

I made an equipment jump into Camp Mackall from a C-123 (earplugs were mandatory) with my class to start the exercise. I saw one or two malfunctions on any given drop. Someone was going to cross over the top of another parachute. In that case, the upper canopy would collapse because the lower chute was stealing the air from the one above. The top person would have to immediately "run off" of the lower canopy or slip off the side to get his canopy reinflated in time. Murphy's Law dictated that somebody was going to land in a tree if there was one nearby.

Originally named Camp Hoffman but, on February 8, 1943, it was renamed Camp Mackall in honor of Private John Thomas (Tommy) Mackall. He served in Company E, 2nd Battalion 509th Parachute Infantry Regiment. During the World War II Allied invasion of North Africa, Tommy was mortally wounded. He had been struck down on November 8, the day that construction began at the Post. Historian Stephen E. Ambrose described the Camp as a "marvel of wartime construction," having been converted from 62,000 acres of wilderness to a Camp with 65 miles of paved roads, a 1,200 bed hospital, five movie theaters, six huge beer gardens, a complete all weather Airfield with three 5,000 foot runways, and 1,750 buildings in just four months. Virtually, all of this was gone except the footprint of the airport complex by the time I arrived in 1970.

As soon as we assembled on the Mackall Drop Zone and stowed our gear, we marched over to a small Tent City next to the old runway complex. Our area of operation was on the Northeast corner of the World War II abandoned Airfield where we were all assigned cots. Likewise, our daytime classes were in large Army tents. The only wooden structure was our "ammo dump." It was full of flares, blank ammunition, real detonation cord (det-cord), fuses, igniters, flash bang, and smoke grenades. It was supposedly a secure area.

We shaved out of our helmets (steel pots), had, at least, one hot meal a day and ate C-rations for the other meals. Trading food items found in C-rations was part of the mealtime ritual. Everyone washed their mess kits in shiny 24 gallon galvanized trash cans full of boiling water facilitated by gas heaters. The first can was soapy where you used a long handled coarse brush to scrub your mess kit and the second can was filled with clean actively boiling water to rinse and sanitize the gear. We were busy from sunrise to sundown and frequently well into the night on various types of Military training exercises.

We began each morning at 6:00 a.m. with physical training (PT) and a six-mile formation run around the Mackall Airfield, rain or shine. We wore t-shirts, bloused fatigue pants, and combat boots. During the run, we called out the tempo with a rhyme or song like the classic C-130 cadence:

Here we go
All the way
Sign my name on the dotted line
'cause all I do is a double time.
Up the hill,
down the hill,
on the hill,
around the hill
C-130 rollin' down the strip
Airborne Daddy gonna take a little trip.
Stand up, hook up, shuffle to the door
jump right out and count to four!
If my chute don't open wide
I got another by my side.
And if that one should fail me too
look out below I'm coming through.
Here we go
all the way.
If I die on a old drop zone

box me up and send me home.
Pin my wings upon my chest
tell my Momma I done my best.
Here we go
all the way
PT PT.[25]

There was one constant in PT formation every morning without fail. We all sang the Ballad of the Green Beret; the 1966 hit song written by the late Barry Sadler. Like the Pledge of Allegiance, it was part of our indoctrination and ritual. It was also the theme song from the movie, *The Green Berets* starring John Wayne:

Ballad of the Green Beret

Fighting soldiers from the sky
Fearless men who jump and die
Men who mean just what they say
The brave men of the Green Beret

Silver wings upon their chest
These are men, America's best
One hundred men will test today
But only three win the Green Beret.[26]

The Q-Course was a pass/fail exercise, and the historical attrition rate was 75 percent. We had baseline physical performance tests to pass and a rigorous and demanding Confidence Course, in which we were expected to improve on each time we repeated it to advance in SF. The program included a no frills hazardous zip line, in which we hung on only with our hands and NO safety equipment was available

---

[25] Army Fitness, Physical Fitness Standards for the Army, Army Running Cadence, http://www.army-fitness.com/Army-Running-Cadences.php.

[26] Ballad of the Green Beret by Staff Sergeant Barry Sadler and Robin Moore, copyright 1966.

or used! The Confidence Course was more than a mile long with over 20 serious obstacles. The barriers included: underground tunnels; 35 foot tall widely-spaced, committing and awkwardly huge timber ladders; balance beams; a bulky rope swing over obstacles; monkey bars; extensive two-inch free rope climbs; rope bridges to negotiate; and high exhausting cargo nets to confront. It was a timed endurance test of balance, agility, strength, technique, and pure physical stamina.

The Confidence Course at Mackall was likely the most punishing obstacle course the U.S. military had to offer. Now it's referred to as the "Nasty Nick," named after Colonel James Nick Rowe, one of only 34 American POW's to escape captivity during the Vietnam War. Colonel Rowe was credited with developing the rigorous Survival, Evasion, Resistance, and Escape (SERE) Training Program taught to high-risk military personnel, such as Special Forces and Aircrews, and to the U.S. military doctrine that institutionalizes these techniques and principles to be followed by captured personnel."[27] During the month-long exercise, we were expected to improve on our previous performance, to up the ante each time the challenging event was repeated.

There was daytime introductory classroom exposure to each of the five Military Occupational Services (MOS). These MOSs defined your primary job in the military. They included: (1) Weapons - light and heavy, and how to operate and maintain all types of weapons both foreign and domestic, (2) Engineering - which meant the explosive annihilation of targets and construction of field fortifications and notable topographic survey techniques, (3) Communications - you were assigned the Team radio, were responsible for sophisticated long-wire base communications, encrypted satellite communications systems, and even the old-style high-frequency Morse Code system, (4) O&I - which was Operations and Intelligence, and lastly (5) Medic - you were the field doctor, surgeon, dentist, veterinarian, gynecologist (yes, we even delivered babies), dermatologist, ophthalmologist,

---

[27] James Nicholas "Nick" Rowe by Michael Robert Patterson. http://en.wikipedia.org/wiki/James_N._Rowe.

psychiatrist, and all around resident medical expert. Medicine was my chosen field.

You had to know how to prioritize and treat battle wounds, triage patients, and resuscitate young men during the fog of battle while under enemy fire. We were taught to maintain a calm demeanor during the chaos of a firefight as our teammates lives depended on it. I learned to keep my head on a swivel and have positional awareness during my waking hours. The Combat Medic had the highest casualty rate because he was constantly exposing himself to enemy fire in the attempt to save his buddies as well as the "friendlies." The SF presenters made each subject interesting and germane to the main topic. Wow, if I only had more time and a little more sleep I could honestly absorb this stuff. There was so much to learn!

One of the specialty tasks that we were exposed to in the field was river crossings (engineering). We learned how to build makeshift rope bridges to span a river or a gorge. On one of those exercises, I caught a Water Moccasin (Agkistrodon piscivorus) swimming in the river. I was able to capture, kill, skin, (no time to eat it) and send a full-length, tanned snakeskin home to my parents where they kept it displayed for many years in my bedroom!

Throughout the medical lecture on the use of atropine syrettes (a small disposable device to inject medicine into the muscle) for the treatment of nerve gas poisoning, the presenter was sitting on a table at the front of the lecture tent. The Special Forces Sergeant demonstrated the use of the syrette by removing the cap that protected the 1 1/2 inch single-use needle. He squeezed a few drops of fluid out of it, so we could see how it functioned and, in the same motion, thrust it into his thigh right through his fatigues! Next, he gave the tube a final squeeze to inject the fluid into his quadriceps muscle and kept on with his lecture uninterrupted. All the while the syrette was still embedded in his thigh. I was stunned and shocked but very impressed. The medic had nerves of cold steel and, at that moment, I wanted to be just like him!

In that same class, we learned to give shots to each other. We paired up, and I first tried to give a shoulder injection to my classmate. Mind you, I had never done this before, and the fine needle bounced off the patient's skin! I knew I could do this. Now, with much more determination and applied force, I felt the needle easily penetrate the skin, muscle, and contact bone. Well, maybe that was too much force! In the artillery, they call that "bracketing." Yes, I knew I could get the hang of this.

During the night when I was not on Guard Duty, they found other things for me to do. If we had a timed long-distance land navigation exercise during the day including a heavy pack and weapons in hilly wooded terrain or swamp, we would also have a long distance land navigation exercise to repeat at night. These fundamental skills were all individual and timed, and they were pass/fail to boot! I guarded my compass for the valuable tool that it was. We learned small unit tactics at night which certainly meant crossing through a swamp in the pitch black. It resulted in being wet, cold, and moving with extreme noise and light discipline. These nocturnal follies did not exempt us from our regular duties and classes the following day.

We were trained in hand-to-hand combat with rubber knives (not with the actual V-42 dagger), guerrilla warfare, rubber boat operations, free rappelling, real survival or SERE training and, of course, we were expected to give 100 percent to the daily training sessions. Our class was a highly motivated group of pugilists, but some individuals voluntarily withdrew because of the stress and abuse. Others were eliminated due to a variety of factors or they simply ran out of desire. Some of the candidates did not understand that it was as much mental as it was physical toughness. I wasn't as big or as strong as most of the macho guys, but I was in charge of my brain. I had the moxie. I had the drive. I had the willpower. I had the mental toughness and a "can do" spirit. Later, those who did not continue to improve or meet established objectives were terminated from the program and sent back to their units. Those were the guys who thought the progam was FUBAR!

So, what exactly is **mental toughness**? Mental toughness is the ability to drive forward and accomplish your intentions in spite of contradicting forces – be they internal ones like fear, anxiety, or an external force such as a person opposing you. Fear is usually the main "opposing" force.

A 2007 paper discussed the components of mental toughness. A performer's attitude or mindset was profiled, specifically his focus and self-belief. Three dimensions were outlined, and they included training, competition, and post-competition. These individual components contain attributes of mental toughness that pertain to their use at clearly defined time periods.[28] Elements such as handling pressure, contending with failure, and pushing yourself to your physical limits during training, all are part of developing resilient mental skills. Mental toughness helps improve flexibility and the very ability to think on your feet. It is the capability to switch on a mindset and still maintain a high state of alertness. It is the capacity to overcome and control your fear and make it work for you. The very power of visualization helps develop a winning mindset. It is the attitude of a winner.

Along with mental toughness and constant physical stress came sacrifice. My personal hope and sacrifice, the suffering of self; all were for my buddies and the Team. It was a willing conscious to subconscious indoctrination, and it fueled the patriotism in a 20-year-old eager for learning, adventure, travel, and combat. Since this nation was founded on Judeo-Christian principles, and it's well known that there are no atheists in foxholes the Military spirit is in concert with the Bible.

> Not only that but, we rejoice in our sufferings, knowing that suffering produces perseverance; perseverance, character; and character, hope. And hope does not put us to shame….
>
> —Romans 5:3-5

My aviation and skydiving interests culminated in all things air and space-related, even jumping from space like Captain Joseph Kittinger, later Felix Baumgartner, and most recently Alan Eustace. Unbeknownst to us while isolated from the real world at Camp

---

[28] Jones, G., Hanton, S., & Connaughton, D. (2007). A Framework of Mental Toughness in the World's Best Performers. Sport Psychologist, 21(2), 243-264.

Mackall on April 14, 1970, an explosion on board Apollo 13 caused a critical situation in the U.S. Space Program. It placed the lives of astronauts Lovell, Swigert, and Haise at extreme risk. The detonation occurred in the fuel cells of the spacecraft's service module 56 hours following lift off. The accident resulted in the loss of Apollo 13's main power supply which meant that oxygen and water reserves fell critically low.

NASA frantically worked on contingency plans for the astronaut's survival. The strategy was to "slingshot" Apollo 13 around the moon and fire the spacecraft's last booster engine to break free from the moon's orbit and return safely back to Earth.[29] However, if they entered Earth's orbit too steeply, they would burn up; too shallow, and they would skip off the atmosphere back into space on a one-way trip to infinity. It was a risky operation, and there was no backup plan.[30] American ingenuity eventually won the day, just like our personal hard work was developing highly skilled and motivated soldiers to combat the spread of Communism in Southeast Asia.

On May 1, 1970, at Camp Mackall, we stood guard and were on extreme alert because of the perceived Communist threat. In Russia, May Day is a very patriotic time and is celebrated as International Worker's Day. We were instructed to be highly vigilant as it was an opportunity for the "Hammer and Sickle" to strike. Heightened security was all part of our indoctrination, and I remember personally being very concerned about this at the time. We had heard all about the deadly surprise Tet Offensive in January 1968 during the lunar new year holiday in South Vietnam. We must learn from these lessons written in blood to become ever mindful and never be caught flat-footed by the enemy. The Viet Cong and the North Vietnamese Army (NVA) took the Americans completely off guard on the Vietnamese New Year. Remember how George Washington had crossed the

---

29 Mission Operations Report Apollo 13 (PDF). Houston, TX: NASA. April 28, 1970. MSC-02680.

30 "Saturn 5 Launch Vehicle Flight Evaluation Report: AS-508 Apollo 13 Mission" (PDF). George C. Marshall Space Flight Center (Huntsville, AL: NASA). June 20, 1970. MPR-SAT-FE-70-2.

Delaware on Christmas to surprise and defeat the professional Hessian forces? I was learning to be extremely proactive with my beliefs.

> "Your belief's become your thoughts. Your thoughts become your words. Your words become your actions. Your actions become your habits. Your habits become your values. Your values become your destiny."
>
> —Mahatma Gandhi

Once accepted into SF and assigned to "Group," add-on schools including SCUBA and HALO could be chosen. HALO is High Altitude Low Opening jumps that are conducted for effective clandestine insertions. Usually, small teams of special ops soldiers freefall from 30,000 feet and land together for a particular mission. The aircraft may be as far away as 10 miles from and never cross the drop zone at altitude. It would be entirely undetectable from the ground. The six or twelve-man team mission most likely would occur at night. Upon exit from the tailgate of a C-130, everyone would follow the team leader. Referred to as the "Rabbit," he was the only one with a red light on his helmet, and the team would form up on him for safety and organization. The opening altitude would depend on winds aloft, their spot, and movement across the ground. Today with ram-air canopies, much greater distances can be covered, and teams can even change DZ's during the jump if required.

My class had one final mission to complete the Q-Course successfully before graduation. It was an Escape and Evasion (E&E) maneuver back to Fort Bragg which was a distance of about 45 miles. We carried our fully loaded rucksacks and were assigned checkpoints to make. Of course, the aggressors (the enemy was, in fact, our own cadre) knew our route and were waiting with harassing fire at first then a full on L-shaped classical ambush. We had to demonstrate fire and maneuver tactics and how to "get off the X" in the simulated combat. That is, how not to become a casualty. I was not going to allow my Team to become "Dead Men Walking," on our final exercise! We carried M-14 rifles and had plenty of blank ammo.

I covertly modified my weapon into a "full auto" version to give us an edge during the exercise. Everyone gave me their extra magazines because I had the firepower that the aggressors did not expect. I fired so many rounds through my M-14 that my barrel turned cherry red in the broad daylight! I needed someone behind me just to pick up my empty magazines. Fortunately, I didn't have to clean my weapon when I turned it in. I'll bet the next guy to fire it was just a little surprised at its modified fully automatic and very abused condition!

All I could think about on this last operation was how Audie Murphy, the most decorated soldier in World War II, would have done it. What changed the balance of power for us, and, no kidding made the bad guys seriously back off was our aggressive use of signal flares as direct-fire weapons. I liberally distributed the personal handheld missiles to my A-Team. I broke into the Ammo Bunker and requisitioned multiple items that I thought would be helpful on our final mission. Hell, we aimed the flares right at the bastards using them like Rocket Propelled Grenades (RPG's). The aggressors went crazy; we weren't supposed to have that firepower! Believe me; you don't want to take a magnesium flare in the chest at any distance! Maybe we escaped because they had to put out all the brush fires we were starting. No one ever said playing fair was part of the rules of engagement (ROE). There were no rules here just as there were no rules in actual combat. We didn't care about singeing Smokey Bear's fur at that point!

For all the times that I was wet, cold, tired, hungry, or just plain scared, I had a blast! I loved the challenge of not knowing what they were going to throw at me next. It was demanding, but it was a good kind of tough. I was learning lifelong lessons and experiencing real-time what others may only see at the cinema. Not quite *Apocalypse Now* but close enough. Over time if humans have suffered yet endured and survived the same then I surely could…it was the pioneering spirit of my forefathers in me. After all, I had three separate families in my lineage that came to America on the Mayflower: Fuller, Brewster, and Hopkins. It was survival of the fittest. I grew up on a farm and could handle, figure out, or improvise most anything. I was living by my lifelong personal philosophy of "toughness is between your ears."

I was learning the SF creed. It was the code of conduct that I was to live by, fight, and possibly die to uphold. It was the warrior's moral code, the very values that we shared with the SEAL's, Rangers, Marine Corps, the Samurai, and the ancient Spartans. For the Green Berets, it was "De Oppresso Liber." Our motto was a constant reminder of our mission and the very reason that we trained to fight. It was a tournament with self…a certain competitiveness that I had been denied in Elementary School; an aggression that I had been exposed to in High School, and a Military orientation that I was thriving on with the Special Forces training.

According to the great Native American warrior Tecumseh, the real soldier must learn to live his life…and be able to die like a hero going home.

> "So live your life that the fear of death can never enter your heart. Trouble no one about their religion; respect others in their view, and demand that they respect yours. Love your life, perfect your life, beautify all things in your life. Seek to make your life long and its purpose in the service of your people. Prepare a noble death song for the day when you go over the great divide. Always give a word or a sign of salute when meeting or passing a friend, even a stranger, when in a lonely place. Show respect to all people and grovel to none. When you arise in the morning give thanks for the food and for the joy of living. If you see no reason for giving thanks, the fault lies only in yourself. Abuse no one and no thing, for abuse turns the wise ones to fools and robs the spirit of its vision. When it comes your time to die, be not like those whose hearts are filled with the fear of death, so that when their time comes they weep and pray for a little more time to live their lives over again in a different way. Sing your death song and die like a hero going home."
>
> —Tecumseh, Shawnee Chief, circa 1780

Tecumseh's words are timeless and were directed straight to my heart. It was a supremely wise philosophy for anyone. These were genuine words to live and die by and became ingrained in my psyche. For I knew that if I followed his counsel, I too would be proud and have no regrets in the end. The ideology was the very nature of Special Forces and the Warriors Ethos.

Formal graduation followed for the ones in my class that completed the first phase. There were 20 of us out of the 89 that had started at Camp Mackall. The next day, we listened to a motivational speech while in formation. Paraphrased, it was much like the talk from Class 286 and included the following three points: 1 - the world is as complex, ambiguous, and uncertain as any time in our history and it will require a special type of problem solver to wade into that uncertainty and figure things out. 2 - you are an elite Soldier, born of your experiences forged in the conventional Army. Never forget where you came from. And 3 - the Green Beret was difficult to earn, but it is even harder to wear. It is a symbol of excellence, a badge of courage, and a mark of distinction in the fight for freedom.[31]

Then we were individually awarded our personal Green Beret. I will never forget the physical presentation; I was extremely proud to serve; it was almost spiritual! The Q-Course had been exciting, challenging, and rewarding. I wanted more, Oh, how I wanted more….

I qualified for MOS training following the Q-Course, better known as Phase II of my SF experience. While in isolation, we performed tick checks for possible Lyme disease on each other while we contemplated the future. One by one, we met with Staff and discussed what MOS the Armed Services Vocational Aptitude Battery (ASVAB) had indicated that we were most qualified to perform. They told me that my strength was in communications. I already knew that I didn't want to carry the bulky 23.5-pound PRC-25 radio with multiple spare hefty batteries. The ten-foot antenna conveniently pointed down to the victim, which was me, for all the enemy to target. At that time, there were no critical MOS's to fill. Therefore, we were

---

31 http://www.specialforcesassociation.org/current-graduating-class/.

allowed to choose an area of interest. Reflexively, I wanted to know what their longest school was. Subconsciously, I guess I had been thinking about my options since Mackall. It was the 52-week combat medical training course and, just like that, I was headed to the 91A Combat Medic School right there in Fort Bragg! Currently, it is called 18 Delta (18D).

The Combat Medic was the longest school in the Army with the most severe training, it had the highest dropout rate, placed the individual under the most pressure, and required the greatest discipline to graduate. The Medic also had the reputation of having the highest casualty rate in combat. It all started with the **Combat Medic Pledge**:

> As a Special Operations Combat Medic, I pledge my honor and conscience to my country and the art of medicine.
> I recognize the responsibility that may be placed upon me for the health and lives of others.
> I confess the limitations of my skill and knowledge in caring for the sick and injured.
> I promise to follow the maxim Primum Mon Non-nocere—first do no harm and to seek the assistance of more qualified medical authority whenever available.
> Those confidences come to me in my attendance of the sick I will treat it as a secret.
> I resolved to sustain and improve my medical capabilities throughout my career as a Special Operations Combat Medic.
> As a soldier/sailor/airmen, I will place all considerations of self below those of my team, my mission, in the cause of my country.

I understood what the oath meant and the first day of school started by learning medical terminology. Our instructor was a young doctor, and the very first thing that he wrote for us on the blackboard was: bilateral-salpingo-oophor-ectomy. Then he took us by the hand and broke it all down. Bilateral-both sides, salpingo-fallopian tubes, oophor-ovaries, ectomy-surgical removal. Now that indeed made sense to me. You could also call it a total hysterectomy.

> As Socrates once said, "The beginning of all wisdom is the definition of terms."

At the same time, we started on patient histories and physical exams, the basis for medical diagnosis. It was, in fact, an accelerated Medical School! We memorized the list of key questions to ask for all the relevant human systems. I had to know and understand all the elements to pose the correct questions, to make a differential diagnosis and then finally the appropriate diagnosis. I learned the mnemonic TIM. It was a way to organize my reasoning, and it stood for Traumatic, Infectious, or Metabolic category. If I used deductive reasoning, it helped organize my decision-making process and rule in which one of those three areas held the correct diagnosis. Next, it was trauma, surgery, orthopedics, and jungle medicine.

The only problem with school was that we were also assigned guard duty at night or KP starting at 3:00 a.m. Some evenings I expertly ran the floor buffer down the endless hallways at the United States Army John Fitzgerald Kennedy Institute for Military Assistance Center (USAJKFIMA), now referred to as the U.S. Army John F. Kennedy Special Warfare Center and School (SWCS). Everyone in SF called it the White House because of its size and color.

I had many pages of notes that ended with an indiscernible scribble across the paper due to extreme sleep deprivation. I never went so far as to fall out of my classroom chair but I'm not sure why I didn't. After all, I wasn't wearing a seatbelt! I was learning to deal with chronic fatigue, not ideal for critical learning of a complex subject. During a visit home, I showed our family physician notes from my SF medic classes. He told me that it looked like the notes that he took in Medical School only in a much more compressed style.

There were 42 students that started in my class. They included friends like Robin Cox, my Class Sergeant and later my ticket for getting into the very selective Salt Lake City Physician Assistant Program (MEDEX). SF Classmate Alan Rodman was a large guy from Bakersfield, California, who always wore cowboy boots when dressed in civilian clothes. He said that it was much easier to kick someone in the mouth with pointed boots! Alan had a barrel chest and a perpetual smile but unusually small teeth. Edward Nash was a quiet, unassuming guy, and you never did quite know what he was thinking, but I felt his name was "chic."

Tim Brewer was soft-spoken, pleasant to be around, and slightly overweight. Joseph Butta was from Philadelphia and made sure that you knew he had deep-seated Mafia family connections, but he had never spent a single day in prison! David Currie was tall, handsome, always smiling, married, and I was very disappointed when he did not make it through 300-F1 and into the SF Dog Lab with me. Daniel Fawcett, Jim Flemming, and Larry Sarratt, and sometimes Mike Rozell were all skydiving buddies who made many trips to Austin, Texas to jump together at Lowman Field. Sarratt's faded blue 1964 Chevy Chevelle seemed to know the way and was always available for a drive-in movie such as *Night Of The Living Dead*, or for the trip from San Antonio to San Marcos for skydiving.

The most quirky guy in my class was John Mason Gilbert IV. He had a 1954 pink Cadillac during our SF schooling but had never acquired a Driver's License. He thought because he didn't need a permit to drive in Texas he didn't have to bother with it! He was born at a wide spot in the road along the Pecos River in West Texas named Iraan…it was pronounced, "Are-Ann!" He never had the need to use a razor either. His facial hair was virgin, unkempt, extremely delicate and very effeminate for a soldier. Terry Henderson and Michael Finn were both big but gentle guys that you wanted on your side in a fight or carrying a stretcher.

Rick Cormier, who I write about in my "time loss" travel adventure, is well described in Chapter 10, The Long And Winding Road. Richard McCarthy was a popular guy in my class, and I wonder whatever happened to him. I'm sure he was a success at whatever he did when he was discharged from the Army. I believe that Carl Whitmore was the only African-American in our group of students, about my size, and a very smart and likable fellow.

My buddy Jerome Benson and I developed a little chant when we were headed off to Raeford for some skydiving. It was in two parts. I started out, and it went like this, "Hi, I'm Ben, (and then he would chime in), and I'm Ben (and then in unison) we're Ben and Benny Benson." Then we would laugh; we were just having fun and skydiving was an integral part of it!

Randy Lippincott in Freefall, photographer unknown.

It was on the Raeford DZ, jump number 79 on May 24, 1970 that I jumped my very first used Para Commander (PC) sports parachute. It was called the Church Window because of its colored design. I made my first dead center (DC) and jumped my first Military helicopter. The Huey UH-1H had nice big doors, was fast to altitude, and could easily haul 12 jumpers. They were comfortable to ride in although the transmission sure had a high-pitched nearly deafening whine.

I remember one particular load in a Cessna 182 at Raeford, jumping with an old Sergeant (old to me most likely meant that he was 40). He was smoking in the airplane, exited with a cigarette in his mouth, and landed with the same lit cigarette still in his mouth!

What's the big deal about a few cigarette burns on your canopy? You know, it adds a little character, and it is self-limited! Who ever heard of a parachute catching fire? He was the epitome of one tough hombre and the visual equivalent of the Marlboro Man!

My first jumps at the Raeford DZ were in May, but during July, I made an elementary mistake. A new competition pit was being constructed, and I was anxious to hone my competitive edge with my new PC. I had never been up to it on the ground and didn't realize that it had not been completed. The area was nicely laid out even with an obligatory target disc but, unfortunately, it was not marked as closed or unfinished. The ten-centimeter white disc in the middle on a lanyard was inviting and contrasted nicely with the unyielding red clay just like a piece of cheese in a trap for an unsuspecting rat. The only essential component lacking was the actual impact absorbing pea gravel.

As I tried for the dead center on my 101st jump, I stretched out in my best competitive horizontal and athletic form. The first thing that I came into contact with was the cement-hard unforgiving clay surface. I didn't have any indication of danger until just before impact. There I was, unable to move, writhing in pain, and I could feel my heart pounding in my ears and infernal pain shooting down my left leg. Unable to move, the Church Window prophetically settled over me, covering my crumpled body. The resultant back pain from a bulging lumbar disc was nearly incapacitating. I hobbled my way to the Emergency Room at the Pope Army Hospital for evaluation. Eventually, I was prescribed Darvon, Soma, and crutches. While on "Profile," (the military terminology for light duty) I didn't march to class with the rest of the students for several weeks while my very painful back and left leg were mending. Because of their sedative effect, the Darvon and Soma apparently did not help my studies! Once again, I had sections of notes that were a complete mess, ending in a diagonal line off the edge of the page. There was a pharmacologic disconnect between the lecturer and my notepad. All of the narcotic effects were augmented when I took the medication on an empty stomach before class; it was all so counterproductive!

As students, we thought Boones Farm Apple Wine was a sophisticated drinking experience but best of all it was affordable. Beer, cigarettes, and marijuana were always available. So, no matter where you were, someone had a stash and was happy to share it. Some of the guys thought LSD was a superior distraction, but I preferred my "one-way trips" on a jump plane. I could see the profound effects that the little yellow paper dots of Sunshine had on my classmates, and that was not for me! Yes, I drew a line in the sand and never did cross it. Alcohol and pot were mind-altering enough for me. That, along with the music of the 60's, an eclectic variant known as rock and roll was my "thing." Later on, rock in its purest form was gradually overtaken by pop rock, beat, psychedelic rock, blues rock, and folk rock, which had all grown in popularity.[32]

In August 1970, I was transferred to Fort Sam Houston, Texas. It was the start my 91B training as a Special Forces Combat Medic at Brooke Army Medical Center (BAMC) which was the Army Burn Center in San Antonio. It was my new home. Our studies focused on laboratory values, how to operate the equipment and perform the necessary basic lab tests. We learned how to use the microscope that included the dark field examination for spirochetes (bacteria causing Syphilis, Lyme disease, and Leptospirosis). We also rehearsed skills training for suturing, tying surgical knots, placing chest tubes, giving all types of shots, starting IV's, cut-downs, placing Foley catheters, nasogastric tubes, and casting bones for fracture treatment among many other clinical talents. We practiced most of these skills on each other in the same way I cut my teeth at Mackall.

Okay, start with some teenagers, tear them down, teach them to follow orders, seriously train them to kill other human beings; and then expect them to behave in a civilized fashion. I witnessed that unruly covert behavior in SF. Someone in my class made an unorthodox statement of protest to the staff at dawn. That morning at Formation, the First Sergeant discovered the symbolic steaming protest in the CO's parking space and then "it" did hit the fan. I'm sure Rozell did it; he liked to push the envelope. I don't recall the exact grievances

---

32 http://www.allmusic.com/explore/style/singersongwriter-d197.

or even if I ever knew what they were. But since we maintained a "code of silence," the whole Company was punished for that mischief.

My only real misbehaving was of a self-destructive type. I saw it in the movies so I thought it must be cool to chug an entire fifth of whiskey while the other guys dropped acid! I failed to read the fine print about acute alcohol poisoning and liver failure. No wonder I don't recall much about that time of my life…I didn't plan to live much past 30 regardless! Now I ask you, how could you be an undercover trained killer and not be just a tad rowdy in your off time? Oh yeah!

Molon Labe

"Whatever you do you must pay the price."
—Angelika Castaneda[33]

[33] In the Heart of The Extreme Athlete, https://www.oonausa.com/interACBW.html.

CHAPTER 9
Into the Mist—Gravity Is So Overrated

Christmas 1970. I was home on leave from Fort Sam Houston, and I had been skydiving out at the farm in Nebraska. My fifteen-year-old brother Loren was doing his best to convince Dad and me that he was ready to make his first jump. It was perfect weather and mostly I was the only one jumping and having fun. At some point, I guess we discussed that my brother Loren would make a jump even though he was underage. He knew that I had all the student gear for him to make a static line jump right there at home. The more we talked about it, the more natural it seemed. I knew all the fundamentals but had never performed them or been certified as an actual jumpmaster.

Loren did his best to convince us he was ready; it was more like begging and on the verge of badgering! You know how children can be once they get an idea in their head, and the chatter can be constant enough to wear you down. Dad was equally complicit because he was supervising us as the pilot of the jump aircraft. It just so happened that my mom and my sister, Ronda, had gone into town for a day of shopping. We had selective amnesia regarding Steve's broken leg from the previous Christmas, as it was never discussed on the traumatic anniversary.

I laid out all the gear needed for Loren, and together we packed his surplus B-4 rig and set up the static line with an 80-pound cotton break cord. It was just like the student parachute that I had used. Now this activity was only possible because our father had become so familiar with the skydiving scene that removing the aircraft door was no longer an issue. We weren't a rogue operation since we had the approved paperwork for door removal on that aircraft to make it legitimate.

As part of the introduction to skydiving and the progression into freefall, the student must first be poised while standing on the wheel and hanging onto the strut. From that position, a hop backward, and an exaggerated spread-eagle should place the pupil in a stable face-down position in preparation for controlled freefall or to pull his ripcord. A controlled exit was the beginning of stable freefall and helped build confidence for the student.

Just like that, and it was Loren's day of reckoning. Again, we talked about everything as I had lectured and demonstrated to Loren nearly 100 times before, all in preparation for this day. Then I had him go through the motions with the plane still on the ground. I described steering the canopy and landings, specifically the PLF (do as I say, not as I do). We also reviewed the necessary emergency procedures, the cutaway in the case of a main canopy malfunction along with tree, power line, and water landings—all which were conceivable but unlikely. After I was comfortable that he had, in fact, assimilated all the information that would be necessary for a successful jump, I helped Loren gear up and then I put on my rig.

Dad already had the right seat, door, and control column removed from the Cessna. I had Loren back up to the door, and I attached his static line to the seatbelt anchor, just as my jumpmaster had done for me. I silently repeated all the last minute equipment checks for both the student and me. The excess static line was neatly stowed under the main container bungees with the strict instruction for Loren to guard his reserve ripcord handle at all costs. Twenty months earlier, I had been the student in the same position, and I knew what he was feeling.

Rolling past the big orange windsock, we took off to the north over Prairie Creek from the grass runway at the farm, climbed to 2,800 feet and was set up for the jump run. Loren looked quite serious but not tense or worried. The reality was sinking in just a little bit for the fifteen-year-old as he stared out the very open door of the aircraft. I repeated some key instructions as a distraction in the loud and windy cabin. Dad was focused on flying the airplane and was apparently confident in my abilities. Loren took every word out of my mouth as gospel. I had the life of my little brother in my hands, and it was all just for fun! When I was satisfied with our position, Dad slowed the airplane, and I gave Loren the command to "Get out." Mechanically, he did as I instructed. I handled the static line to ensure a positive opening. When I saw that he was comfortable and ready, I slapped him on the thigh and said, "Go!" With only a slight hesitation, he was off!

In his logbook on that momentous day, I wrote, "Good exit, fine arch, good canopy control." As jumpmaster, I watched his canopy, which I had packed only an hour before, open flawlessly, and then I hauled in the static line without fanfare. Although this was my first time in that role, it went off without a hitch, just as I had planned. No, he did not have his mother's permission. Yes, he was underage. No, Loren had never undergone formal schooling. Yes, I was not licensed to jumpmaster anyone, let alone a first jump student!

Dad circled to the right as I continued to observe Loren maneuver the parachute and finally land. It took a total of two and a half minutes. I stowed the static line out of the way in the back of the plane. I had Dad climb a little bit for the next pass. I exited with a five-second delay and deliberately landed between Loren and the staging area. It was an impressive effort on everyone's part, and within the hour, we were doing it all over again. A real bonding event had occurred for the three of us, in no small part due to the positive outcome.

As I've said before, my philosophy is that it is easier to ask for forgiveness than it is to ask for permission. That's just what happened when Mother returned from town and discovered the mischief that we had been creating. My dad didn't mind taking the heat. In retrospect, I think that he unquestionably started living just a little bit through his boys. We were pushing the envelope and having an excellent time of it! My father was not your typical man. In fact, he was an extraordinary man. Not only was he a father and husband, but he had fought in World War II, came home, built up the farm by himself where I was raised, and eventually earned his pilot's license. Dad had a scantily clad vintage Vargas pinup on the inside of his closet door during my growing years and subscribed to *True The Man's Magazine* during the 1960s. He was honest, well-spoken, with a great disposition, good sense of community, and a steadfast work ethic.

Loren's first freefall was recorded on June 5, 1971, under my tutelage. He demonstrated acceptable performance on the first static line jump that day, which was followed by his initial freefall, that is,

Loren's first "hop, and pop." He made 28 total jumps between the farm and the LSPC over the next few years. Eight were static line jumps due to the length of time between experiences. His highest skydive was from 12,500 feet with a 60-second delay over his three-and-a-half year endeavor.

Into the Mist

While stationed in San Antonio for jump pay purposes, my military static line jumps were at Hondo DZ every two or three months. My civilian jumps were over the San Marcos Lowman Field just South of Austin, Texas. Usually, three or four of the guys from school would drive up for the weekend and be back on base Sunday night. The one jump that stands out above all others, literally, was above and into a single cumulus cloud. Texas can display some textbook meteorological phenomena in a big way. That day, Mother Nature chose to exhibit widely scattered towering cumulus clouds literally from the horizon to horizon, as far as the eye could see. Individually, they were miles apart. The bases were uniformly at 3,000 feet above the ground, without any cell towers, and the tops were at 13,000 feet. The desire was too great! The majestic vapor pillars were alluring and begged to be penetrated. We coaxed our pilot into flying over the top of the towering cloud nearest the DZ at 13,500 feet. It was all very legal right up to the point of our exit over that sinister white mass.

Three of us "cowboys" naively planned to assemble inside the cloud. How hard could that be? We had plenty of time. On top of the very friendly-looking fluffy cloud, we thought that we could easily make a three-man star in the allotted 70 seconds in freefall. Little did we know it was not only a shot in the dark but also a foolish plunge into the great unknown. After our exit, we were quickly enveloped in the mist, and even minimal visibility was futile. It was a billowing cumulus after all! My judgment is what had been clouded, and I was unquestionably flying blind! My goggles instantly fogged up and started streaking water droplets in the 100 percent humidity. Any possibility of seeing either of my friends was quickly replaced with a defensive 180-degree turn, and I hoped like hell no one was doing the same thing right below me. The plan was to exit the cloud and enter clear air before opening. To deploy a canopy under an unsuspecting jumper would be lethal with a potential 120 mph collision. I would never see it coming, and it would be super quick! Maybe, just maybe, the rules had some merit after all! Could it be that the studies at the National Institutes of Health indicating the part of the brain that restrains risky behavior, bad judgment, and poor thinking skills are not fully developed until the age of 25 had some credence? "Stupid is as stupid does." Now I can say that my hindsight is 20/20 in the meteorological arena.

The big friendly fluffy cloud quickly turned deadly. Although the penetration of the chalky mass was novel and enjoyable at first, it was not without impactful anxiety. In a few seconds, I could start to feel the moisture buildup on the front side of my jumpsuit and, more importantly, it impeded my vision. I had the same optical sensation as driving down a fog-laden road at 120 miles an hour, with scattered flashes of limited visibility mixed with a dense veil of bright light. It was mesmerizing with strobe-like qualities. Although I didn't have to worry about running off the road, there would be no way of stopping if I suddenly saw one of my friends on a collision course. It was just like playing Russian roulette, and I had already pulled the trigger several times. Any impact would have instantly resulted in two deaths. In my naïveté, I didn't even consider the possibility of precipitating a lightning strike. All of the components were present.

Clouds**:** A short film about dreaming before the main feature… Infinity.[34]

Inside the mist, a dramatic occurrence in the form of a small circular halo appeared below me. The sunlight refracted around my falling body and cast a shadow in the cloud with a dazzling rainbow ring around it called a "glory." This optical phenomenon resembles an

---

34 Allure of the Seas, aft staircase, port side, level 11.

iconic saint's halo around the shadow of the observer.[35] The glory was ironically prophetic and a bad omen for me. I didn't want to see a halo around my head just yet! I was not feeling all that angelic; apparently, my wings were not working very well either.

Relying on my faith and altimeter, after suddenly erupting from the cloud base at 3,000 feet, I quickly located the other two jumpers and set myself up to land on the DZ. All three of us had fortunately maintained good separation, and there was never a risk of collision. Check that box! I was happy to have made the jump but never had the urge to repeat it…ever! In retrospect, it was a willfully reckless act, but boy was it a fun ride; 10,000 feet of fluff! The mocking paradox was that I was signed off for my C-license on that exact jump. I had recently made my first planned night jump, and number 137 was necessary to qualify for the coveted jumpmaster rating that came with real adult responsibilities. I had come a long way since first jumpmastering myself on my 11th, 12th, and 13th jumps in Kansas. Luckily, I didn't have to prove good judgment or impeccable moral fiber to be eligible.

Adventure is the essence of life.
—Dick Rutan

When someone asks me if I have ever been injured while skydiving, my pat response is, "Why yes, I had my feelings hurt once because the aircraft left without me!" But the truth is that I had a severe right ankle injury. It was due to an untimely turn near the ground at dusk on that same San Marcus field. I didn't have a good excuse for the miscalculation. Frankly, I was surprised that I could even sustain such a freak injury. At the time, I was convinced that I had broken my right ankle. The swelling was immediate, extensive, and the pain was excruciating. I didn't think to elevate my ankle or use ice and a compressive Ace wrap. The severe injury caused me to finish my 91B class on crutches for the second time due to skydiving. It was just part of the whole package that was an acceptable risk for a high adventure sport.

---

35 "Does the glory have a simple explanation?" Opt. Lett. 27, 1379-1381 (2002).

CHAPTER 10
The Long and Winding Road

I sat down at the bar to the left of Command Sergeant Major David L. Clark. It was my last day of skydiving at the Raeford DZ, and I was in the Green Beret Sports Parachute Club to say my goodbyes at Fort Bragg. No one else was there that early afternoon. Sergeant Major Clark was the consummate SF leader, accomplished jumper, and skydiver. His awards and decorations spoke volumes. John Wayne had even mentioned that he wanted to be like Sergeant Major Clark! Recently, to conclude his 56 years of federal service, he was inducted as a distinguished member of the Special Forces Regiment.

That spring day in 1971 as I struck up a conversation about skydiving, I mentioned that I had just received my overseas orders. He asked me where I was assigned, and I told him that Europe was my destination. With a straight face, Sergeant Major asked if I was interested in a position on the 7th Army Parachute Team. My actual answer was, "Will it require more than my first born?" He replied with, "Now don't get excited son, but I think they can use you." Sergeant Major Clark told me that First Sergeant Don Strickland was at the National Parachuting Championships in Tahlequah, Oklahoma. Clark promised that he would contact Strickland when he returned to West Germany. My feeling was one of quiet elation. I was to go home on leave, and my mission was to complete the requirements for my D-license before I arrived in Europe, as the Sergeant Major suggested. I fully embraced my new assignment with dogged determination.

I made the uneventful 1,400-mile trip home in my 1968 burgundy four-door Peugeot. It took 24 hours, and I drove straight through the night. While in Fort Bragg, I had purchased the little car from two local nurses. It averaged an honest 35 miles per gallon on the highway with regular gas, and I never had one bit of trouble with it. Well, not exactly...I did have one "situation" with the little French sedan. A fellow SF classmate of mine, Rick Cormier, and I planned a weekend getaway to Myrtle Beach for a little R&R. You know guys and bikinis have a way of attracting each other!

We took off after class on a Friday without a firm agenda or reservations anywhere. We were playing it strictly by ear. Rick had a terrific voice and loved to sing. He also had a portable cassette tape deck, and we played the heck out of the ten-minute version of the 1970 Grand Funk song "I'm Your Captain" (Closer to Home). Strangely, we also played some Creedence Clearwater Revival on that tape including the 1969 Midnight Special. No, the cassette tape never broke, but maybe it was a foreboding sign in retrospect.

Stay with me on this.

The two of us were having a great time on the first part of the road trip. The weather was beautiful and the forecast for the weekend was the same. Absolutely no alcohol or drugs were involved but somehow after sundown we got turned around. It was still early, about 9:00 p.m. and I was driving on an isolated two-lane blacktop country road. The mostly straight and level highway was through a heavily pine forested area. Without warning, the car suddenly lost all electrical power, and I coasted onto the shoulder in the profound darkness. If you ever saw the prologue of *Twilight Zone, The Movie*, then you have an idea of the possibilities for two guys in a stalled car on a deserted road. We got out and looked under the hood. Maybe the battery cable or fan belt had come unhooked or something. I carefully checked all the fuses. We had no tools, and it was pre-cell phone days. We had plenty of gas, so that was never an issue.

Rick and I talked about different things that could cause an abrupt and total electrical failure in the otherwise reliable car. He was not a mechanic, but he had his own Corvette at home and was experienced at troubleshooting car problems. Since I had grown up on a farm and was around machinery my entire life, I knew a thing or two about such issues. We were miles away from any country houses, buildings, or any light source whatsoever. We were experiencing a complete blackout. It did not occur to us to try to play the battery operated tape deck to see if it had power because we were focused on the problem at hand.

However, my wristwatch was mechanical, not battery operated, and it was working properly. I did not have a flashlight so we could not testify to the complete absence of any electrical source. There was no answer to the mysterious problem, and we were simply not going anywhere soon. We had no intention of walking for help, and there was no traffic on that remote country road. In retrospect, the strange, subtle thing was that there didn't seem to be an urgency of any kind to our situation. It all seemed routine. We were just killing time waiting for nothing to happen.

Thinking back, as I can recall the odd "insignificant occasion," it seems that I, in fact, watched the entire occurrence from 100 feet above, behind, and slightly to the left of the parked car. With good night vision, I could see the empty road stretching out ahead of us into the dark forest, and the surrounding woods. There was a nearby small open meadow that was slightly up-sloping, about five acres in size. At the crest was an area to the left on the very edge of the field where there were likely buildings and a power line. Nothing was distinguishable to me, there were no lights, but I could clearly see the parked car below me in the dark. We had been enveloped in the night under a moonless inky black sky. We didn't realize it at the time, but we were being held in limbo by some entirely unknown force! I have a mental picture from somewhere in the air but no detail of how I could have possibly gotten there.

After 2:00 a.m. the following day, the next thing that I was aware of, we were undeniably headed down that same remote blacktop; however, now we were on the return trip to Fort Bragg. Suddenly, it was Sunday morning and the weekend was coming to an end; we were released from the "force field" that must have held us captive. Strangely enough, we were pointed in the same direction as when we had pulled over; I never turned around. No, we did not get a tow truck. A "Good Samaritan" did not stop by to give us a jump. We did not hike down the road for help. There still was absolutely no traffic on the road. Abruptly and without explanation, we were just driving without speaking. The car was running perfectly…it was as if nothing had happened, as though we had never even stopped.

I had no memory of the lights coming on or cranking the starter and finally getting it to turn over—nothing! The return trip was straightforward, and we just seemed to know how to get back to Fort Bragg after being stranded. I never referred to a map. We didn't speak of it again nor did I think that a time loss event was "unnatural" at that point. It was like our power of reasoning had been temporarily suspended too. There was no possible rational explanation regarding the unexpected complete power failure and the sudden resumption of travel heading home without fanfare. It strangely seemed to be a "nonevent." We made absolutely no repairs on the car. There was only one assumption to be made that combines a suspension of electrical power and spontaneous loss of memory. It was the possibility of some form of extraterrestrial intervention.

We hadn't even heard of the concept of an electromagnetic pulse (EMP) nor did we consider a transient electromagnetic disturbance that could theoretically emanate from a UFO. We had no reason to believe that we were in some top secret area that the military was using to carry out trials with "experimental weapons."

I had no recollection of any strange colored rotating lights in the sky or pale, wide-eyed bodies on the deserted road walking mechanically toward us. We neither saw nor at least remembered anything unusual. It was a complete blank! I recalled only the total loss of power, pulling over to the side of the road, and viewing it from above. The otherwise reliable car had suddenly and completely stopped, we stepped out to look under the hood and then around 29 hours later we were driving down the same road, in the same direction, without any explanation! We weren't hungry and never stopped to eat. If Rick remembered anything, he never mentioned it to me. We never made it to Myrtle Beach that weekend, and we completely missed out on Saturday. This experience remains a bona fide puzzle for me in my later years. What happened that night in the remote backwoods of the Carolinas? I have never felt the need for regression therapy…well, maybe a little. Nor have I ever had another "time loss" event or out-of-body experience. But shouldn't it make me a little bit curious?

CHAPTER 11
My Date with Destiny

During my leave home in June 1971 before rotating to Europe, my singular objective was to qualify for my D-license. The aim was to bolster my resumé for possible membership on the 7th Army Parachute Team. I had no guarantees at that point and only my brief unplanned conversation with Sergeant Major Clark. First, with my dad's help, I had to make 17 additional skydives to bring my freefall total up to 200. The D-license called for five 60-second delays, night and water jump, a demonstration of accuracy, a barrel roll to the right and left, and an in-flight witnessed "Chinese series." This last task consisted of a timed front loop, back loop, right 360-degree turn, and a left 360-degree turn. All tasks needed to be done with utmost precision and control. To get the official sign off for the highest United States Parachute Association (USPA) License, I would have to jump with the club in Lincoln, but 100 percent of these qualifying jumps were signed off by the jump pilot or another jumper.

It was the end of the week, and Dad set aside time to fly for me at the farm. The convenience of having our own plane, runway, and built-in DZ was huge. However, the time had gotten away from me when I noticed that it was 6:30 and I had a 7:00 p.m. date with my high school sweetheart, Ginger Uzendoski. She lived 17 miles away, the last seven of which were on a gravel road. I conferred with Dad, and he agreed that the quickest way to get there was by air.

With the modified transportation solution, I estimated that I would be only 15 minutes late. I called Ginger with the new plan but gave no real explanation. I told her just to stand out in the middle of the yard at 7:15 and I would be there. Hurriedly, I showered, dressed, and drove the short distance back out to the runway and the waiting Cessna. I threw on my rig, and we were in the air in no time. It was to be my sixth jump of the day! Dad knew right where to fly, and we were soon at 5,300 feet over Ginger's farm at the prescribed time. Since I had been jumping all afternoon, I knew how to gauge the winds. I gave Dad a couple of corrections and then he cut the engine to make it easier for me to open the door for a clean exit. In a flash, I was out on a 20-second delay and uneventfully deployed the old 28-foot steerable canopy. After my exodus, Dad did a wingover and headed for home low-level where he was most comfortable flying. I easily landed in the horse corral, a little short of the big tree-lined farmyard with power lines where my date was waiting for me.

Ginger was thrilled and impressed by the uniqueness of my little escapade! In just a few minutes, I field packed my parachute, zipped off my jumpsuit James Bond-style, and threw them in the trunk of her car. Not thinking anything of it, we headed into Fullerton and then on to dinner and a movie in Grand Island. Halfway into town, we met the entire Volunteer Fire Department, EMS, and Rescue trucks full-throttle on the way to a serious accident. As we pulled back onto the gravel road, we turned to each other and said that we hadn't seen any indication of a fire anywhere. We wondered what the emergency was. Wow, whatever it was, it must be big to demand that amount of fanfare!

As it turned out, the next day Ginger called me with an update. A neighbor had called in the emergency report saying there was a catastrophic airplane crash because they heard the engine abruptly "stall," saw the pilot bail out, plunge through the air, and deploy his emergency parachute. At the same time, the plane suddenly turned and dove toward the ground. They thought the plane must surely be close by, but didn't know exactly where it had impacted. I guess the fire chief thought they would just drive around long enough until they spotted a guy hitchhiking with a parachute over his shoulder or a column of black smoke from the wreckage. Everyone knows that airplanes always burst into flames and black smoke when they crash. After all, it shouldn't be that hard to spot in broad daylight! What they needed was another airplane to "find" the site of the accident. Hey, you can't make this stuff up!

Needless to say, I never pulled that little impromptu stunt again in Nance County. I didn't relish the idea of dealing with the Polish authorities or get my name in the paper. I knew that with enough time they were going to figure it out and be red-faced. As it turned out, that was excellent training for hundreds of other jumps that I was going to make in many tight and desperate places, not only in the United States but also in major European cities. I found it to be very exciting and challenging. I knew that each and every jump had the same risk as the first...death, or worse, crippled for life.

Although I joined the Army to do battle, I had always tried to avoid fights in high school. If I had been bigger, there were occasions that I would have demanded justice. However, there were several incidents from my past that could have ended in disaster:

As a sophomore, I had my license and drove to Fullerton one Saturday night in my red 1960 Ford Starliner that cost my brother and me $1,200. It came equipped with a boss 352 cubic inch engine, four-barrel Holley carburetor, three-speed Hurst shifter on the floor, and Astro Mags. Yes, it was a sweet muscle car and could haul some serious ass! I understand that it was also the widest production car ever made.

That evening, I pulled into an abandoned gas station and was surprised when Francis Morgan appeared at my window and tried to pull me out of the car in somewhat of a drunken stupor. Well, that would have been a truly Herculean event because, although my window was down, I still had my seatbelt on! I had no idea what had provoked him other than girl or car envy. Although I had gone to country school with Francis, I didn't recognize him under the influence, in his aggressive, ill-advised, and artificially "macho" state.

I could have started the Ford and driven off, but that didn't enter my mind. Instead, I reached down to undo my seatbelt and threw the big heavy door wide open. My reaction surprised Francis, and as soon as he regained his composure, being the much larger, taller, and older person, he came after me with a vengeance. Then, after I had deflected a few of his suboptimal jabs, he tackled me. Once on the concrete, it was easy for him to keep me on my back. As he tried to punch me in the face, I was able to block his less than precise blows. As he started to fatigue I grabbed his shirt with my left hand, pulled him close, and started to pound away at his face with my right fist, jackhammer style. I aimed directly at his nose, and the blood ran everywhere but mostly on me and my shirt. I was able to pummel him at will, and at last, he seemed to have had enough and rolled off of me after not landing a single blow. Somehow, I doubted that he had learned his lesson that night about drinking and fighting!

Not wanting to wait around for any of his Navy buddies, I hopped in my car and drove off. On the way out of town, I ended up at Rhonda Christensen's where I cleaned up and washed most of the blood off. Since I was wearing cutoffs, I didn't realize that both knees and elbows had suffered significant abrasions on the rough and broken concrete in the "fight club" arena. My wounds were lightly bandaged, and I headed home never to mention any of this to my parents.

> I won't be wronged. I won't be insulted. I won't be laid a hand on. I don't do these things to other people, and I require the same from them.
>
> —John Wayne, *The Shootist* (1976)

Not all fights with the Fullerton thugs were with fists or bigger opponents. Late one night, there were three of us in my car when we were run out of town for no particular reason. If I had to guess, it was most likely alcohol-related on their end. Yes, I had dated Ginger, one of their cheerleaders all through high school, and I suppose they were resentful. The aggressive act came with the threat of gunplay; yes, we saw muzzle flashes coming from their car. Fortunately, they did not follow us very far into Merrick County nor were they very accurate shots. I did carry a revolver in my glove box but did not have to use it that night; it would have been so ugly! Unfortunately, I believe that it was another one of my country school classmates in the chase car. What had I done? I guess those guys held grudges but couldn't hold their liquor.

The next great car chase was during my senior year. This time it was in Merrick County driving my dad's new tan Ford pickup truck. Somehow I fell into the crosshairs of a guy by the name of Hotchkiss. I had no idea what I could have done to upset him. Maybe he thought that I was someone else. He chased me westbound through Central City and out of town to the north trying to run me off the road. Fortunately, I was by myself. Funny thing, I didn't even know the guy. Plainly, I could not lose him and figured that alcohol must have been involved. My next idea was to head out past Hord Lake where I could cross the Platte River. It was on the old one lane extremely narrow and about a quarter mile long wooden plank bridge at speeds in excess of 65 mph. I had unwittingly trained for this, just for fun over the years, and now I hoped that it was going to pay off.

The gravel road at the south end of the bridge was a T-intersection. I kept him on my tail along the rickety bridge. My whole being was focused like a laser on the last plank and the end of the railing on the long, precarious, ancient bridge. I slammed on the brakes as hard as I could and made the 90-degree right turn at the last possible instant. Sliding sideways, spinning tires, I threw gravel into the darkness. I recovered control of the truck as I accelerated as hard as the six-banger would take me through four gears. His headlights were still on my tail. He had managed the hairpin turn and was in hot pursuit, but I had grown up on country roads and was able to push the envelope.

Very quickly, a left turn came up. Caught in his personal desire to close in on me for a pit maneuver, Hotchkiss veered into the ditch as I managed the next 90-degree turn. I can still see his lights in my rearview mirror, bouncing up and down in the tall reeds alongside the road behind me. I did not wait around to discuss current events or see if he was going to call AAA. I'll bet he was pissed! He had a nice long walk into town to cool off, but his car was still stuck in that muddy ditch. Frankly, he was lucky as he could have just as easily rolled it. Either way, I was headed home unscathed, and I had no plan of returning to the scene of the crime!

It wasn't more than a week later that I watched *Cool Hand Luke* at the Central City State Theater. When my date and I came out after the movie, all four of my truck tires had been slashed. Next, I expected to see a pile of parking meters on the sidewalk, also the handiwork of some intoxicated vandal (review the opening scenes of the movie with Paul Newman). I had parked in a lighted area in front of the theater, and an eyewitness disclosed to me that Ron Hotchkiss did it. My Dad reported the crime to Sheriff Dan Schneiderheinz. Apparently, Hotchkiss had an existing "rap sheet," was on parole, and ended up back in prison for his unprovoked act of aggression.

Why were all of these people after me? I believe that it was mostly fueled by women, alcohol, and a long-standing town rivalry. In the case of the Hotchkiss road rage, I think I was in the wrong place at the right time. I had never even spoken to the guy. Was I going to have to move to Germany to get away from all of this violence? As it turned out, West Germany was where the Baader-Meinhof Gang and the Palestinian group, Black September had chosen to terrorize. Yes, I lived there during the Munich massacre of the Israeli Olympic Team during the 1972 Summer Olympics.

While still on leave, I successfully planned and executed a water jump at McHargue Lake for my D-license. I scheduled it just before heading into Lincoln as I knew I would need to have my reserve canopy aired out, inspected, and repacked. I found that a second jump on the main parachute was just the ticket to dry it instantly! BAM, 120 mph wind blast dried out ripstop nylon in a split-second! The opening even sounded different and was accompanied by a pleasing light mist.

My next qualification jumps were over Agnew, Nebraska. Cliff Dobson D-1193 signed me off for my Chinese series and my final certifying dives for the D-license. I made it, and I could hardly believe that I had reached that important benchmark! All of the stars were aligned, and my ambitions were coming to fruition. I had put in the time and effort, and everything was turning up roses. I thought to myself, next stop, Europe. I was anxious yet confident in thinking that I could be qualified and lucky enough to be assigned to the prestigious 7th Army Parachute Team. The sky was the limit, and I loved the possibilities!

I had safely driven all the way home from Fort Bragg in my 1968 burgundy Peugeot 404 with a sunroof. Then Steve Steckmyer and Dan Hord helped me celebrate by standing up in that sunroof, half out of the car making loud animal noises and drawing serious attention to us as we drove through the University of Nebraska Campus. Somehow, I recall open alcoholic containers in the vehicle. Yes, miraculously the campus cops understood the significance of qualifying for my D-license, and they let me off with just a warning. Being in the military seemed to be paying off! My only instructions were that I try and keep it between the ditches and hold it down.

Qualifying for my D-license was a crossroads in my career and made the pursuit of all my aspirations possible. The license demanded respect and did show a high level of technical competency. At the time, there was only one higher rating, and that was the Instructor/ Examiner (I/E) Certification. Later, I earned my FAA Master Rigger and Instructor ratings. I felt like I had arrived. It was a goal that I had been working toward and it was all made possible through my father's support.

CHAPTER 12
The 7th Army Parachute Team

June 1971 West Germany. My arrival at Rose Barracks, Headquarters and Headquarters Company, 8th Infantry Division was unceremonious. I spent that first 24 hours going back and forth between my bunk and the latrine. I didn't know if it was the flu or food poisoning. After 48 hours, the company clerk, Terry Patterson, showed up with my 7th Army Parachute Team orders. I was impressed with his distinctive black jumpsuit and Garrison cap. Assigned to the Second of the 509th in Mainz (Tom Mackall's Unit), I was attached to Headquarters and Headquarters Company, 8th Infantry Division, for special duty with the 7th Army Parachute Team. Just like that, I was in! Sergeant Major Clark was good with his word and made my assignment possible.

My official rank on the team was sergeant. I was an acting sergeant or the slang we used was an "Act'n Jack." My rank was E-5, but my pay grade was still E-4. I guess the Army knew they had the upper hand since I was officially "special duty," and exempt from typical Army rules and hardships. After my arrival in Europe, I was never given the opportunity to take my E-5 Boards. The specialist rank was related to a job assignment, and I was a trained combat medic.

Since I was not married, I was assigned a cot and locker at the Rose Barracks on post. Bruce Groff was my first roommate. Patterson drove me down to the airfield where I met the commanding officer (CO) Captain Gordon (Mike) McPherson, First Sergeant Don Strickland, and most of the team members (a total of 16 skydivers and one officer). I was issued my parachute gear: brand new French jump boots, several black Pioneer jumpsuits to be embossed with my name and a 7th ATP patch (used ones for every day work and brand new ones for show), a new white Bell helmet with large black USA letters on the front, gloves, goggles, and a locker in the hangar to store my gear next to the packing tables. We were also issued several ubiquitous aviator kit bags for general-purpose organization and military-style travel luggage. We had gray sweats for physical training (PT), and Olympic-style athletic warm-ups for casual wear during competitions.

In addition to our jump gear, we were issued dress blazers with an embellished pin-on 7th APT crest for the breast pocket. These were worn on formal social occasions. We were "freefall" ambassadors and were expected to look the part. I had traveled a long road from my first jump in the spring of 1969 to this day. Now my real skydiving journey was about to commence. I had reached the enviable status of a "professional," and the path that I would travel would be more than I could ever imagine.

7th Army Parachute Team Crest.

The hangar was where all the Team work activity in Bad Kreuznach took place for us. It was where we did our trip planning and maintained our gear. Captain McPherson's office was in an enclosed room on the south side of the hangar. However, I was never invited or ordered to enter this room. I have no idea how I dodged that bullet. There were many occasions where I could have been called on the carpet or even fired from the team!

The central space in the hangar was occupied by a half dozen of the nearly 50-foot long packing tables. Another sizable room on the north side was where all the team trophies were displayed on the walls and under glass cases. I don't remember if I ever counted them, but they were prolific; they were all different, impressively beautiful, and from all over Europe. These awards were not like sports or car trophies in the United States; some were of fine cut glass, others hand carved wood, and many were engraved metal cups and such. Banners and small flags of all types were displayed to document dates and places. It was a conspicuous show of pride. I loved it and was anxious to make my contribution!

The routine workweek was as follows: show up at the hangar after breakfast by 8:00 a.m. in sweatpants ready for physical training (PT). The first thing the entire team did in formation was military-style calisthenics, and we did this every day. One of the senior NCOs would lead the workout and call cadence. Afterward, team members went for a jog around the airfield at different intervals and at their own pace. I don't know why but we always ran counterclockwise around the inactive runway.

On one of those outings, a team member, Sam Alston, was late and ran by himself. On the west end of the far north side of the field, an elderly German couple was walking on government property in the opposite direction. As Sam approached in his gray sweat suit, the couple's German Shepherd broke loose and charged him. Sam was startled and back peddled in an attempt to avoid the dog. The Shepherd attacked Sam, biting him and puncturing his scrotum. Apparently, Sam did not suffer any permanent disability; he has a child but does not have a dog that can jump above his knee. You see, it certainly did take balls to be on the team!

7th Army Parachute Team, Circa 1971. Photo Courtesy US Army. Back row Left to Right: Command Sergeant Major Harold B. Stanley, Sgt. Pete Zadick, Sgt. Terry Patterson, Company Clerk, Sgt. Cal Callaghan, Sgt. Steve Bienert, Captain Gordon (Mike) McPherson. Front row Left to Right: Sgt. Mike Wasley, Sgt. John Cutts, Sgt. Ronnie Walker, Sgt. Pat (Rip) VanBibber, Sgt. Randy Lippincott, Sgt. Bill Waters, Sgt. Hershel Fisher, Sgt. Rob Robinson, Sgt. David Layne, Sgt. Guy Leverett, Sgt. Moe Mohundro.

During the week, we received air support from the 350th Aviation Company (18th Aviation Battalion USAREUR) out of Fliegerhorst Kaserne Hanau that appeared around 9:00 a.m. I could always identify the "whop-whop" of the incoming Huey miles away before I could ever see it. When I first arrived in West Germany, we made our practice jumps at the Baumholder DZ. It was the same place where Rommel trained and indoctrinated his 15th Division Afrika Korps World War II tank commanders.[36]

Later on, we were approved to jump at our own airfield in Bad Kreuznach. There was no commuting involved, and we had our own pea gravel pit for compitition. However, we didn't mind the Baumholder trips because we typically flew low level over a nudist colony! The flight was a recurrent and laconic distraction for us! The standard day was about five jumps, but I occasionally logged up to eight skydives. During the week, we worked on our show or any specialty jumps, and almost every weekend we flew somewhere for a demonstration or competition.

Now I was a freefall professional! First, I was trained as an infantry soldier, next as a paratrooper, and then I received advanced training as a Special Forces Combat Medic. For my tour of duty, I was attached to the 8th Infantry Division (ID) for Special Duty with the 7th Army Parachute Team (APT) as a Freefall Exhibitionist. The titles were a bit confusing, but I loved it! It's so great when a plan comes together!

We frequently flew with the doors open, and eventually the temptation overwhelmed me. In flight, I would climb outside the helicopter, stand on the strut, walk up to the pilot's window, knock on it to get his attention, and when he lowered the window in a nonchalant demeanor, I'd ask, "How much longer?" Sometimes I got a look of surprise and other times of disgust. The initial disbelief was usually followed by, "Please come back inside the helicopter and sit the hell down…."

As a pilot, I understood the center of gravity (CG) and the weight and balance effects on aircraft performance. So, I started an innocent

---

[36] Part 2: War Comes to Baumholder. http://www.ww2onyourown.com/Baumholderhistwarcomes.html.

game on long trips to break the monotony. Without fanfare, we would all slowly shift to one side of the helicopter. After the pilot had trimmed the aircraft (adjusted the pressures on the controls for straight and level flight), we would all quietly move to the opposite side. The subtle changes would cause him to have to re-trim for the gross change in lateral CG. Most of the sharp aircraft commanders quickly caught on to what we were doing and put a stop to it. We were just breaking in a new pilot!

Randy Lippincott in Freefall, photo by Mike Wasley.

Shows were primarily in West Germany, but they could have been anywhere in Europe or, in the case of Berlin, behind the Iron

Curtain in East Germany. We boarded a C-141 to Great Britain, took a C-130 to Aviano, Italy, drove to Austria, Belgium, Switzerland, and France, and hopped a C-119 to Pisa, Italy. However, we took the Huey "H" model helicopter almost everywhere in West Germany and Luxembourg. The Huey was a nearly perfect jump platform because it could carry all the people and equipment for the show. Also, it could land and takeoff conveniently on the demonstration field, which typically was a sportplatz or soccer field in a village or city center.

Before my arrival, the team had just returned from a show in Morocco, North Africa. While I was there, I was disappointed to have trips canceled to Rome and another to Normandy for the D-Day celebration. The latter was an especially bitter pill for me to swallow because those beaches were hallowed ground fought for and won by the blood of the "Greatest Generation." I felt like I was missing a crucial opportunity to pay my respects and help celebrate all of those young American lives.

The typical demo team consisted of eight men, with two on the first jump for the baton pass, and one man out of each side of the helicopter for good separation, trailing smoke, then coming together for a hookup, followed by a slow spiral for a candy cane effect with red smoke. Upon landing, one of the jumpers would present the official memento to a VIP. The second pass at 10,000 feet AGL would be the four-man formation jump. Four jumpers would assemble as a diamond, track or move across the sky as a tight formation, and then separate in a dynamically outstanding bomb burst effect. We would open our canopies simultaneously and still land directly in front of the onlookers. The last solo jumper was the cutaway. He had three parachutes: the cutaway canopy was a disposable reserve (we tried to recover it, if possible, to be reused), his main parachute to maneuver in front of the crowd, and his actual emergency reserve of last resort. The eighth man was the announcer and ground control.

Bill Waters always wore his parachute when we traveled by air, earning him the nickname Bailout Bill. He jumped the Delta II Wing with a masochistic vengeance. The canopy was shaped like a triangle and did not open consistently. He had about an 80 percent success rate for that idiotic thing to work properly. I wish I knew how many total reserve "rides" he had because of it. Regardless, I'm sure he didn't mind walking back to the DZ when he had a malfunction.

Because of the Wing's poor track record, there was serious potential for injury. I never felt compelled to jump it as it did not fulfill my personal objectives and it was too risky. In our travels throughout West Germany and Bad Kreuznach, we occasionally saw Bundeswehr (German Army) World War II veterans on the street. They were about my dad's age and commonly recognized as amputees in a wheelchair or on crutches with missing limbs. Secretly, when identified, we referred to these senior veterans as old "Wing jumpers." The stigma was more to make fun of Bill and his favorite parachute than the disabled former Nazi soldiers.

Large groups of these battle-scarred troops had been guests of the U.S. Government as POWs. I recalled my dad telling about German POW camps in Nebraska during World War II and that the prisoners were typically used for farm labor. Camp Atlanta was established next to the town Atlanta (in south central Nebraska) as a German POW camp. As with many detainee camps, the site was chosen because it was located well into the interior of the United States and escape was futile. The location housed 3,000 German prisoners and most had been captured in the North African Campaign.[37]

Many of these POWs underwent critical medical care and received antibiotics that were unavailable to them in their home country due to war shortages. Overall, they were treated extremely well in the United States; after repatriation, about 5,000 German POWs nationwide immigrated to the United States. Thousands of others returned later to visit.[38] My father was stationed in Germany during World War II to fight the Germans; now I was in West Germany in many of the same places, ironically, to entertain them and as a goodwill ambassador.

I had been on the team only five days when I was assigned to jump in my first show. That Friday, we had two separate venues. Since I was the new guy on the demo team, I was last on the schedule and slated to

---

37 Glenn Thompson, "Prisoners on the Plains." Nebraska Prairie Life Museum.

38 Garcia, Malcolm J., "German POWs on the American Homefront," German Smithsonian.com, September 16, 2009.

jump the cutaway rig. It was designed as a solo jump from 10,000 feet AGL depending on the airspace and weather. The prime directive, as always, was to land in front of the fans no matter what you did or did not do in freefall. This jump was the second demo of the day for me. The first show had been at the nearby Strasbourg Kaserne for a change of command ceremony inside the post where we had to land on the unforgiving cobblestone courtyard. Even though it was good practice, it turned out to be just as dicey as it sounds.

My second jump at Wiesbaden (West Biebrich) was for a civilian beer fest sponsored by Binding Beer (pronounced Bending). I had a good idea where the spot was but not a good handle on the winds aloft that would play a crucial role in the jump's success. I was unsure how they might affect my drift in freefall under the open disposable canopy.

We all used one or two smoke grenades for every demo jump. As soon as I exited and was clear of the aircraft, I pulled the lanyard connected to the pin on my red smoke bomb mounted on my right foot (the pilots frowned on smoke in the helicopter). I felt the grenade fire and heard the "pop" of the igniter. All of this was to make me more visible while in freefall. I did a few spins and a delta (freefall position with legs extended and arms back to initiate a horizontal move across the sky) to an improved upwind location. The time was used mostly to judge my drift and determine exactly where I needed to open. I didn't want to screw up the demonstration jump...and it was my birthday. All the while I was thinking of how to decelerate to lessen the painful opening shock that I knew was coming.

At 3,500 feet, with some trepidation, I eased the cutaway ripcord handle on my left side out of its pocket. I surveyed my position to make any final adjustments for the spot, tried to think of a reason not to pull the ripcord and gritted my teeth. After the momentary hesitation I put my right hand over the extra large commemorative mallet that was under my jumpsuit to keep it away from my face. The opening shock of the unreefed (unimpeeded or slowed down) reserve canopy peaked at 12 Gs over a period of much less than a half second. BAM! I was sitting "in the saddle" at 3,000 feet under the all white "throwaway" canopy. The opening shock of the cutaway parachute is traumatic, and it takes a few moments for the brain to recover. On the ground, our announcer Sergeant Patterson was setting me up for the handwringing part of the show finale.

Due to inexperience, I was not that sure of myself and did not feel comfortable with the sizable distracting mallet in my face. The extreme forces generated at the instant of the opening could have slammed my face into the hard block of wood or knocked me unconscious. Maybe a mouth guard would have been a good idea. The entire cutaway apparatus was tricky and fraught with potential terminal snags. The artificially complicated situation was exponentially more dangerous than a straight forward skydive. It was baptism by fire!

The cutaway was the top parachute in the typical reserve position on the "piggyback" system that also housed the much larger main parachute immediately below it. My actual emergency chute was in the front chest location nearly covering the commemorative wooden mallet. As soon as my wits returned, I slipped my left arm through the very short modified cutaway riser and activated the Capewell device, releasing it from my harness. Then, with my left elbow bent at 90 degrees, I was effortlessly clutching onto half of the cutaway canopy with one arm. I quickly sized up my position and reevaluated my spot. Should I go lower because I was too close to the target? Or should I stay high because I was too far away from the crowd? I needed no further adjustment so now I could play. I simply let go of the left riser, and in a few seconds accelerated to 90 mph in the vertical position, while the deflated fabric whipped madly overhead. Now, what could I do to keep suspense high for the audience? I knew that our announcer was playing up the fact that my parachute had "unexpectedly malfunctioned" and collapsed. To the spectators, my circumstances started to look dire as they could easily make out the figure of a man under the mass of fabric.

Next, I reached up with my right arm, placed it through the riser and "cut it away." Then, using both hands to hang on to the wildly jerking collapsed canopy (also known as a cigarette roll), I struggled to maintain positional awareness and timing—exactly what was my altitude and my critical orientation to the crowd-line? Falling in the vertical position, I was approaching terminal velocity. Then, when

I thought that I had milked it enough, I completely let go of the cutaway parachute at 2,200 feet. Again, I was back in freefall when all other team members had been under fully functioning sport parachutes. The crowd could see my body and facial highlights. I was no longer a dot in the sky; they could plainly see the features of a real person—of me!

Terry, the announcer, started talking faster than his English could be translated. The audience had been whipped into a frenzy. All eyes were focused on a human in freefall accelerating toward Earth in some irrefutably grave situation. Hopefully I was the only one that had not forgotten that this was a show. I demanded their complete attention. As alarming as it may sound, the audience was spellbound by the potential catastrophic scenario. Painful seconds were ticking away, but it was all so captivating. At that moment, I was the center of their world, and my life hung in the balance!

Yes, I was focused on my job with more than casual interest as I zipped through 1,800 feet above the ground. I appeared larger by the instant to the spectators. Now they could see my face. Was it truly a hopeless situation? At that point, I sat up smartly, and deliberately picked up the ripcord handle, which was on the right side this time, and yanked it with conviction. The canopy cleanly deployed as designed. I was comfortably in the saddle at a very "up close and personal" 1,400 feet above the ground. For safety's sake, there was no reason to go any lower. In less than 80 seconds, I would be securely on the ground in front of the stunned audience!

My attention turned to the spectators. I did a wind check and evaluated exactly where I should prepare to touch down. All of my skill and planning paid off, and I comfortably made a small hook turn for a perfect standup landing 25 feet in front of the gallery. I made it all look so easy even though the demands of the jump were extreme. As I shed my helmet and my harness, I realized that the crowd of 5,000 was singing "Happy Birthday" to me in German. I was 22, and for the first time in my life, I was truly a "showman." I reveled in the moment. All eyes were on me, and it felt sensational!

My 22nd Birthday and first demo jump, photographer unknown. Left to Right: Teammate Sgt. Jeff Devon, Sgt. Terry Patterson, Sgt. Mike Wasley, and Sgt. Randy Lippincott wearing the native costume and holding the Mallet to begin the festivities. The jump was in Wiesbaden (West Biebrich), West Germany July 2, 1971.

As a team member for less than a week, I was as elated as anyone could be. I accepted the Burgomaster Hat with a "Chief Pin" to compliment the native blouse that I was wearing over my jumpsuit. I presented the commemorative mallet that I had carried on the jump to Helmut Reuter to tap the keg and initiate the festivities. It had been an unexpected thrill ride for me and surely was a time to remember.

The other team members secured their gear, and we were escorted into the beer tent sponsored by Binding Beer. We had VIP tables directly in front of the show along with complimentary bottomless three-liter mugs of beer. I had never seen a beer-stein that big! We had all the food and beer we could consume, and I was like a kid in a candy store! Like they say in the Air Force, "all thrust and no vectors!" Yes, it was the "perfect storm" brewing, no pun intended. The only portion of the show that I recall today was a female contortionist. I couldn't believe anyone could do what she did with her body—in a word, flexibly incredible! It gave me perverse thoughts and visions that I had never had before. I wondered if she was dating anyone. I don't remember much after that.

However, I do recall that Burgomaster Helmut Reuter was a great host and looked out for me since I really couldn't function on my own. I had way too much dark beer as I celebrated. His charming wife was beautiful but as Shakespeare put it, "Alcohol increases the desire but diminishes the performance." I'm sure that I took advantage of Mrs. Reuter, but it was because she had to clean up after me, and not the manner in which I had fantasized. That experience was my liver's first real introduction to vast quantities of strong German beer. Also, it seemed that drinking excessive alcohol demanded smoking cigarettes along with it. The more alcohol, the more cigarettes. I never purchased a pack, but they were always there when I was drinking. Smoking soon became a bad habit while I was on the road, but only in conjunction with alcohol. Soon I was on a slippery slope. It was an innocent enough start. I just wanted to fit in with the guys, and we were all having fun.

The Reuters were gracious enough to extend an overnight invitation to stay at their home although my base was only 30 miles away. It was the next afternoon before I found myself at the Bahnhof and ready to board the train home. Somehow, in all the intoxicated confusion, I retained my costume, Burgomaster hat and pin, the large three-liter beer mug (in one piece), and the commemorative mallet. I even asked permission and received the large heavy brass tap struck by the wooden mallet to open the huge wooden German beer barrel. Wow, if I collected this many souvenirs at every show over the next year and a half, I was going to have a truckload of stuff to take home! Reality and time were blurred by that gigantic mug, but with a little help from my friends, I made it back to Rose Barracks. This trip was the beginning of a marvelous adventure and a truly golden period of my life. A year and a half and 800 freefalls later; I returned to Nebraska already having lived two lifetimes, more than fulfilling my dreams!

One of the senior team members, Mike Wasley, showed me the ropes at the hangar and helped instill an interest in becoming a parachute rigger, and I completed my training while on the team. The Rigger License qualified me to pack reserve parachutes as a professional, and my Seal Symbol was GA6. Mike also enlisted me in helping him produce the octagonal hand finished, stained, wooden batons that were passed in freefall and presented to VIPs at the different demos. They were about fourteen inches long and two and a half inches in diameter. With a little practice, we could pump out enough for one year on a Sunday afternoon. The shiny brass plate inset on each baton was inscribed,"Passed in Freefall by Members of the 7th Army Parachute Team." Mike also had an interest in photography and taught me to develop black and white film in a military darkroom. He was my best friend, a kind soul, hard worker, and he loved to jump. Mike and his wife Judy Wasley took me into their home and welcomed me as one of the fellow team members.

The Wasleys were very family-oriented, but Judy was a genuine domestic goddess and the glue that held the family together. I often watched Judy meet Mike at the door, take his jacket and hang it up. She would fix him a refreshment, and as soon as he sat down, would kneel at his feet, remove his shoes, and start with a marathon foot massage. Judy was such a kind and gentle woman. She frequently fed me and asked me to stay at their home. She not only cleaned up after me but invited me to return and never uttered a critical word. I loved both of them and felt they returned that love to me in a multitude of ways. Judy was the epitome of grace personified and still treats me the same way to this day.

During that time on the Team, I admit that I was working a little too hard at trying to fit in and have fun. On a typical evening, four or five of us would load into teammate John Cutt's car, find a quiet area to toke on the ganja-filled bong until we couldn't see out the windows. I was getting used to the very potent European hashish because it was all we had available to smoke. When everyone was satisfied, we would drive around the corner to the Italian restaurant for a terrific meal. My absolute favorite food was cannelloni in a white sauce at the Ristorante Marco Polo on the West side of Bad Kreuznach.

I suppose my participation was partly peer pressure, but I was a willing participant. We never made the connection that our drug habit was potentially supporting criminal activity, or worse yet, terrorist organizations! The recreational drug use wasn't as innocent as we would have liked to believe that it was. At the height of my excesses with booze and dope I had gained a painful 25 pounds, and I noticed it every time I landed under a parachute. I had to quit eating so much!

Terry Patterson was the company clerk. He was a "leg," which was what anyone in the Army called a non-airborne trooper. We referred to him as "Tire Pressure," which was taken from his initials as a mechanism for teasing by the other team members because he was not a jumper. One day after I left the team, Terry was working in the hangar, and his duties took him up a ladder to the area above the trophy room. Somehow he became disoriented and fell from the loft, landing on the concrete floor, and resulted in a severe hip fracture. It was a traumatic injury for a young man to sustain, and he required surgery and an extended time off work for rehabilitation. I guess if you spend enough time on a parachute team, you run the risk of breaking a leg—but as the announcer? That was just bad luck! He was replaced with someone who was airborne-qualified but ridiculously terrified of freefall and was never able to make the transition. Like Terry before him, he stayed on as the company clerk and the ground announcer.

Recently I learned from multiple team members that someone on the team had suffered some serious bad luck. It was "our" drug dealer. I had no clue at the time where the hashish was coming from and never asked. They were playing a serious game and eventually was incarcerated by the German authorities for both dealing drugs and counterfeiting.

I preferred to play with parachutes.

The Great Divide

This story would not be complete without an explanation of the undercurrent at that time that ran rampant through the entire Army. The war in Southeast Asia was still being fought. Although all members of the team were Regular Army (RA), meaning volunteers, we were obligated for a minimum of three years. There were no draftees (which indicated only a two-year commitment) on the team. The constant atmosphere of "us and them" was between the "lifers" and the three-year guys. Lifers were in for the long haul and a pension; volunteers were there for the short term, by choice. Like our first sergeant, most lifers had, at least, one or two tours of duty in Nam. Another division within the ranks consisted of the "juicers" who drank alcohol and the "stoners" who used dope. We worked and performed as a team but socialized separately.

Rigging Grenades

On slow days, in preparation for jump demonstrations, we would rig the military-issue M-18 smoke grenades in the hangar. To enable us to activate the M-18s in freefall, we had to remove the handle, known as the spoon, which depressed a stout spring-loaded point striker. Otherwise, the handle would become falling debris if we did not remove it. (Normally when you throw a grenade at someone, the spoon is not a concern.) When the pin was pulled, the lever handle was released, which kept the striker from igniting the primer. I would work on an entire case of 24 grenades at one sitting. First, I carefully extracted the pin and, at the same time with my index finger, held down the spring-loaded point striker. The maneuver allowed me to remove the handle and then replace the cotter pin that had the familiar ring on it. The small pin kept the striker adequately depressed. To the cotter pin, we attached a lanyard made out of gutted 550 parachute cord to enable us to safely "pop smoke" in freefall after exiting the aircraft.

On rare occasions during this rigging process, the technician's finger could slip, resulting in a pronounced "snap" as the freed striker hit the primer and ignited the short fuse. The unfortunate person had less than three seconds before smoke started to spew uncontrollably out of the grenade and it became too hot to handle. So, lest he fall into disfavor with the team, the unlucky guy made a mad scramble for the door to get rid of the grenade before the team hangar filled with red smoke. We used several colors of smoke when available. White was never used because it burned too hot and did not provide adequate contrast against the sky. Red was the best color and showed up well. Frequently, our white socks and underwear would forever be stained a pinkish color from the direct exposure to the red smoke in freefall.

Some of the guys who smoked cigarettes would light up when traveling to different locations; however, not on the way to altitude on a demo jump. I was told a story about a team flying a British Army Wessex in England. As they settled into their climb to altitude, some of the Yanks lit up. The British sergeant, who was piloting the aircraft, turned around and, with a look of terror on his face yelled "Fire, Fire!" Apparently, smoking was frowned upon in the British Army's aircraft. At that time in the U. S. Army, it was up to the aircraft commander.

Not All Fun and Games

On my first "square canopy" jump on skydive number 294, Bob Harman, a fellow Red Devil from Great Britain, let me jump his new Paraplane. I suppose it was okay now that we were "mates" and all. The small Paraplane seemed to perform well enough although it was impossible to slow down for a satisfying landing flare. Therefore, it was not feasible to use for competition accuracy jumps. It was a lot like today's small canopies used for swooping.

On August 14, 1971, I had my first demonstration jump in Great Britain at Alconbury. The airbase was the Royal Air Force (RAF) Bomber Command during World War II. Alconbury, along with RAF Molesworth and RAF Upwood were considered the "Tri-Base Area" due to their close geographic proximity and interdependency. From Alconbury, the 92nd Bombardment Group engaged in attacking strategic targets including shipyards at Keil, ball bearing plants at Schweinfurt, submarine installations at Wilhelmshaven, a tire plant at Hanover, airfields near Paris, an aircraft factory at Nantes, and a magnesium mine in Norway.[39]

I was visiting the heart of the defense for Great Britain and the very source of the crushing blow to Nazi Germany. "Per ardua ad astra"...through adversity to the stars[40] is the motto of the Royal Air Force, which dates back to 1912 and was used by the newly formed Royal Flying Corps. The Latin phrase expresses the sentiment of British willpower in defending themselves by air. Facing overwhelming odds, the RAF held off the superior Luftwaffe (German Air Force). During the intense nine months bombing of London, 40,000 civilian lives were lost. Due to the British resolve, the Battle of Britain was the turning point in the war and the first resounding defeat for the German Air Force.[41]

For the show at Alconbury, I was assigned the cutaway in very windy conditions; by design, I was the only person on the final pass from 9,800 feet. We were not cleared to fly above 10,000 feet. That day I was the only one from the team to land on the airfield in front of the onlookers. After observing everyone else getting blown away downwind on the preceding passes, I was determined to make an enormous correction. It was my first sport jump from the tailgate of a C-130 Hercules, and I enjoyed it to no end. It was like my own private C-130 Turboprop, and the British Isles were at my beck and call!

---

39 Maurer, Maurer, ed. (1982) [1969]. *Combat Squadrons of the Air Force, World War II* (reprint ed.). Washington, DC: Office of Air Force History. ISBN 0-405-12194-6. LCCN 70605402. OCLC 72556.

40 "Frequently Asked Questions." RAF. 2013-04-26.

41 http://www.raf.mod.uk/history/thebattleofbritain.cfm.

The 9,800-foot ceiling was not considered high altitude, so once the tailgate of the C-130 was lowered, we orbited with it down until I was the only one left on the last pass of the show. James Bond, eat your heart out! The loadmaster had on an emergency parachute, but he was tethered to the plane for safety. As jumpers, we "freely" roamed around the cargo area, but as the designated jumpmaster I was calling the shots. First, the pilot communicated that we had airspace clearance to jump and that we were over the DZ. As jumpmaster, I fine-tuned the situation, made visual confirmation when I got the green light and decided exactly when to go after making adjustments for the wind.

Since I was jumping by myself, I was the final authority and could run, walk, fall, or flip off the back ramp whenever and however I wanted. It was exhilarating! I was totally unsupervised at that point. Did I mention that I was having the time of my life! And yes, it was still imperative to land in front of the audience. Multiple adjustments to timing and distance from the target were made on the fly. Thoughtful judgment was refined for each segment: under the fully-deployed cutaway, then under the streamer, back into freefall, and, at last, under a fully deployed main canopy. They all added to the dynamic complexity of the jump in a critical high wind environment. The window for a safe and accurate landing decreased in size exponentially with each added knot of wind. As it turned out, winds at 10,000 feet were blowing at 60 knots or 69 mph.

I was delighted to be the only team member to land in front of the crowd, and I think that my First Sergeant was grateful that someone from the Team landed on the DZ. If any team member ever had a bad jump, the standard retort was, "Well, at least, I looked good headed to the aircraft!" It all went rapidly downhill after that...pun intended.

That summer, I had the opportunity to do a subterminal (falling at less than 120 mph) cutaway at a demo. What a pleasure to not be pummeled by that little 24-foot reserve canopy! There is a considerable difference between 5 and 12 Gs of "snatch force," or instantaneous deceleration. The 12 Gs was like hitting a brick wall at 120 mph. Even for a 22-year-old, it was brutal. You had better consciously shut your mouth and Valsalva (to exhale forcibly against a closed windpipe and tighten your abdominal muscles) when you pulled that ripcord because what happened next was nothing short of raw violence.

During my travels that first summer, I attended many air shows at a lot of different venues. One of my favorites was the green, lush, and scenic Singen, West Germany demo along with some beautiful sailplanes. The gliders were so elegant and gracefully perfect while in flight. I had never seen such precision flying before. They could stay up in the air a lot longer than we could under our parachute canopies. It was idyllic Bavarian West Germany—scenic, historical, and aesthetically-pleasing. It was a scene right out of *The Sound of Music*!

The Germans love their air shows and all things aviation. In September of 1971, Bad Tölz, West Germany, was a beautiful place to visit. I was part of the team that won second place in accuracy. We would probably have won first place except for my one poor jump of 1.94 meters; the rest were 0.00, 0.14, 0.44, and 0.50. Skydive number 339 was my first practice formation jump. I was the right wingman, and that was my position for every subsequent diamond formation jump while on the team. My immediate action drill after the leader's wave-off was a diving hard left 90-degree turn.

Although we didn't jump anywhere on Independence Day 1971, we felt redeemed by a large celebration in Frankfurt over the 4th of July in 1972. Our next demo was at Grafenwöhr for a military "Show of Force." The enormous American tanks and big guns firing downrange were a fearsome sight. Now those were some real fireworks! They could easily hit moving targets over a mile away. We put on a small demo at a military soccer field and then flew to Bruchsal for a competition with the Bundeswehr. I was on a fantasy vacation! I was completely taken care of and my every need was all planned out to the "nth" degree. All I needed to pay attention to was my hygiene, dressing myself, and packing my parachute. Yes, I had my name sewn right on the riser, so there was no mistaking it; I took care of her, and she took care of me!

That first year on the team was exciting, fun, and a great learning and travel experience! I acquired practical knowledge in competition, including style, accuracy, and formation flying. However, the dangerous "tight spot" demos and canopy flying presented the greatest risk of injury. Overall, I had been very critical of myself but I never really screwed up enough to hurt anyone—myself included. Later, roommate Sam Alston and I thought we would head out on a little adventure and jump in a very special place of our choosing. We didn't know that we were going to set a Swiss record.

He that will not sail until all dangers are over must never put to sea.
—Thomas Fuller

CHAPTER 13
Swiss Record Jump

My only scheduled vacation in Europe started with Sam Alston on December 26, 1971. Sam and I departed Rose Barracks in Bad Kreuznach under gray skies and headed south towards Switzerland in his blue Volkswagen Karmann Ghia. It was to be our brief "voyage of discovery" and we had little more than necessities for the trip. Our personal checklists were complete: Military ID, gas vouchers, parachute gear, kit bags, log books, change of clothes, and a camera. We carried enough money for fuel, food, and a few jumps. Although we paid in dollars, we received change in Swiss francs. As I recall, the exchange rate was a little confusing for me. At the time, I thought that I got the better end of the money trade. We had grown accustomed to having Uncle Sam furnish the aircraft, so paying for our jumps was painful. I knew, in this case, that the experience would be well worth the money.

As we pulled onto the Autobahn heading south toward Switzerland, it was overcast, and the roads were wet. We hoped that we would find good weather at our destination 360 miles to the south and deep within the Alps. It was a full day's drive in the little VW. Time quickly passed as we talked about our future adventures and what we planned to achieve in the landlocked country well known for its neutrality during World War II. We planned to drive through Geneva and then head east toward Agarn, a small village that would be our base of operation. With some effort, we found the airfield where we would meet the next day to organize our jump. The airport was in the valley north of the iconic and majestic Matterhorn in the Pennine Alps. The breathtaking view would be the backdrop for all of our jumps there!

We checked into a local youth hostel and walked across the street for a lovely dinner. Up early the next morning, we prepared for our adventure. We had a Swiss pilot for the Pilatus Porter, and we would be jumping from an altitude of 15,500 feet. We made a single jump on the 27th and two jumps on the 28th. The first jump on the 28th, we completed the first-ever certifiable eight-way international star (formation skydiving with a ring of eight interlocked jumpers while in freefall) in Switzerland.

Swiss Star Record, Team Members, and Pilatus Porter. Photographer unknown.

The eight-man-star members were: Back row Left to Right, Swiss Pilot unknown, Captain Sam Nilson, American; Gilbert Zurbeiggen, Swiss; Charly Crettaz, Swiss; Berner Daniel, Swiss; Front row Left to Right, Don Stiles IE, SCR 552, American; Sam Alston, American; Randy Lippincott, (I received my SCR 1151), American; Roberto Hirzan, Italian.

Our celebration was short-lived because we had to return to work and more jumping. We took pictures and signed logbooks. "Veni, Vidi, Vici." It wasn't long before Sam and I were headed back home to Bad Kreuznach after our 48 hours of fame in the incredible Alps. We felt a great deal of satisfaction and a legitimate sense of accomplishment. This trip also proved uneventful because we did not hit a deer with the Karmann Ghia like we had on our trip to Bad Tölz.

I became a Star Crest Recipient (SCR) number 1151 in Switzerland that winter. I had reached another major goal, but it wasn't until the following summer that I had an opportunity for the Star Crest Soloist (SCS). I earned my SCS number 415 on July 19, 1972, out of a Huey over Hoppstädten, West Germany. The SCS is awarded to a person who enters eighth or higher into a timed freefall formation. The larger the star, the more skill required to match the rate of the falling cluster and be able to engage it horizontally. At first, as jumpers connect with each other, the star accelerates; then as it builds, it starts to float or decelerate. The skydiver must pay attention to and anticipate the speed of the falling star. The jumper must be able to adapt quickly and adjust his vertical pace as needed, "on the fly," so to speak.

The Bob Buquor Star Crest Memorial

The eight-way star was one of the early yardsticks in freefall, and the basis of the Star Crest award. The necessary number of skydivers (eight or more) not only reflected the level of difficulty in skydiving at the time but also the size of available aircraft. Typically, a pair of four-place Cessnas (like the Cessna 182 Skylane) were used in formation to allow four skydivers from each airplane to exit at the same time and attempt geometric formations in freefall. Skydiving is all about freefall, and the freefall is all about the relative work (RW). Working with others in freefall introduced another level of complexity to the individual skydiver. He was no longer falling through the air by himself but was "relative" to several other jumpers.

7th APT Eight-man SCS photo July 19th, 1972, photo Courtesy US Army. Left to Right: Command Sergeant Major Harold B. Stanley, Sgt. Pete Zadick, Sgt. Steve Bienert, Sgt. David Layne, Sgt. Pat (Rip) VanBibber, Sgt. John Cutts, Sgt. Randy Lippincott, Sgt. Bill Waters.

The skydiver had to develop skill in controlling vertical and horizontal movement simultaneously. Total control meant that the last person to exit the plane had to stand on his head or dive to accelerate fast enough to catch the first jumpers. He also had to judge when to slow down so as not to zoom past the existing formation. He would have to be able to "stop" at the level of the other jumpers and then dock successfully by moving into the structure horizontally, which was also changing velocity. If you did not anticipate these dynamics, you would "fall below" the star and be unable to "float" back into position in time to make it into the formation.

The late Robert H. Buquor helped promote early aerial photography and RW (two or more jumpers in freefall building a planned formation). Bob made his first jump in 1958 at Elsinore, California. He was instrumental in filming the black and white TV series *Ripcord* and other commercial productions, including the 1964

World Parachuting Meet in West Germany. On July 27, 1966, Bob Buquor drowned in the ocean off Malibu Beach while filming an MGM production starring Tony Curtis and Sharon Tate. Ironically it was titled *Don't Make Waves.*[42] Bob had been married less than a year.

His pioneering contributions were memorialized with the Bob Buquor Star Crest Memorial Award that was initiated in 1967 by Bill Newell (RIP). The perpetual Star Crest Awards were formed to honor the memory of Bob Buquor and to recognize relative work skydivers for their freefall achievements. **STAR CREST** is a mnemonic for **S**elect **T**ype **A**ccomplished **R**elative worker **C**ombining **R**eliability **E**nthusiasm **S**kill and **T**eamwork.

Over more than the last four decades, the Star Crest Awards have been instrumental in the promotion and development of skydiving relative work worldwide. The program grew from the original Star Crest Recipients (SCR) in 1965, to include the Star Crest Solo (SCS), and Night Star Crest Recipient (NSCR) in 1971, the Star Crest Skydiver Award (SCSA) in 1975, and the Night Star Crest Skydiver Award (NSCSA) in 1978. In 1984, the Bob Buquor Memorial Star Crest (BBMSC) introduced the Universal Skydiver Award (USA). In 2002, two new vertical/free fly awards were incorporated into the program; the Vertical Star Crest Recipient (vSCR), and Vertical Star Crest Solo (vSCS)."[43] The patch to memorialize a man has now grown to have a life and a history of its own.

A second record that I was involved in came a short time later. I don't remember how we conned the pilots into taking us into positive controlled airspace (above 18,000 feet you must be on an IFR flight plan, have clearance, and be in communication with Air Traffic Control), but they did. Most likely it was a case of beer! We wanted a team record jump, but everyone was thinking way too slowly when we exited. We believed that somehow we could will ourselves to get by without oxygen. We simply did not have provisions for supplemental oxygen in the helicopter. They were not outfitted to operate in the

---

42 *Who Was Bob Buquor* by Bill Newell, http://www.starcrestawards.com/history/history_bob_buquor_who_was_he.html.

43 Ibid.

flight levels (above 18,000 feet). A little more time at altitude and people would have started passing out from hypoxia especially the smokers among us.

Even though it was a strictly prohibited operation, our team record was 19,400 feet MSL (mean sea level, measured from the surface of the ocean, not from the local ground) out of a UH-1H over West Germany. We were not cleared into the airspace, had no supplemental oxygen, and no one was really in charge of the jump. I can only surmise that the pilot turned off the altitude reporting function on his transponder to avoid self-incrimination. I can imagine a "Farside" cartoon with the commercial jet pilots in the cockpit turning to each other and asking, "Now what's that mountain goat doing up in the clouds?" Only they would be asking just before impact, "Now what's that Army helicopter doing up here above 19,000 feet?"

The published service ceiling for the Huey H model coincidentally is 19,400 feet. The fully loaded UH-1H was struggling to maintain altitude at 19,000 feet in the thin air. It was hardly climbing at 100 feet per minute for the last 15 minutes. It had taken an extended period to get there, and everyone on the aircraft was very low on oxygen and ready to bail out. The doors had remained closed, so we didn't freeze along with the self-imposed suffocation. I could feel the effects, and there was no escaping the mental status changes—it's just that I didn't care.

Euphoria and lethargy are both deadly precursors to frank hypoxemia and ultimately loss of consciousness. I had no idea who was spotting, what the exit point was supposed to be, or where we were going to even land. I just went when the doors opened, and everyone else was bailing out. It was like "monkey see, monkey do." Everything is better in freefall and breathing more dense air was no exception! I'm sure that we didn't think to close the large doors behind us, in our oblivious state, for the already-chilled pilots.

Left to Right: Sgt. Randy Lippincott, Sgt. Mike Wasley,
Sgt. Sam Alston. Photographer unknown.

The record jump failed to come together with our intended 12-man star. Nobody even made an effort to put together a formation. We were just happy to be breathing a little easier and to be able to land within walking distance of our DZ. All I wanted to do was stay out of everyone's way and avoid any mishap. I felt sorry for the pilots because it took them much longer to get down, with or without a violation. They were exposed to oxygen starvation for a more extended period and had to deal with actually operating "heavy equipment." But they survived, and we had our unauthorized team altitude record over West Germany.

Soon the team was headed to my favorite place in West Germany, Bad Tölz. We were guests of the Army Special Forces and made additional high altitude jumps under their supervision. Starting with skydive number 423, I made three HALO jumps on Schweiganger (Sweet DZ) just outside of Bad Tölz. The name Sweet DZ referred to "cow pies" because it was in a pasture for cattle when not being used as a drop zone. We jumped with equipment (rucksacks) and oxygen from altitude. The aircraft was an old World War II C-47 just like they used on D-day at Normandy. We lowered the heavy gear that we parachuted with on a 15-foot lanyard. The tether transferred the weight of the equipment and lessened our impact with the ground, just as I had learned in jump school. Fortunately, they were all daytime skydives, and we landed on the designated DZ and not in the trees. It was fun, educational, and we felt privileged that our training was hosted by the original unit that had started it all in 1952, the 10th Special Forces Group. The scenery, equipement, and logistics were just like what you'd see in the movies!

We were fortunate to have an accomplished Senior HALO Instructor as the First Sergeant on our team. Command Sergeant Major Harold B. Stanley trained Captain Joseph W. Kittinger in the art of freefall for his record-setting jump from 102,800 feet on August 16, 1960. Stan told me that he made over 50 practice jumps with him, and Joe never did become proficient in controlling his freefall before the record balloon jump that stood for 53 years.

Sam Alston wrote the following account:

> I (Sam Alston) was working with Command Sergeant Major Harold B. Stanley, the inimitable consummate results-getting NCO, and listened while Stan told about HALO Training when he first came to the 7th Army Parachute Team as the Non-Commissioned Officer in Charge (NCOIC). Stanley was truly the most unassuming NCO ever in all the armies, in all the countries, in the whole world, since the dawn of time. Sergeant Major said that during HALO Training while level at the jump altitude of 30,000 feet MSL as the mission allowed, he would have the HALO candidates take off their oxygen masks. Stanley said that they, of course, would immediately pass out. He would leave their masks off for a minute or so then reach over and let the team member get a breath of

oxygen to revive them. As soon as the student came around, if they were in it for the jump and fully intended to go, they would jump up and head for the door. If they just dawdled around and pretended to be coming out of it, he said you knew they did not want to jump. Stanley said that was his best way of busting HALO candidates out of the program because no one was able to fake that scenario. You either wanted to go or not. Go to the door, and you were HALO-qualified. Lollygag and you were busted out. He was a storied fascinating guy. Command Sergeant Major Harold B. Stanley was a tremendous leader and was so quietly able to make people work their hearts out for him. What a privilege to have served with him.

—Sergeant Sam R. Alston, 1972

CHAPTER 14
Piancavallo Ski Resort

The team rotated to scenic Aviano, Italy, in February 1972. The favorable winter conditions allowed us to jump in fair weather year-round. It was an American Air Force Base and home of the F-4 Phantom, the loudest fighter jet in the free world, and we coined it the "1958 Air Plow" for the way it looked. The Phantom was the definitive answer as to how the Air Force could convert jet fuel (JP-4) into noise. Our quarters were small; Pat VanBibber was my roommate and a "Salty Dog" was our domesticated house pet. On occasion, we would stoop to a "Greyhound" (gin and grapefruit juice without the salt). For some reason, we decided that gin by the gallon was the way to go, and it became the mainstay of our diet. You see, we didn't have much money, and we didn't go out often or fraternize with the locals. We thought we were having fun even if it was only with each other!

Each morning, we all rode to the airfield together in a large Air Force step-side van. Some of the senior NCOs took turns driving. First stop was the mess hall and then our DZ for a round of military PT in our sweats. From our Area of Operation (AO), the runway was close enough for us to watch the landing traffic with an unrestricted view, but we were far enough away that our jumping activities never interfered with the flight operations. We could land and take off on our grass field because we used helicopters and never came close to the end of the active runway. We were in a large area on the south side of the airfield complex. It was a supremely scenic DZ with the snow covered Italian Alps bordering us to the immediate north.

I remember seeing my first C-5A Galaxy take off to the west from that runway; it was like watching a building rising in slow motion on a tether. I couldn't believe the massive size of the airplane in relation to its surroundings. If it landed again, I was sure that the airport would tip over! In a word, it was "ginormous." How could something that big get off the ground? I couldn't wait to see one up close or even walk through it, let alone jump from it in its unique double-deck airborne configuration.

Aviano in Northern Italy is at the base of the Italian Alps, which offers excellent skiing in the winter and beautiful scenery year around. Some of the guys on the team had cars and scheduled some time off to drive to Piancavallo, the nearest ski resort to the north. Since I was from Nebraska, I had never been snow skiing before, except behind my dad's pickup truck in a cornfield. I knew all about the leg fractures that novice skiers suffered, and I wanted no part of it. That would have jeopardized my perfect job, and I was simply not going to risk it. Why tempt fate? I never even contemplated the trip to check it out. I had made plenty of judgment errors up to this point, but skiing was not going to be one of them. Today, however, I would love to spend the entire winter in Piancavallo and ski every day for months on end, waiting for my next dose of fresh powder snow.

By the end of my first season, I was confident in my ability to touch down on the target. Regardless of what happened in the air, the prime directive was to land on my feet in front of the audience. Proximity to the crowd was essential, and a well-finessed standup landing was impressive. After a point, I felt that I had mastered these skills and thought about spicing up my personal showmanship. First, the conditions had to be just right with about a six-knot steady breeze parallel to the crowd line. I needed an opening spot that never left landing in front of the onlookers in question and an opening altitude that gave me plenty of time to reconfigure. I also had to plan my traffic pattern so that I would not be crowding anyone else in the air and that no one would possibly interfere with my critical final approach, flair, and the touchdown. Any midair incident could knock me out of the harness and to my death.

All the while I had to maintain positional awareness and set up my harness to enable me to step smoothly out of it. Of course, this is extremely dangerous at any altitude because I was completely unattached to my parachute and could effortlessly fall out of the parachute harness to my death. After opening, I would unhook one side of my chest reserve and sling it out of the way. Next, I would pull my harness down under my thighs to sit securely on it like a swing with my back comfortably supported against the container. When I was satisfied with my configuration and my progress to the target, which was the epitome of multitasking, I would finally unclip my leg straps, and then my chest strap was the final commitment. The procedures left me virtually free of any connection to my parachute harness. I was sitting in the saddle like a vulnerable swing at 1,000 feet off the ground with absolutely no protection or safety net. I was only grasping the toggles for directional control of the canopy, indisputably unattached to anything other than my self-preservation.

At that point, I had to lay aside my tenuous configuration and focus on landing in front of the spectators. I would set up my approach making from a 90 to an 180-degree hook turn and flare for the perfect featherweight standup landing. My goal was to make it look ridiculously easy. My presentation was everything! To an airplane pilot, a left turn to land seems more natural, and that is how I would typically set up; after all we are creatures of habit.

Once I flared and lightly touched down for a perfect tiptoe landing, I simply let go of my toggles and nonchalantly walked away from my rig as if I had just stepped out of a phone booth. I didn't even look back. I was that confident. The canopy would remain stationary and hover in position by itself for nearly a minute, fully inflated and held in place by the steady light breeze. The still-attached reserve and harness gave it just enough weight so it would not drift off like a kite. It was an impressive sight and gave me a great sense of satisfaction because I had never seen anyone do it before or even after that. It was not for the faint of heart! I loved to do this original maneuver on special occasions in perfect conditions. I don't believe any of my teammates ever tried to imitate it, and I was just happy that I had successfully mastered the avant-garde maneuver.

While in Italy, we worked on all areas of competition. I was issued a new canopy called the Papillon, which means butterfly in French, so now all I had to do was learn how to sting like a bee! For competition purposes, I thought that its performance was superior to the American Para Commander (PC). The fabric was zero porosity; it did float like a butterfly and was seemingly more responsive.

Randy Lippincott in the pea gravel pit on an acuracy jump Aviano, Italy; with the Italian Alps in the background. Photographer unknown.

This was my second season in Europe, and I wanted to focus on my competitive skills. I felt that I had mastered the demonstration jump since landing in front of the onlookers didn't have to be all that precise. We had no designated coaches but tried to improve with simple trial and error and self-critique. My logbook is replete with self-flagellating analysis. Unfortunately, our team was "self-taught" through endless repetition. We did not have organized professional coaching to develop individuals for international competition.

Much later I learned "there are four key attributes of a world class athlete: desire, physical ability, psychological orientation, and technical execution. It's just as important to plan a training program for your psychological orientation and plot out your mental training program with the same attention to detail as you do your other training activities. In time, the mental training will become second nature, and you will do it automatically. Most of the guys beating you aren't that much better physically; they are usually better technically and, more importantly, mentally."[44]

The team didn't have a program oriented toward serious competition. We were there to represent the U.S.A. as goodwill ambassadors, so sometimes losing was part of the program.

British teammate David Layne related a story about nearly biting the dust while training in Aviano. During March 1972, he logged it as "Three-man with Waters and Van Bibber." In addition to the RW, he was performing the cutaway, a jump that was always a solo demonstration jump. I was never sure why anyone intentionally practiced the brutal cutaway, but this story illustrates my point. The modified rig was designed with two complete sets of parachute quick release assemblies in a tandem configuration. One set was for the standard main parachute that David planned to land with, and one set was for the designed cutaway parachute. I can't fathom how you could confuse the two unless you pulled the wrong ripcord without thinking. Once he deployed the cutaway, it was self-evident which quick release assemblies were part of the open parachute. After all, it was holding your entire weight.

Somehow in the excitement, David partially cut away the incorrect canopy and then his confusion turned to panic. Next, he incompletely cut away his good main canopy, further compounding the problem. Somehow he ended up with two hideously large collapsed canopies overhead that were not arresting his descent in any significant manner. To impact at that velocity would have been fatal. It was an unfathomably grave situation; indeed, a skydiver's worst nightmare come true. It was the dreaded double malfunction, the beginning of the classical curse and final jump for many skydivers. Time was

---

44 http://trackandfieldathletesassociation.org/site/a-world-class-athlete-what-are-the-key-attributes/.

racing by that could never be retrieved. Those were very busy and tense seconds in which David had to get rid of two malfunctioned canopies and go back into freefall. Only then was he able to activate his emergency chute—and he did so just in the nick of time. He used up eight of his nine lives in those split seconds! Everyone was so relieved that David survived the unthinkable double malfunction that we took off early to celebrate his good luck. It's still scary to realize how close he came to becoming a statistic!

While in Italy, my next challenge was one of airborne navigation. I learned about the Cross-Country Patch, and that it was designed to test my route planning capability from aloft. No one had ever studied this skill for the parachutist. I had to be ten miles away from the target when I exited the helicopter. The actual bulls-eye was no more than ten feet across, and I was not allowed to be higher than 10,000 feet above the ground when I started. Winds tend to change speed and direction at different altitudes, and that is just what happened on this jump. About halfway down, the wind direction shifted, but I was able to anticipate it and stayed on course.

Under the canopy, I made only slight adjustments to maintain my heading. I pulled my arms and legs in and put my head down for the duration to streamline my body and decrease aerodynamic drag. I needed to eke out every foot of distance for the ten-mile venture. My first attempt at this was with a second generation small ParaPlane, and my journey ended a disappointing two and a half miles short of the target. They had to send the helicopter to find me!

Using my first attempt as a gauge, the task, seemed impossible, but I was determined. On the next jump, I waited for more favorable winds, used the much larger Cloud parachute, and deployed it as soon as I was clear of the Huey. I was excited for the second attempt and anxious to discover if I had learned anything. The Cloud had a much better glide ratio than the smaller ParaPlane. I quickly took up a compass heading, picked a spot on the horizon to aim at, and tried to identify the DZ area within the first five minutes. I immediately made myself as aerodynamic as possible. The ten minutes from 10,000 feet seemed more like thirty! I made a few minor adjustments for parachute efficiency and continuously checked my heading and track across the ground. I did adjust my heading mid-flight due to a slight dogleg or shift in wind direction aloft.

After only a few minutes I was considerably higher than the other team members who jumped with me. Ten miles was a long way! The winds were good to me, the weather divine, and my pilotage was on the mark; however, my range was still not assured at the one-mile point. I could tell that it was going to be close. In the end, I was barely able to make a small left turn to base leg, quickly apply the brakes, and land within the required ten-foot target. I earned Cross-Country Patch number 67. It had been an excellent exercise in canopy work, pilotage, and was a challenging fun jump!

Nearing the end of our stay in Italy, I had worked hard on all aspects of competition. I cashed in on my efforts at a small local meet in Udine, Italy. I won the Individual Accuracy Competition with three consecutive dead centers. My performance gave me a perfect total score of 0.00. The last jump was my 42nd dead center out of 538 jumps. Wow, this was fun, and I was surely getting into the competitive spirit!

> Anyone compelled into the competitive arena will encounter the greatest challenge a human being can face: the current of our own thought. Although we possess an awesome power to create our reality, few ever learn the simple mental techniques that accomplish outrageous results. If we can perfectly envision our mastery, then mastery becomes our domain.
>
> —Ellen Reed from
> *Mental Training for Skydiving and Life*

I loved northern Italy, but my stay had been unconditionally focused on jumping. My experience with food was not so great. I was so busy practicing my craft that I didn't give much thought to the cuisine. My young and impatient palate was unrefined and unappreciative of the celebrated Italian food. However, I did take advantage of my proximity to Venice. One weekend I traveled by train to the historic city with two of my buddies. I enjoyed the world class venue, the scenery, and most of all, the old world history. I stood in St. Mark's Square and saw the Basilica and traveled The Grand Canal that ends near the Venezia Santa Lucia Railway Station. I wish that I had spent more time there. Even though Venice was a beautiful city, and I enjoyed it, I kept thinking about the demo in Rome that I had missed, which would have been a fantasy come true. It had been on the books but was canceled at the last minute, and I never knew why.

When we left Aviano, most of us drove back to West Germany. I remember traveling over the famous Brenner Pass and also taking the Brenner Railway through a tunnel. The journey was a unique experience where we drove our vehicles onto a flatbed railcar and stayed inside the automobile for the duration—at least we were supposed to stay in the car. It was exciting but very dark and wet in the sizable and very long tunnel. We entertained ourselves while en route by exiting our car and messing with the guys ahead of us in the pitch dark on the dangerous and moving train. The weather on the Italian side was rainy and stormy when we drove onto the train, but when we exited on the Austrian aspect of the mountain, we were greeted by a calm magical winter wonderland.

In no wind conditions, the exceptionally large snowflakes fell vertically in slow motion. The power lines already had a perfect two-inch coating that completely encased the wires. The scene was spectacular and impossible at the same time. It was amazing! I had never seen anything like it! Quite simply, it was breathtaking in the calm conditions, remarkably rare and unspoiled. We were in the Austrian Alps! Years later while living in Fairbanks, Alaska, I witnessed the same kind of phenomenon and learned to understand it. Due to "creep," the snow would eventually encompass the entire wire because of gravity and the fluid nature of the material. As more snow fell on the old organized snow, it slowly moved to the side and off center. Then as more gathered, it consolidated with the old snow and continued to advance to a lower position on the wire. Eventually, the horizontal wire or power line was completely and uniformly encased in snow. This action took place because there was no wind to interfere with it during the long process. I will always hold this memory as a truly classic and pristine winter wonderland scene, perfect in every detail.

CHAPTER 15
EPL EGO The Wings of Icarus

We were competing as a squad at the European Parachute League (EPL) in Bruchsal, West Germany, in April 1972. When I woke up that morning, I didn't know that before nightfall, I would look death in the face and not know why. I had been a member of the 7th APT for ten months. We jumped every good weather day, and it felt very natural to me. I was living the dream! As team members, we were competing in the EPL Division. We had just returned from Aviano, Italy, where we held our intensive Winter Training Camp to take advantage of the great weather. Our objective that day was to gain eligibility as individuals participating in the U.S. National Parachuting Championships stateside. We would also represent the 7th APT at the Major Civilian Tournament. I was competing in both main events—style and accuracy.

Style is a series of spins and loops done from 7,500 feet above the ground. It was a combination of a 360-degree turn, a back loop, another turn, and another back loop; in a predetermined combination. The score was calculated on the contestant's overall time and precision of movement. Overshooting or undershooting into the turn caused additional time to be added to the score. Usually, the time from two or three jumps was added together for the final score. The lowest overall time won the competition.

For accuracy, the size of the skydiving target was ten centimeters in diameter or approximately four inches across. A hole in the center of the disc allowed it to slide on an anchored lanyard so that it could be brought back to its exact starting position in the pea gravel pit after being disturbed. The jumper would try to strike the disc with his heel or toe for a perfect score—a dead center (DC). The job of the judges was to mark the jumper's first point of contact with a number nine gauge wire fichét. Once the official point of impact had been determined by consensus of the judges, the disc would be re-centered with the lanyard. The official score was the distance measured in centimeters from the precise point of impact to the edge of the disc.

Therefore, if you missed the target by 15 centimeters, then your score was 0.15. There was no instant replay to review a strike or contest the score. To land on the target with the toe or the heel was a dead center and was scored as 0.00. Often, when the disc was inspected, a skid mark would be evidence of the first point of contact and verification of hitting the bulls-eye. If you made ten dead centers in a row from an exit altitude of 2,500 feet, you were extremely competitive. I managed perfect scores on several occasions during my tenure, both from round canopies: the Para Commander (PC), made in the United States, and the Papillon, a French parachute.

That morning, we all had breakfast together, the weather was good, and I was in a positive mood looking forward to the Regional Contest. When my teammate, Mike Wasley ordered orange juice and coffee I discreetly called the waitress aside. I instructed her to bring the two drinks mixed in one tall glass—"orange juice and coffee." We had just reinvented the Arnold Palmer breakfast drink. We all had a big laugh, and Mike took it all in stride.

The meet started on time and proceeded in an orderly fashion. Our team was competitive, but I totally blew my first attempt. Perhaps I was overconfident. My subsequent jumps had some redeeming value, and we all were having a big time. After the official jumping had ended for the day and the competitors dispersed, Mike Wasley, John Cutts, and I talked the helicopter pilot into a "fly-away" just for fun. We figured that since the aircraft was in the air, we might as well be jumping out of it. The three of us stood there, packed, and eager to go into the fading light.

We loaded and quickly took off in the large green aircraft. As we made the turn coming back across the runway complex, we only had 2,000 feet AGL. Our young egos were writing checks that our bodies were unable to cash! It would have been something else altogether if the three of us were proficient in getting a three-man formation as we exited the door; that would have been realistic and doable. But we had never attempted anything like that, especially starting at 2,000 feet above the ground to begin a relative work (RW) jump. The official rules were that you were supposed to be under an open canopy at 2,000 feet, not just starting a formation jump. Oh, and did I mention that the sun was setting?

Mike was unnecessarily in the left door of the helicopter, and John and I went out the right door. The artificially imposed separation was simply too great to overcome in the allotted seconds. It was a typical half-baked idea. We simply didn't have enough coordination and airspeed to make a spontaneous three-man star. Since the helicopter was only climbing out at 80 mph, it would take more than four seconds to accelerate to 120 mph to gain maximal control in freefall. We hadn't even thought this through since it is less than seven seconds to 1,000 feet and about six seconds for the remaining 1,000 feet, right up to the point of impact. The fading light of late dusk didn't help make visual contact easy for this idiotic three-man star attempt. Had we been serious about this planned SNAFU? I wonder what the helicopter pilots thought about our "plan," or if they even really cared. They mistakenly believed that we were "professionals."

After the gross failure of our twilight three-man formation attempt from 2,000 feet, I was only concerned with locating Mike and John to avoid the deadly mid-air collision. Typically, a singular event rarely causes an accident; rather, it is a cascade of events that lead to a fatality. I could count two strikes against me from where I was—low light and an extremely meager exit altitude. In the semi-darkness, it was easier to look for the canopies versus looking for the falling bodies. I waited as I searched with a conflicted gaze into the darkness above me knowing that the ground was looming large and quickly rushing up from below. The seconds were painfully ticking away…tick tock, tick tock! I thought fleetingly about Steve Steckmyer who had been in the same position when he fractured his femur and nearly became a fatality.

From my exit altitude, I had a maximum of thirteen total seconds before impact and ten seconds until I clearly had to have full canopy deployment. It would take two seconds for a perfect opening sequence with a one-second leeway. The "fudge factor" was to maneuver the canopy before slamming into the runway. I rationalized my intentionally excessive delay and felt assured that no teammate was above me; surely no one would be so harebrained to go that low. I was already "sitting up," to increase air flow over my back and maximize my body position for a quick opening. I knew, with certainty, that I was only getting this one chance. I was betting the farm that no one was above me, so without a wave-off, I gave a swift tug on my ripcord handle. There was no plan "B" if this didn't work!

Then, as time slowed for me, as it had done on other occasions, I focused on the runway directly below me. It was unmistakably getting bigger and coming up faster than I had planned. Perhaps it even made me a tad uncomfortable and was distracting, which was a gritty and visceral response. Why couldn't I have been over a forgiving soft grassy area instead of that, huge, imposing, steely blacktop? Oh, the pain! I would have a chance of survival if I were over that merciful grassy area. I remembered that the team commander, Captain McPherson, had a malfunction over a similar runway situation that crippled him for life. There was no time for panic, just finely calculated cockiness and I was ready to pull the trigger. Was I on a convergent trajectory with destiny? Could I have been secretly looking for an excuse to discover just how close I could come to taking a "dirt nap" and still walk away? Had the murky evening light fogged my judgment? Was this the best way to forcefully siphon ice water through my veins? The answers were all forthcoming.

My attention was sharply drawn to the large and imposing but indifferent runway below me. Thoughts and images flashed vividly through my mind as I hurtled toward the runway: I knew that I was not ready to give up the warm summer evenings in Nebraska, sitting on the porch sipping Mother's iced tea and listening to the omnipresent crickets. I still wanted another sunrise over the windmill, the ubiquitous icon of my birthplace. I had grown fond of the full-bodied German beer and wanted to enjoy more. I wanted to spend Christmas with my entire family one more time. I needed the obligatory muscle car and a stereo system when I returned to the good old US of A as an authentic Army veteran. I wanted to watch a hundred more episodes of Johnny Carson and watch Johnny Rodgers and Nebraska beat Oklahoma in football just one more time!

No! This jump would not be my last. I was not ready to cash it in with a malfunction, pilot chute hesitation, or midair collision at 120 mph. I was going to die with my boots on alright, but not like this-and not on this jump. I had no problem walking a tightrope or living on the razors' edge. I was neither frightened nor did it give me pleasure to stand on the very fringe of the void and look directly into the all-consuming irrevocable emptiness. As Elvis Presley would say, I was just "taking care of business." And the air don't care!

"Air: an invisible realm that endlessly makes way right up to the point of impact."[45]

I sensed the parachute container on my back partially relax, which was the first indication of potential success. The canopy opened flawlessly, and I was elated to hear its reassuring cacophony. The uniquely fleeting quality of fabric being whipped by a blast of air, snapping, popping briskly as each panel reacted, designed as my intrepid speed-brake and life preserver. Not only was it the dubious sound of deliverance; that day it was also the resonance of life. I was still breathing so I knew I was alive. My butt was firmly in the saddle under an open canopy for the planned three or four seconds. Four seconds times 16 feet per second under an open canopy is 64 feet, plus 300 feet or about two seconds for the parachute to open equals 364 feet above the ground. My unwitnessed landing on the runway was anticlimactic other than I was obliged to land facing the same direction in which I had opened. There was no time for a turn to avoid any landing traffic on the runway. It would have been paradoxical to be sucked into the jet engine of a landing KC-135 after surviving the freefall.

Feeling somewhat sheepish about my artificially self-induced critical low-pull, I gathered up my rig and headed over to where the other two guys were going to land in the next minute or so just as the runway lights turned on in the twilight zone. John and Mike were still well above me at a reasonable altitude. They didn't feel the need to

[45] Allure of the Seas, aft staircase, port side, level 11.

"smoke it" for the sake of an unreasonably delayed opening. Coming close to death gives you the best opportunity ever to try to live a better life and to focus on what is supremely relevant. It was just another one of the many ironies of my life. As it turns out, hubris is a drop zone in Germany.

> You only live twice. Once when you are born and once when you look death in the face.
>
> —Ian Fleming, *You Only Live Twice*

The next day, I was consumed in self-reflection on the flight home. Maybe, just perhaps, I should consider this game a little more seriously. After all, there were consequences for poor judgment. I had just completed a formal instructor course with Bill Jones immediately before the meet. Shouldn't that make me a more competent skydiver? When was I going to behave like I had given any mature thought to longevity? Okay, so it's a rhetorical question.

The following month we had an international competition in Bruchsal, Germany, against the Russians, Germans, and French. I made six consecutive dead centers, was on the first place team, and earned the number one individual position. I had been a dark horse, and that felt good. Life is good! As guests of the Bundeswehr we stayed and ate Army chow on the military post. On most trips, we consumed the traditional oversized schnitzel and chicken, but one of the West German Army dishes that I grew to love was the extremely thick split pea soup. It was the most hearty meal available, and I ate mine with a fork!

CHAPTER 16
Prince Philip and Miss Great Britain

April 1972. The team flew to England in a C-141 Starlifter, and we were staged out of the Burtonwood Army Depot. In its heyday during the Second World War, Burtonwood was an enormous and significant base. The perimeter fence around it was an incredible 70 miles in length. Eventually, it had the biggest warehouse in Europe consisting of three million square feet on a mind-boggling 47 acres under one roof![46]

From the airfield, we took a taxi to our hotel. We were in heavy traffic in Chester and stopped at a red light when suddenly one of the team members called out "Chinese Fire Drill!" We burst out of the automobile, ran around it in opposite directions whooping and laughing and jumped back in just in time for the green light much to the bemusement of the cab driver, motorists, and pedestrians. We were just having some fun and happy to be skydiving in Great Britain!

Our demonstration was scheduled for the marvelous Royal Horse and Carriage Show, and we performed both days. The Duke of Westminster, one of Britain's most wealthy men, Prince Philip, and Miss Great Britain, the beautiful Carolyn Moore, were all in attendance. During the show, we met and shook hands with each of these remarkable dignitaries along with Lady Leonora Mary Grosvenor, the Duke of Westminster's daughter. Royalty walked and interacted in a most natural and relaxed matter, and we all felt comfortable with them; however, I did maintain a strict military presentation. We were all in awe of their presence but sincerely appreciated the time and effort they made to greet us individually. Although they were not rushed, their presence was strictly orchestrated, and they wasted no time or movements.

---

46 http://www.bbc.co.uk/liverpool/localhistory/journey/american_connection/burtonwood/intro/facts.shtml.

On April 22, 1972, the weather was marginal and the show that we put on that first day was from 4,500 feet. The relatively low altitude didn't matter, as everything was up close and personal. I was assigned the cutaway on the first demo, and in moderate winds of 20 knots, I landed nicely in front of the spectators. It was a reliable test of my spotting ability and altitude management. Unlike the other jumpers who deployed their chutes at the prescribed height over the opening spot, I had three variables to deal with—time, altitude, and distance. I had to manage each element for a successful jump under two separate canopies. Each stage was adjusted accordingly with every phase of my jump. I had to calculate dynamically the horizontal drift under the open canopy and also my horizontal movement even while using it as a streamer. I needed to determine when to release the cutaway canopy. After the canopy had been ejected, I went back into freefall, and only then could I make final adjustments to the deployment equation. If I opened too near the patrons, I would land on them or behind them. If I opened too far away, I would not make it back to the audience.

The jump was a success although I later learned that my cutaway canopy might have spooked a horse in the competition. The *Driver's Grand Prix, Horse and Hound* reported that "Jack Collinson had a nasty turn when one of the parachute team got off course and grounded right in front of his team."[47] It was much more likely that the spent cutaway canopy drifted onto the field of play rather than any one of the team members landing in front of the horses. That would have been unsatisfactory on our part and quite avoidable for any of our expert jumpers.

The exhibition was in honor of the Fifth Duke of Westminster, Sir Robert George Grosvenor. On the second jump that day, I was selected to present the official 7th APT baton to Lady Leonora Mary Grosvenor, who was my age. It was quite exciting, and a privilege to interact with her in such a personal way! Today, she is the Countess of Lichfield, and I am retired. She has since married, divorced, and her

---

47 *Driver's Grand Prix, Horse and Hound,* dated May 12 1972.

ex-husband died in 2005. Since 1979, the countess has had the title of Extra Lady-in-Waiting to The Princess Royal.[48]

As it turned out, my teammate David Layne was a native of England and his parents and sister came to see the show. He was visiting with them when he realized that the faint sound in the background was the distinctive whine of the jump helicopter firing up. David was half a mile away from the loading point and frantically hailed a vintage car, a Vauxhall Prince Henry, and arrived at the helicopter in style. Rather than being rewarded for his initiative, he was the recipient of a good old-fashioned ass chewing. David made the second cutaway jump that day, and his discarded canopy may have been the one that accidentally spooked the equines at the royal event. He also told me that he attempted to get the Duke of Edinburgh to sign his logbook, but his bodyguards would have none of it. David was categorically told that the Duke did NOT give autographs!

On the second day of the show, at the end of the demo, the team fell in at attention and Prince Philip, the Duke of Edinburgh, was introduced to each one of us individually, and he gave us a sincere handshake while looking us straight in the eye. He was only a year older than my father and quite likable. The Duke was also a decorated military man and he had served as a commander in the British Royal Navy. His military background helped give him a well-rounded world view. To this day, he is the oldest surviving male member of the British Royal Family. Now he has been married to Queen Elizabeth for seven decades.

Previously vetted, the entire team was invited to attend a formal affair at Eaton Hall, Park Cheshire. The estate was the sprawling country house on the 1,100-acre private domain of the Duke of Westminster. As we approached the royal structure, the landscaping was grand, classic, and breathtakingly beautiful. The sweeping, lush panorama was just like in the cinema! The driveway was long and bordered by flawlessly manicured old growth shamrock green shrubbery, bold fountains, lakes, and statues. I felt like I was in

48 http://en.wikipedia.org/wiki/Leonora_Anson%2C_Countess_of_Lichfield.

the presence of opulence as we approached the historic grand stone structure.

Once inside the austere rock edifice and past the foyer, butlers directed us toward a 15 foot tall, huge rustic pair of iron-clad heavy wooden doors. We were uniformly dressed in our finest blazers, 7th ATP Crest attached to our breast pocket, and a strict military presentation. As we entered one at a time, our name and rank were announced on the landing at the top of the stairway. As we made our entrance into the Great Banquet Hall, we paused momentarily for the formal presentation and then marched ceremoniously down the sweeping grand staircase and into the regal onlookers. We were among world-class British royalty!

As we mingled with the royal elite, including Miss Great Britain, we were approached by exquisitely dressed beautiful young ladies in very formal attire. The maids wore the classic short jet-black frilly dresses and starched pure-white matching intricate, sexy aprons. The cookie-cutter servants could just as well have been professional models walking the runway. They would alternate sterling silver trays full of cocktails served in crystal and various traditional English delicacies. It was very much like being in a King Arthur film without the claymore or broadswords. I had died and gone to heaven for that one night, and now I knew how the other half lived and entertained! The setting was breathtaking, the company was majestic, and the evening divine. I was star-struck and felt fortunate to have a backstage pass to see how the one percenters partied. Somehow, I knew enough to mind my "Ps and Qs," a very British saying referring to any alcoholic drink consumed in the volume of pints and quarts. You see, I was as disciplined as I wanted to be and this was one of those times. I didn't want my name affiliated with an international incident or embarrass the 7th APT!

As I looked around, taking in the stunning medieval decor, I noticed two wonderfully imposing, larger than life-sized original Rembrandt's on either side of the massive rock and timber fireplace. They were perfectly "at home" in this stone chamber constructed during the seventeenth century. I was getting the idea of how the very British James Bond spent his weekends at home—and I rather liked it. All pomp and ambiance. I could picture Bond's family mansion by the name of Skyfall as being equally grand when entertaining the crème de la crème.

However, as the night waned, four of us young Americans received an invitation to continue the party at the private residence of two jewelers from Chester. Soon after we were received at that impressively vast mansion, we realized the host's ulterior motive. My most vivid memory of that visit was locking myself in the huge main bathroom to avoid unwanted advances. The ostentatious privy was the combined size of the dining and living room where I had grown up. To steer clear of any impropriety before it occurred, we eventually fabricated an excuse and awkwardly departed for our hotel in a very sober state. It had been an uncomfortable experience, to say the least, and did not suit my lifestyle.

Skydiving Is No Accident

On tour, we were always treated like nobility, fed like farmhands, and given enough dark German beer to founder a horse. One of my favorite demonstration events in West Germany was in a rural farming village celebrating its 700th anniversary. It was exciting to be part of such an event. In this case, our DZ was the sports platz or soccer area and just past the outskirts of the Berg to the southeast on a small hill. However, the playing field had been neatly cut out of the surrounding towering old growth forest with just enough room for the sports platz and a crowd of onlookers. The audience had gathered, and our air show was nearly over. Most of the jumpers were safely on the ground, but VanBibber was the last one on my load to land on the dubious and secluded DZ.

Some of us were jumping brand new Ram-air canopies, and an inexperienced Pat had extended his flight path a bit too far downwind. As he rounded his base turn with his Cloud parachute onto a final approach to the soccer field, he discovered that he was shallow and too fast. At that point, the trees were quite tall and very stationary. Then, there was nothing to do except brace for impact. The parachute canopy was barely visible above the tree tops when Bibber disappeared into the dense green forest. After a seemingly endless pause, we heard cracking, snapping, and popping noises that could never be misconstrued as good. To this day, I can still see Bibber exploding out of the tree line, canopy twisting and surging, his tall frame oscillating back and forth with his hands faithfully on the control toggles, spraying pine boughs onto the unsuspecting public below. His momentum had carried him through the wall of dense branches about 40 feet above the surface and onto the playing field. Fortunately, no one was injured, and Bibber shrugged it off as a "typical" jump. He did, in fact, land in front of the spectators—right after he showered them with the freshly cut foliage! I had never seen anything like it.

Often, we would be invited to stay overnight for multi-day events or if we were en route to another show. Sleeping accommodations in local guesthouses were always the same in the rural German "bergs and villages." The second-floor bathroom was at the end of the hallway, and the small but clean rooms were never heated. The beds were cozy and covered with bulky down comforters in our individual rooms. The feel of the white, crisply starched, coarse, duvet was uniquely fabulous and unforgettable. Once in bed, I would do a few minutes worth of full leg peddling exercises causing enough friction between the covers to start to warm things up! Fairy dust followed within minutes, and then it was the magic of the night for a young skydiver. No one on the team expected it, but we were all treated like rock stars wherever we went. It instilled a sense of pride in my unique and once-in-a-lifetime job.

On October 22, 1971, we put on a demo for Secretary of the Army, Robert F. Froehlke at Lee Barracks in Mainz. The demo was on post in the midst of various two and three-story buildings. I remember that we all safely landed on the cobblestone surface without any mishaps. The following year, on May 12, 1972, at Lee Barracks, David Layne was not so lucky on the Delta II bad luck canopy. David reported the details of a malfunction on that jump. The weather was poor with low clouds and moderate wind; however, it was a maximum pressure demo and a mandatory military show.

Layne told me that the notation in his logbook recorded the jump from 2,000 feet but was well below that. The recording of 2,000 feet was to keep it "legal." Jumping the Delta II, two of David's last ten jumps had been malfunctions. On that day, he exited the aircraft, immediately deployed his parachute, and the canopy instantly went into a violent diving spin. The failure was caused by a hung up steering line. Layne had stowed the excess brake line in a rubber band at the top of the canopy that became snagged. He started out low and spent too much time trying to deploy the canopy. David knew it was too late to use his reserve, and that he was just going to have to ride it out and hope for the best. David was in a hazardous and exceedingly compromised position over the extremely precarious landing area. The prospects did not look good!

David later described the blur of spinning buildings below and the sound of screaming women just before impact. He was aware of two shrieking mothers on the sidewalk, both pushing baby strollers. Fortunately, Layne crashed into the middle of a street and not on a steep slate roof. He hit with so much force that his smoke bracket was mangled and gouged a hole in the pavement. That smoke bracket most likely saved him from serious injury and kept him out of the "broken leg club."

Steve Bienert and other team members were on the scene in no time. After checking that nothing was broken, they helped David to his feet and made him stand in the team lineup to complete the ceremony as if his malfunction was part of the routine. He reported that he was still in shock and shaking like a leaf when the introductions were made at the end of the demo. However, this would not be his only narrow escape while skydiving on the team.

We were all consumed with a love of jumping, but my first season on the demo team was very demanding from many standpoints. Some exhibition jumps had "catastrophe" written all over them, especially if you missed the DZ or did not end up in front of the crowd. On May 13, 1972, Michael J. Povlsen, (FNG) jumping a demo with the 7th APT landed on top of a boxcar at the German-American Fest in Kaiserslautern. He suffered a severe right leg fracture on his 204th jump. Mike was interviewed at the Second General Hospital in Landstuhl, West Germany. The *Stars and Stripes* reported: "As the winds shifted, Povlsen drifted over a (rail) freight yard north of his

DZ and landed on top of a boxcar. The wind pulled him over the edge and down between two cars. 'My body fell between the cars, and most of me hit on one side of the rail, but my leg hit on it (the steel track). When my leg made contact with the rail, I heard the bone snap,' he said."

I had a serious premonition of the same thing happening to me in Bremerhaven, which I describe in "The Infamous Missing Man Formation" Chapter 19.

Teammate John Cutts broke his leg jumping at a demo in Strasbourg, France, after my tenure. They took him to a nearby French hospital and wanted to operate on him. He was having none of that "French butchery!" In due time, he was drunk enough to control the pain. They splinted his leg, loaded him into a car, and his comrades drove him the two and a half hours back to Bad Kreuznach for treatment at the military hospital. He survived the ordeal to jump again.

Long before I came to the team, Captain McPherson D-2330 had a malfunction over a runway resulting in a severely fractured leg. After a lengthy rehabilitation, his dedication led him to return to the team. He walked with a limp and often used a cane for ambulation on his bad days. He only made one or two jumps with the team during my time in Europe.

CHAPTER 17
Italian Sports Camp

The team was invited to an Olympic-style tournament for a skydiving competition alongside a multitude of other sporting disciplines. It was held in Italy's President Giulio Andreotti own horse racetrack just outside of Pisa during the first part of July 1972.

N° 37934

FIRMA DEL TITOLARE

Il SGT. LIPPINCOTT RANDALL

nato a CENTRAL CITY il 2-6-1949

Distretto CENTRAL CITY matr.

ha conseguito la qualifica di « paracadutista abilitato al lancio » il 10-7-1972 presso il Scuola Militare di Paracadutismo

IL COMANDANTE DELLA SCUOLA

(Col. Vitaliano Gambarotta)

Timbro

Esercito Italiano Scuola Militare Di Paracadutismo Brevetto
The Italian Army Military School of Parachuting License No. 37934

I remember the large venue and that the photo for my Military School of Parachuting License was taken with a long telephoto lens from about 50 feet away. It seemed strange at the time, and I suppose the cameraman had forgotten his portrait lens. The international competition was well-organized and intense but very friendly.

Our journey to the competition was a bit circuitous. First, the team drove north from our home base in Bad Kreuznach to Schaffen, Belgium. At their Parachute Training Center, we boarded a vintage prop plane with the Belgique team, who were also attending the camp. From there, we flew southwest to Paris and picked up the French team at the Le Bourget Airport where Charles Lindbergh landed following his historic 1927 transatlantic solo flight. In essence, we were hitchhiking with the Belgium team.

The flight started out midday, and on the last leg of our trip, we were flying over the Italian Alps at sunset in a Belgium Air Force C-119 Flying Boxcar. Any direction you chose to look was perfectly breathtaking; the scenery was right out of *National Geographic*! From our vantage point, we could see only mountains and snow covering the Earth. The low evening light on the Alps painted the peaks in stark contrast to the valleys, and both were bathed in soft pastels that hinted of alpenglow. Snow-clad summits were endlessly connected by a milky sea of low lying clouds. In the crystal clear air, there was no sign of man. We might as well have been on the moon. The excursion was one hell of an all-expense-paid field trip with more to come!

The skydiving competition on the racetrack lasted the entire seven days. I made a total of 18 jumps including one practice and one exhibition jump. Consistency was everything, and I was using my new Papillon for the competition. Although I made three dead centers, I didn't quite have the French canopy dialed in, and one bad jump put me out of the running in the international competition. I placed twelfth in style, seventh in individual combination, but was on the second place team overall with Callaghan, Leverett, and Fisher.

We stayed on campus at the sports facility, but I had an opportunity to travel to the coast while in Pisa and try my hand at surfing in the Ligure Sea on the Mediterranean. The waves were not that conducive, and I had no formal instruction, but at least I returned unscathed! It was important to me to avoid injury. I had denied myself the opportunity of downhill skiing in the Alps, I had no plans to scuba dive in the Mediterranean, and rock climbing in the Dolomites was out. I certainly didn't want to hurt myself while attempting a little surfing. Later, I visited the Leaning Tower of Pisa, but we had little free time for sightseeing in the historic city.

Most of our parachute drops for that competition were in an anemic UH1-B helicopter, but I did get an opportunity to jump a Piaggio while in Italy. I didn't realize it at the time, or I might have freaked out, but it was on my 666th jump! The Piaggio 166 Pusher Turbine Prop is an Italian-made mid-sized civilian aircraft, and it was different from any other aircraft I had ever jumped. It was a small twin-engine high wing aircraft with eight seats, and the exit door was on the left side in front of the propeller. Yes, you read that correctly. Although the propeller did not extend that far below the underside of the high wing, it was still intimidating. The wing was moderately broad, thick, and angled upward, but the presence of the spinning blades was still a bit disconcerting.

Running at flight idle, we approached the aircraft from the front, which made communication impossible above the sound of the turbines. The left side door was the entrance and our exit in front of the whirling propeller. As the host team, the Italians held out no animosity toward us and, of course, nothing merited an international incident with a messy fatality. It was not only a novel and very fast aircraft but fun to have jumped from as well. However, we did insist that the Italians make the first jump!

The awards ceremony was on the last day of the competition, and we headed home the following morning. On our return trip to West Germany, the legs were reversed. From Pisa, we took off in the C-119 and headed to Paris with all three teams on board. We all rode in the back wearing Belgic emergency parachutes per the Belgian Air Force protocol. The return flight had been as bucolic as the arrival had been beautiful. But as we approached Paris, the weather deteriorated drastically. It was so worrisome that I even opened the back left door during the flight in case it was necessary for an emergency bailout. However, by that time we were at a relatively low level of 800 feet over the beautiful rain-soaked, green, lush, countryside.

Piaggio 166 Turbine Pusher Prop, with the Italian Team. Sgt. Cal Callaghan far right, Sgt. Guy Leverett below the prop, and Sgt. Randy Lippincott holding his white helmet. Photographer unknown.

The pilots were scud running (flying under and around low-lying clouds), and we were getting severely bounced around. As a pilot myself, I realized the dangers involved in the ill-advised activity. The closer we got to Paris, the more violent the weather became. It started out with heavy rain and lightning, then just before landing at the Paris Le Bourget Field, we flew through the middle of a savage hail storm. We were in a 1950 "Tin-can," and it sounded like Thor was trying to pry us out of it! The noise was deafening, the ride was brutal, and the outcome was continuously in doubt. I was perilously ready to use my parachute even at that ridiculously low altitude! I had a vision of *Flight of the Phoenix* and did not relish an "off airport landing" in the antiquated Boxcar even if it was a successful movie!

Wet microbursts are associated with thunderstorms and tend to be deadly around airports. Just before landing, the wind shifted 180-degrees. Yes, it was the proverbial, deadly, unpredictable, severe low-level wind shear. That's the thing about emergencies; you never know when they are going to occur. Now we were in real trouble! If the pilot stalled the airplane that close to the ground, we would all be killed in a massive fireball. There would be no chance of recovery, and a crash would be inevitable. I mentally calculated that I could still successfully exit at 300 feet! The sudden tailwind caused us to land at almost double our planned touchdown speed. Fortunately, it was a very long runway because we took up all of it to get stopped. It was a miracle that we didn't run off the end because of the wet conditions and excessive momentum due to the wind shift. The smell of rubber and hot brakes drifted into the cabin as we turned off the rain-soaked concrete at the extreme end of the runway.

I was surprised that the tires had not blown or that the pilots had lost control during the crisis. It was very scary because the outcome was seriously in question. I vividly remember how visibly shaken up both of the military pilots appeared after we had all deplaned. After all, they would have been the first casualties. The airplane, however, was in much worse shape. It was hammered into an entirely different machine by the severe hail, and it wasn't going anywhere for a very long time. Most likely, it was destined to the scrap metal heap. All the aluminum of the leading edges was grossly deformed, and nearly all of the forward looking glass had been broken out. We made it home that day but it was by train, and we were thankful to be on it. We were not hanging around for the "Phoenix" to rise from the ashes!

CHAPTER 18
Weinsheim 750th Anniversary

Little did I know how the next exhibition was going to change my life. John Cutts approached me to jump in his place on that demo. He had made other plans for the weekend, and I accepted his offer without hesitation. I only had four months left on the team and wanted to log as many freefalls as possible, and I was closing in on my 750th jump.

It was almost going to be a local show as Weinsheim was less than a five-minute flight from the Bad Kreuznach Airfield. The show was a celebration of the 750th anniversary of the tiny nearby berg. I knew nothing about the small village, but that would all change soon.

We made the demo on July 22, 1972, at the prescribed time, and upon landing, I recognized a familiar face. It was my conversational German language instructor. He happened to be the Village Burgomaster and enthusiastically greeted me with, "Come Randy, there are American girls!" Reluctantly, I agreed to humor my teacher, although I had no interest in meeting his friends. He escorted me to a picnic table where there were, in fact, Americans. He introduced me to Phyllis Updegrave, whom he worked with at the American Military School in Bad Kreuznach, and her daughter Melea who was sitting next to her. Melea was blond, 19, outgoing, and very attractive. It was hard for me to take my eyes off of her. I sat at the table directly across from the young lady, had some traditional German chicken, and tried to behave. Before I left, I had a date for the following day. I almost couldn't believe the serendipity of what had just happened!

Time couldn't pass quickly enough for Sunday to come around. I had to find out more about this beautiful women that I had just met. It didn't take long, and I talked Cutts into letting me take his black 1954 Harley Davidson motorcycle back to Weinsheim the next day. After all, it was his fault that I was in this predicament! Melea and I spent a serene afternoon in a grassy field south of the village on a secluded hillside. She had prepared a picnic lunch, and we shared a bottle of local Rhine wine together. The sun shone down on our faces, but it was my heart that was warmed. The gentle breeze played with strands of her blond hair and the tall grass. I remember that conversation was easy, and I hung on every word that she spoke as we reclined on a blanket in the isolated, fragrant field. I thought that Melea was a goddess sent to make me a better man. That day, for the first time, I held her sweet dimpled face in my hands, and I left my heart in that meadow. Being with Melea was an unexpected special tenderness come true! I was quickly growing very fond of her.

Although Melea had just graduated high school, she spent the first part of that summer in Majorca on the very romantic and historic Mediterranean Sea. She seemed more worldly than me, for I had not been with nor dated anyone the entire time I was in Europe and was not looking for any relationship except with my parachute. I was on my best behavior, but we soon became romantically entwined. I had gone steady in high school, had courted girls in college, and had been with other women, but this was very different. Melea was special, and I did not want our relationship to end. If I was not jumping or out of town on a trip, you could bet I was in Weinsheim. If I was off work in the afternoon, I was in Weinsheim. If I had a free weekend, it was spent with Melea. Fortunately, I had unlimited use of John's motorcycle. Everyone on the team noticed the change in me and commented on it. Suddenly, my life had real purpose.

She was so pleasant to be with, and communication between us was open. We were honest with each other and held no secrets. The relationship was innocent in the purest sense. Day by day, our genuine feelings grew for each other. It was sheer magic for me whenever I was around Melea! I was working at 10,000 feet and living on Cloud Nine as I fell head over heels in love with her. I would kiss her mouth in sweet slow motion and caress her body like it was my last act on this Earth. She was putting some serious miles on my heart! First Sergeant Stanley had a candid way of asking how a date went. His exact words were, "Did you pop her toes?" The remark honestly was a direct reference to sexual intercourse. Of course, as a gentleman, I would only answer the question with a big smile. After all, he was my boss and had saved my bacon on multiple occasions. There was no way that I could ever be upset with Stan.

Melea had a stunningly perfect angelic face, flawless skin, silky flowing hair, and the body of a Grecian goddess. Mature far beyond her years, she moved like a model, spoke like a princess, and her eyes connected directly to my very soul. She was innocent, but also captivating and seductive; I was completely helpless in her presence. Her smile was mesmerizing, and whenever I was around her, I felt so very incredible. Melea was not only gorgeous, she was smart, and I was nowhere near running out of superlatives. Unfortunately, she was registered to attend college in Ellensburg, Washington, that fall. That seemed very far from where I was headed, but I believed that love could conquer all.

I was smitten. Soon I was spending so much time with Melea that First Sergeant Stanley came up with his new pet name for me, "Honey Bear." The honey bear is so focused on the nectar of the hive that he can only think about licking honey all day no matter how many times he is stung. First Sergeant Stanley even had it transcribed on the plaque I received when I left the team that fall. My name was engraved as Randall H.B. Lippincott. It still proudly hangs on the wall in my library to this day. Freefall was no longer my first and only love!

A thing of beauty is a joy forever.
—Keats

I remember riding a city bus with Melea in Bad Kreuznach. Unsolicited, the woman in front of us on the bus turned and commented that we looked to be intensely happy together. We were a perfect match! Now, what I knew all along was confirmed by a complete foreign stranger. I would do anything for this woman, and I was starting to plan the rest of my life together with her. I only thought about pleasing her. If she was happy, then I was too.

My grandparents, Harvey and Nancy Lippincott, visited the team that summer and also met her. I borrowed their new red Cadillac DeVille to take Melea on a unique date (not on a motorcycle). It would have been to a drive-in movie, but instead, I drove out onto the inactive and dark Bad Kreuznach Airfield. It was a quiet and very secluded place that I was familiar with and that night we spent our time uninterrupted in the backseat with all the windows heavily fogged over. I had never been so in love, so entirely focused on another person. Yes, the physical aspect was great, but that just reinforced the relationship for me. I couldn't explain it. I had been unexpectedly swept off my feet when I was not looking for romance. I was living in a glorious fantasy world that I wanted to last forever. The stars could not have been more perfectly aligned. I did not want that night of sweet romance to end. During my every waking hour, I thought of ways to make her happy. Melea was the woman that I wanted to spend the rest of my days with…always and forever. I was having the time of my life. Skydiving simply no longer held me in its spell.

Stars: overwhelming events occurring at the safe distance of the past.[49]

Sgt. Randy Lippincott and Grandfather Harvey Lippincott next to the Team Huey. Photo Courtesy of Nancy Lippincott.

49 Allure of the Seas, aft staircase, port side, level 11.

On occasion, I was able to break away in the middle of the day, and we would spend hours together in her bathtub in the small upstairs apartment. My fingers and toes were mottled; they had never been so white and wrinkled! We enjoyed each other's company enough that our state of dress—or undress—meant nothing. I could never be close enough to her or be with her long enough. I never felt more alive in my life! It was more exciting than freefall, and it lasted longer!

That summer, we were lost in music together. I distinctly remember the songs that we played: "Crocodile Rock" and "Rocket Man" by Elton John; "The First Time Ever I Saw Your Face" by Roberta Flack; "The Lion Sleeps Tonight" by Robert John; "Nights in White Satin" by the Moody Blues; "A Horse With No Name" by America; "Saturday in the Park" by Chicago; "Sealed With a Kiss" by Bobby Vinton; "Proud Mary" by Ike and Tina Turner; "Wild World" by Cat Stevens; "I Woke Up in Love This Morning" by the Partridge Family; (Your Love Keeps Lifting Me) "Higher and Higher" by Jackie Wilson; and yes, "Love Her Madly" by the Doors. I had been living my fantasy! I hated having to say goodbye that fall and resented the distance that was coming between us. I didn't know how, but I was going to make it work. With Melea's help, everything would be okay. There was nothing that I wouldn't do to show her how much I loved her. I was proud of her pursuing her education and was optimistic about our future together.

CHAPTER 19
The Infamous Missing Man Formation

While Melea was away, I was alone again with only my work to focus on. I was happy to be in Northern Europe at the seaport of Bremerhaven, West Germany. It was that first night downtown in a loud disco that I first heard, "Get It On" (Bang a Gong) by T. Rex. That song just struck a chord with me, and made a lasting impression because I still love it! It is the theme song of skydiving: Get it on! Don't just sit there and talk about it. Let's go 120 frigging mph, screaming straight down, with nothing but a tug of war between gravity and air holding you back. No bravado, no strutting; just GET IT ON!

Without exception, every freefall is the real deal; each and every time you step out the door into nothing but space and consequence. You are taking your life into your hands; you are personally molding your destiny at that very moment. If you jump with others, you are altering the survival equation exponentially. I needed to trust the other team members, but trust had to be earned. Anyone can kill you in a 120 mph heartbeat with a single mistake. It may be innocent or sloppy on someone's part, but nonetheless, you are just as dead. The use of automatic opening devices are routine today, but during this period, no one used "training wheels" unless you were a student.

Okay, so maybe my assessment of risk-taking had changed. I missed Melea, and now that I was making plans for the rest of my life, maybe I wanted to live past the age of 30.

The Four-Man Diamond Formation

Traditionally, the second pass for our demonstration, a jump from 10,000 feet AGL, was the four-man diamond formation. Two jumpers would exit from each side of the helicopter with adequate separation as seen from the ground but quickly came together. The visual effects were possible through the use of smoke bombs attached to each jumper's foot. The bracket was constructed with separation between the white hot grenade and the boot so that the jumper's foot stayed cool. Everyone would form up on the number one man, also known as the designated leader. The lead jumper was responsible for the spot, i.e., how fast, in what direction we tracked (moved horizontally) across the ground as a unit, and the altitudes for separation and opening. The wingmen would assemble on both sides and slightly behind the leader, close enough to reach out and touch the leader's respective foot. The slot man would slide in behind the leader to complete the formation. The unit would move horizontally through the air as determined by the lead jumper. In the diamond configuration, the smoke from the four members would blend into a single column as seen from the ground.

At the designated altitude, the leader would "wave off," which was the signal to stand by to execute your individual maneuver. As soon as the lead jumper did a quick diving 180-degree turn, the right wingman (that was me) did a 90-degree diving left turn, and the left wingman did a 45-degree diving right turn. The slot man floated momentarily and at the instant the traffic cleared, he dove straight ahead. From the ground, it looked like the formation instantly coalesced into a single mass and then dramatically exploded in opposite directions, each jumper trailing red smoke in one of the four cardinal headings. It was the outstanding and impressive bomb burst effect. Each jumper then turned to focus on the leader for his next cue. Everyone had their ripcord in hand, ready for instantaneous activation. Once I saw the first hint of the leader's pilot chute, I forcefully popped my ripcord. From the ground, it appeared that all four canopies opened simultaneously. From beginning to end, it was a breathtaking well-choreographed machine.

I always felt that the formation jump was the "heart" of the demonstration program. It was the most fun to participate in, involved the greatest number of jumpers and was impressively graphic and dynamic from the ground. It clearly portrayed the essence of a classic air show—action, grace, and stunning beauty. In a word, impressive!

Since Bremerhaven is coastal, it is not at all surprising that weather was a dominant factor when we were ready to start our program. We took off in the UH-1H Huey helicopter from the soccer field where the show was to take place and climbed to the requisite altitude of 10,000 feet. The first event was the two-man baton pass with smoke. As the two individuals came together from opposite directions, they united and started a spinning (candy cane) maneuver until it was time to break off to get separation followed by canopy deployment. Upon landing, one jumper would produce the souvenir embellished with an inlaid brass plaque.

The second pass was the diamond formation, which was our trademark presentation. We didn't have radio contact with the ground on this particular day, but the smoke trails indicated that the wind had picked up; we could also see whitecaps on the water caused by the strong wind. The Beaufort Wind Scale confirmed that whitecaps are generated at wind speeds of 20 knots or greater. Nevertheless, on jump run, our leader determined that it was show time, and the fans were not to be denied.

The exit was routine, and we quickly formed up with no problem and had a nice tight diamond trailing a "single column" of red smoke. However, as I evaluated our drift across the ground, I determined that it was incredibly fast. We had a strong tailwind and were rushing toward our target at an alarming rate. I could plainly see that we were going to overshoot our objective. We were way above our bomb burst altitude, and after a split-second hesitation, I unilaterally decided that the only way to make it in front of the crowd was to deviate decidedly from the planned show routine.

There was no time to discuss it with my teammates! Instantly, I made a right-hand 180-degree turn away from the formation to head upwind at my maximum penetration. I had no idea what the slot man was thinking about my sudden and unorthodox departure. I didn't even bother to watch the other three guys because the spot was, in fact, super critical at this point and I was concentrating on it. Honestly, I was banking my reputation on my judgment at that instant. If I didn't land in front of the audience, it was going to be an all-around embarrassment. Now, not only was I going into the wind but I could undoubtedly see that I was going to have to smoke it (open much lower than normal) to possibly even land on the soccer field; let alone, in front of the crowd.

To this day, I can still picture the imposing church steeple in downtown Bremerhaven (Herz-Jesu Geestemünde), and I recall how I gauged my opening on that ominous landmark. Even though I was in the saddle well below my compulsory 2,000-foot opening altitude, I immediately turned my parachute into the wind to try and hold my precarious distance. Everything was happening so quickly, but I needed to check my speed across the ground as I involuntarily raced backward toward the DZ at Bürgerpark, a half mile away. The wind was fierce, and I was on a highway to the danger zone! I had fleeting thoughts of landing on a downtown penthouse, power lines, or a busy intersection in this major metropolitan city. I was aware that when I dropped below the tops of the buildings, there would be a significant wind shear, and I would have to reconfigure to land safely on a street or the sidewalk.

Then suddenly, I was well away from the buildings and crossing the main railway hub and countless unforgiving cold steel railroad tracks, deadly power lines, and running trains. I had moved from the frying pan into the fire! My position was the formula for a plethora of misery! In fact, my final resting place was still "up in the air." Abruptly following a couple of turns and less than 70 seconds after covering a considerable distance, I was the only one on the ground in front of the cheering assembly. A little giddy with my déjà vu; again, I was the only person to land in front of the audience, just like my August 14, 1971, jump in Alconbury, Great Britain. I was quietly becoming the main attraction in Captain McPherson's Flying Circus. After all, it was not my first rodeo!

My team members had landed a considerable distance out of the city limits, and a car was sent to pick them up. Nobody was injured, but some feelings were hurt. This jump was immediately coined, "The missing man formation." I was never disciplined for the deviation, nor was I encouraged or inclined to repeat such an act. On similar days that we had high winds, someone would come in the hangar and announce that the wind was "dropping," - yes, dropping electric line poles, church steeples, oak trees, etc. It seems that all of life has been a double-edged sword for me and my exploits.

The next day in Bremerhaven we again found ourselves in a compromising position at 10,000 feet ready for the diamond formation. However, our team leader was determined not to repeat his mistake and exit too close to the venue. This time, it was the pilot yelling at us to "Get the hell out of my helicopter!" We were headed directly into a hugely majestic and intimidating thunderstorm. I glanced forward and saw that the black cloud filled the entire windscreen of the big olive drab Huey. I knew the helicopter would not survive entering this type of cloud. We were already too close for any real safety parameters, but the pilot wanted to cut his losses. Moments before the pilot peeled off; we bailed out of both doors for the four-man formation. I had visions of *The Man Who Rode the Thunder*! In 1959, Colonel Rankin ejected over a thunderstorm where he was suspended from his canopy over 40 minutes and was nearly beaten senseless in the cloud as lightning flashed all around him. His wild ride turned out to be a seriously brutal lesson for all of us.

As soon as I left the aircraft, my face was sandblasted by vicious razor-sharp drops of water. Yes, it was rain, but not like any rain I had ever experienced. Colliding with the precipitation at 120 mph on my unprotected skin was frightfully painful and distracting. Fortunately, I was wearing goggles, but I still wanted to use both hands to guard the rest of my exposed face. However, I needed one arm to maintain control and to keep me from going completely head down. The rain was uniquely and unavoidably traumatic for the continuous 8,000 feet of freefall.

Rain: a disguise used by clouds to gain earthly insight.[50]

Now it was hail that I desperately wanted to avoid. I had entered the hydrologic cycle quite unintentionally and had no interest in a repeat sequence. The four-member team falling through the rain was

[50] Ibid.

the classic setup for a potential significant electrical discharge or major lightning strike.

Lightning may be released whenever a charge is generated in the air. Traditionally, the friction of individual raindrops or even dust falling through the air creates a collective charge that triggers a lightning strike. The discharge may take place between clouds or from cloud to ground. We were going much faster, and were much larger than a raindrop; and we certainly generated more friction and, therefore, more static energy than a tiny drop of water. It was the definitive setup for a lightning strike.

I didn't like the way this was developing. I could feel the hair on the back of my neck stand up! I was waiting to see St. Elmo's Fire around my gloves or the other jumpers next to me, which is the hallmark of a buildup of an excessive charge just before being zapped by a devastating bolt of lightning. Visions of the recent "missing man formation," flashed through my mind. I thought it unfair to "go out" like this. I knew it would happen fast and we would be in an unconscious or dazed state as we impacted the ground together in our present formation. There was nowhere to go but down in a smoldering mass.

I believe my "Guardian Angel" was on that jump and shielded all of us from a potential deadly midair discharge. The electrical voltage and heat generated would have instantly stopped the heart, seized the brain, and melted our delicate nylon parachutes. The scenario was not a scene from a Roadrunner cartoon! My definition of lightning is God's way of flashing the porch light to let you know it's time to come in.

Nevertheless, in spite of all the distractions and the potential for disaster, we all finished the show on a positive note. Yes, we made our finest bomb burst, and all landed in front of the gathering. Our canopies and jumpsuits were all the cleaner for it!

CHAPTER 20
The Really Big Show

Air shows, unfortunately, are not without real casualties. The site of the second-deadliest recorded air show incident took place in front of 300,000 people in West Germany at the U.S. Air Show, Flugtag '88.[51] At Ramstein, three aircraft from the Italian Air Force Display Team (Frecce Tricolori) tragically collided midair during their demonstration run and crashed to the ground and into part of the onlooking crowd. Three pilots died, and 67 spectators were killed.[52] In the resulting explosion and fire, 346 spectators sustained serious injuries, and nearly 500 others had minor physical injuries, not to mention the psychological trauma of the spectacular event. Over 600 people reported to the Landstuhl Regional Medical Center to donate blood that afternoon for the victims.[53] Ramstein Air Force Base in Kaiserslautern, West Germany, was not far south of my Base in Bad Kreuznach for the 7th Army Parachute Team. My brother, Captain Loren Lippincott, was stationed there attending the airshow on that Sunday, August 28, 1988, 16 years following my tour of duty.

At the time of the accident, one of the damaged aircraft from the group crashed into the Emergency Medical Evacuation UH-60 Blackhawk Helicopter parked on the ramp. The helicopter's pilot, Captain Kim Strader, was critically injured, and he died from burns on Saturday, September 17, 1988, at Brooke Army Medical Center in Texas. Reportedly, the pilot of the aircraft that struck the helicopter ejected and was killed before his parachute opened.[54] The third aircraft

---

51 4 held over worst air show crash, CNN World, http://en.wikipedia.org/wiki/Ramstein_air_show_disaster.

52 1988 Ramstein air crash stirs memories, www.stripes.com.

53 *Trauma, Disaster and Recovery,* Robert J. Ursano, M.D., Carol S. Fullerton, Ph.D., Kathy M. Wriqht, Ph.D. and James E. McCaroll, Ph.D., editors. Department of Military Psychiatry et al., page 12ff.

54 SL Army officer burned in air show crash dies, www.deseretnews.com.

disintegrated in the collision and parts of it were scattered along the runway.

Chaos ensued following the explosion and horrific fires. In two minutes, the fire trucks arrived, two minutes later the American ambulances arrived, followed by the German ambulances. Then, three minutes later, the first rescue helicopter arrived. No one was in charge, and it was complete disorder and utter confusion. Unharmed bystanders were screaming, frantically looking for family members in the flames, debris, and thick choking black smoke. People who were not on fire stood in shock unable to even help themselves. It was pure mayhem!

My brother was a spectator in the audience with his family and immediately left them in a safe area to assist in triaging and helping the wounded victims in any way he could. At one point, he wandered out into the grassy infield alongside the landing strip where there was scattered wreckage, and he discovered the torso of the Italian pilot. It was no wonder that his ejection seat didn't save him; he had been traumatically severed during the high-speed collision. The scene was already horrific, and it was going to get worse. The victims were in various states of impairment, injury, and stunned by the shocking event. It looked like a war zone with smoking rubble and charred zombies in different states of shattered dress and ambulation. It was a scene of unspeakable horror!

At 4:35 p.m., 51 minutes following the initial impact, this is the unedited transcript from the military doctor on call over the emergency radio:

> We are searching for burnt (sic) patients that are pulled and transported unaided away from us by the Americans (spectators). They told us nobody from them are here no (sic) more. Not all the injured people are transported away by helicopter or ambulance. There is total chaos around us and some of the injured are even transported on pickup trucks that are not leaving on (sic) emergency exit, they are driving beside the drifting (stunned) visitors. It was a terrible sight

> to see people with burnt (sic) clothes and sagging burnt (sic) skin, squirming with pain of transfixed and shocked with pain on these vehicles.[55]

After the fires were extinguished and the wounded taken care of or transported away, Loren assisted in moving the dead onto one of two large flatbed trailers for processing at a remote site. Body parts and limbs were scattered randomly among the smoking remains. At one point, Loren reached down to recover a hand in the debris. A simple gold band could have told the story of tragedy and heartbreak. It was all that remained of someone's life, now only a broken family. The smell of jet fuel (JP-4) and burning human flesh was all too familiar for the combat veterans who were present. It was an unbelievably heinous scene right out of *Dante's Inferno.* This account takes me back to the Hindenburg Lakehurst disaster and the immortal words of Herbert Morrison from WLS in Chicago, "Oh… the humanity!"

When Loren first described this event to me, he recounted it in a matter of fact way. However, he was reluctant ever to bring it up again or even write his account of it for me. Indescribable, the massive, tragic sudden loss of life in such an undignified and impersonal way was actively being suppressed. It was as psychologically traumatic for the survivors as it had been physically devastating for the victims. Death is permanent but mental scars last a lifetime.

After hearing of this disaster, I remembered watching the beautifully graceful Italian Tricolor perform flawlessly in Innsbruck, Austria, where I was competing in a parachuting match in October 1972. The mountainous area was a spectacular natural backdrop for the fantastic air show. The jets seemed to play hide and seek with the imposing surrounding rocky peaks. How could anything go so wrong with such a precision group like this? But then, they were piloted by humans.

---

55 "Katastrophen-Nachsorge – Am Beispiel der Aufarbeitung der Flugkatastrophe von Ramstein 1988", Hartmut Jatzko, Sybille Jatzko, Heiner Seidlitz, Verlag Stumpf & Kossendey 2. Auflage. 2001, ISBN 3-932750-54-3.

On a much lighter note, but at the same venue on August 27, 1972, I was dispatched with the team to the Silver Anniversary Celebration and Air Show for the U.S. Air Force. That day, there were over a half million witnesses in Ramstein at the Grand Celebration, and we were only one of the acts performing.

Since I had first started jumping, I found one constant wherever non-jumpers were involved. It was the art of asking imbecilic questions regarding our freefall activity, motivation, or equipment and it verged from the ridiculous to the sublime. We privately referred to them as "whuffos," which is a term for any non-skydiver. It came about due to the often repeated question, "Whuffo you jump out of airplanes?" With 500,000 plus people in attendance, I figured there were plenty of whuffos amongst the onlookers.

The weather was perfect, and the show came off without a hitch. The announcer stated each of our names and where we were from as we descended under open canopies. No sooner than I had landed, I made eye contact with a "whuffo." The small man approached me, emerging from the huge crowd line, wearing a Scottish print jacket and a contrasting plaid fedora. Mr. McGregor was a well-dressed elderly gentleman with a slight frame. I was surprised that the very first question out of his mouth was unrelated to skydiving. Mr. McGregor had braved a throng of a half million people to gain my attention and ask, "Do you know Harvey Lippincott from Gibbon, Nebraska?"

"Why yes I do, he's my grandfather!" I told him. We had a nice visit while I was packing my parachute for the next jump. He was visiting family on the base and was excited to be a witness to the largest air show he had ever attended. Gibbon was a town of about 400 in a very rural and agricultural area of Nebraska along US Highway 30 where everyone knows their neighbor. I will always remember meeting him as an incredibly unique and pleasant encounter during my European stint. I would have loved to have met the rest of the McGregor clan and visited more extensively about his relationship with my grandfather. Later, I received photos from Mr. McGregor of our reunion documented on his little Brownie camera. Mr. McGregor was not just another "whuffo," and I'm glad I had the presence of mind to treat him with respect when he spoke to me. It was a lesson that I would never forget. No matter where you travel in the world, no matter how far from home, one never knows who you might meet, and you always need to be on your best behavior. Under no circumstances can you anticipate when you may meet someone you know, or who knows your family.

Ramstein Air Force Base was about a 15-minute flight from our base in Bad Kreuznach. My only regret that day was that I chose to ride home in a car instead of flying home in the helicopter. The traffic jam leaving the airbase after the show was a protracted three-hour ordeal!

For my brother, Mr. McGregor, and for me, Ramstein had created both high and extremely morbid memories. The tragic Ramstein Air Show accident in 1988 will never be forgotten for so many different reasons.

McGregor and Sgt. Lippincott at Ramstein Airshow. Photo courtesy of D.E. McGregor taken on his Kodak Brownie camera.

CHAPTER 21
Berlin, Tempelhof Airfield

We were tasked with the first military demonstration jump, or for that matter, any parachute jump in Berlin since well before World War II. For the West Berlin trip, some of the guys drove private cars. I had special military travel orders (Flag Orders) and took the train through East Germany and into West Berlin. We jumped from aircraft already stationed at the Tempelhof Airport. I vividly remember the trip through the East German countryside. The buildings were raw unpainted concrete, with no color at all; everything was a pitiful drab gray. There were no billboards or advertisements, and not one sign of individualism, or for that matter, capitalism. It was evident that I was witness to an oppressed state.

Tempelhof Airfield was only one kilometer from the Berlin Wall, so our maximum allowed altitude for the entire show was 2,000 feet AGL. I'm not sure if the restriction was self-imposed or if it was a condition set forth by the East German Government or ATC. Regardless, we didn't want an international incident, and we certainly didn't want to be imprisoned in a communist gulag in the unlikely chance that we landed on the wrong side of the Wall. We were just happy to be jumping over the historic Tempelhof Airfield. We made a series of six low-level demo jumps over two days. They were all team stacks because of the restricted ceiling. The September 1972 air show was our second 25th year anniversary celebration for the United States Air Force. A reported gathering of 250,000 people were in attendance, which was only half the size of the turnout at the Ramstein air show celebration. I had never really thought about it before, but three-quarter million people witnessed my jumps on just those two occasions!

Sgt. Randy Lippincott signing autographs, Berlin air show. U.S. Air-Force Photo By Helga Mellmann.

Some of us made the trip to the small and historical Check Point Charley Museum. I also visited the iconic Brandenburg Gate and was up close to the Wall. My juxtaposition to the division between East and West Germany was a real eye-opener for me. What I had seen on black and white TV as a kid turned out to be true. The only way to show our genuine contempt toward the Russian soldiers was to "moon" the guards from an observation deck. They had weapons, and I'm sure they used live ammunition. After all, we knew they shot their people who tried to escape, so why would they care about killing foreigners?

I visited the Berlin Airlift Memorial in front of the Tempelhof Terminal. It was a moving but unpretentious marker commemorating the British and American pilots who lost their lives during that operation. The three curved ribs that formed the tall monument symbolized the three air corridors used by supply planes during that very busy and tense eleven months. The shrine was reminiscent of the towering Airforce Memorial at the Pentagon and to a lesser extent, the Chapel at the Airforce Academy.

Tempelhof has a well established military history dating back to the Crusades. The site of the airport was originally Knights Templar Land in medieval Berlin; and from this early beginning, the name Tempelhof originated. Later, the site was used as a parade field by Prussian and German forces until World War I. In 1909 a Frenchman, Armand Zipfel, made the first demonstration flight in Tempelhof, followed by Orville Wright later that same year.[56] Tempelhof was officially designated as an airport in 1923. The original terminal became the world's first to be accessible by underground railway. Now it is called Platz der Luftbrücke after the historic Berlin Airlift.[57] The enormous Tempelhof terminal was once among the top 20 largest manmade structures in the world.[58]

During the occupation of post-World War II Germany, the Soviet Union blocked any access to the portion of Berlin under Allied control. The Soviets wanted complete authority over the divided city. In response, the Western Allies organized the Berlin airlift to carry any and all necessary supplies to sustain the people in West Berlin, bypassing the Russian blockade.[59]

Incredibly, an allied supply plane took off or landed in West Berlin every three minutes from June 1948 to May 1949. The planes made nearly 300,000 flights, and the coordination and planning were a mind-boggling and intense exercise.

The sense of history was overwhelming during our parachute demonstration. We landed in the same place where those allied planes had landed 23 years earlier. We were the first jumpers that

---

56 U.S. Centennial of Flight Commission.

57 Take a Tour Through the Mother of All Airports, March 2014.

58 *Airports International* June 1975 (industry magazine).

59 Air Force Story, The Cold War, 1948–1950 (1953). Universal Newsreel. 1953.

most of the isolated Berliners had ever seen. In his 1963 "Ich bin ein Berliner" speech, President John F. Kennedy emphatically declared the support of the United States for Democratic West Germany. All of this came after the Soviet-supported Communist State of East Germany erected the Berlin Wall as a barrier to prevent any movement from East to West.[60] The Soviets, desperate to stop the defectors, needed a formidable deterrent, and to show the West that it meant business.

Our military pulled out all the stops for the Silver Anniversary Program. Of course, the Air Force had many different types of aircraft on static display, but the Army also had tanks and motorized guns. It was a most unexpected treat for me when we were allowed to drive those behemoth machines. We were certainly treated like VIPs! It was a thrilling experience to maneuver those colossal machines around on the expansive course laid out on the concrete apron at Tempelhof. I had driven a D-4 Caterpillar with steel tracks on the farm, but these were considerably more heavily built and had very modern and powerful automatic transmissions.

It wouldn't be until 1987 that President Ronald Reagan would utter the words, "Mr. Gorbachev, tear down this Wall!"[61] Although the airfield closed in 2008, the 909 acre Tempelhof Airfield footprint is still the largest inner city free space in the world. I felt privileged to have made some great memories in such a wonderfully historic venue.

---

60 "John Fitzgerald Kennedy". Scholastic Library Publishing, Inc. 2006.

61 "Remarks on East-West Relations at the Brandenburg Gate in West Berlin." Ronald Reagan Presidential Library.

Command Sergeant Major Harold B. Stanley over Tempelhof. Lanyard in his left hand, smoke has not started to vent. U.S. Air-Force Photo By Helga Mellmann.

CHAPTER 22
Left Behind, Not My Finest Hour

Although I was accumulating fantastic experiences and memories, such as our demonstration tour at Templehof, I was also in an emotional downward spiral following Melea's departure. And I began to make some poor choices. Communication with Melea from Europe was infrequent because she was busy preparing for school and I was traveling and occupied with work. No one made expensive transatlantic telephone calls at my pay-grade. At that point, while I wanted to save my money for our future, I also felt that my fate was uncertain, and that hopeless feeling led to waves of depression. Under the surface, I was reserved and cautious of what lay ahead for me. In my defense, I can honestly say that I was trained to kill enemy combatants and was willing to die for my country. It takes a certain mindset to "know" that my life expectation was short and uncertain at best. That knowledge and thinking process can foster dissonant thoughts and rash behavior in a 23-year-old.

The marginal conduct on my part was certainly not the way that I was raised. In retrospect, it was the classic definition of insanity as I repeated the same activity over and over and expected a different result with the booze. I don't believe that my immaturity ever placed any of my teammates in jeopardy, only myself. My story is clearly intertwined with extreme highs and lows (no pun intended). In the final analysis, I was still that insecure skinny farm kid with the buck teeth and inferiority complex who acted with an outwardly defensive manner when confronted. In my mind, my reflexes were ingrained with the response that I had learned dealing with my much bigger and older brother during my childhood. Because I lacked the physicality, I had to come across as loud, angry, and hostile against a much larger foe. Today, I envy a direct, articulate, and soft-spoken person—which I am not. Skydiving was a great distraction, but I could not jump all the time, and when I was not, the lonely hopeless feelings returned. After the high emotional relationship I had enjoyed with Melea, the loneliness and depression were magnified. My attempts to compensate, or block out, these depressed feelings only led to more problems. I recall one such time in particular:

We were on a routine demonstration jump in West Germany. Everyone made their individual assignments and landed safely. The fans met us with great warmth. We were always loved wherever we performed! I felt like I was a rock star! It was normal for us to still be in our jumpsuits as we adjourned to the traditional beer tent. We were invariably treated like royalty, fed like farmhands, and served beer like it was water. I had been on the team long enough that somehow I felt like a "child of privilege" and thought I knew how to play the game. Of course, along with that came an "attitude" of haughtiness, which was not intrinsic to my character. However, that evening I had worked in earnest to gain an advanced degree of intoxication, and my inhibitions were considerably lowered.

Apparently, we were a euphoric lot, feeling festive with much to celebrate. Luckily, I was still able to walk on my own as we exited the beer tent at the end of the evening. Upon my departure, a Full Bird Colonel addressed me regarding the show that day. I smugly turned to my left, looked right at him and a dismissive, sophomoric response came out of my mouth, "I only speak to generals!" I believe that First Sergeant Stanley was standing nearby, and somehow, God only knows how he insulated me from my own inebriated and uncalled-for insolence. Sadly, I still remember my insubordination all too well. I knew it was wrong then and regret it to this day! It certainly was not my finest hour! I did learn from that experience, and there was never a repeat of that particular ignominious scenario.

When we returned to Bad Kreuznach, I never heard another thing about it. I was never called into the captain's office to get chewed out, threatened with my job, or lost any rank. It's as though it never happened. I was allowed to suffer in silence without being thrown into the spotlight for my unruly conduct! I had already inflicted my own best punishment without a formal reprimand. I would have to wait for my comeuppance, not knowing where or when but most probably in a sober state. All of this had already been at the expense of my liver.

Psychologically, it has come home to roost at this very late date! What goes around, comes around.

I am also not proud of my first "all expense paid" visit to beautiful Luxembourg. It seemed like a repeat of the original West Biebrich trip on my 22nd birthday. With much practice that summer, the Luxembourg show was truly a unique all-time low for me. After a most excellent skydiving demonstration, I let my imbibing run away with me. Early in the evening, I started chasing fine French cognac with full-bodied German beer. It was not pretty. I thought that I was having a great time! The food was abundant and delicious, but I could have died from the amount of alcohol I consumed. The entire demo team ate at the same huge crowded table for dinner. I sat near the middle on the right-hand side of the long table for the feast. Somehow, after the meal, I stumbled back to the helicopter by myself. I never even checked into my room and apparently no one missed me. Did I think we were going somewhere? I passed out on the long porous nylon seat in front of the helicopter transmission by myself.

Unlike the bloody and costly Battle of the Bulge in nearby Bastogne, my battle was self-imposed and without a victor. In the nearby Ardennes Forest, young outnumbered American men had fought courageously and with honor, leaving a legacy of bravery and individual gallantry—all of which my personal battle lacked. At least in Bastogne, the enemy wore a foreign uniform. My conflicts were all from within my mind, and I was metaphorically only two steps from hell.

When I "came to" in the frigid morning air at dawn, still in my damp jumpsuit, I somewhat foggily deduced what had happened. The muted early morning light and mystical haze not only surrounded the helicopter on the ground but also extended into the depths of my mind. It helped dull the "icepick" feeling I had in my forehead. After I had scraped the disgusting dried food off my face, jumpsuit, and the seat, I found a bucket to carry water and finish cleaning up the mess in the helicopter. My disgustingly matted hair was next. I qualified for the role of the unkempt, dirty POW at this point—certainly not an elite parachutist.

My marginal behavior was only act one of my journey down the primrose path and some profoundly boorish behavior. We were scheduled to be part of a show that day, and I still willingly jumped in my completely intoxicated state. Nobody questioned my cognition or got close enough to smell me. I thought that if I could walk to the helicopter, then I could surely fall out of it! Youthfulness can prove to be incredibly resilient. Somehow I lived through that time in spite of making consistently bad choices. Either God was keeping me alive to punish me at some later time, or He had greater plans for my life, and I was exposed to these wild events to build character.

Over the next very long 30 hours, I could feel the toxic ethanol being expelled from my body with each disgusting breath. I had never experienced anything so repulsive, and it had been willingly self-inflicted. As my brain throbbed and my parched tongue stuck to the roof of my mouth, I could feel the poison oozing from my pores. When was it going to stop? It was a most unsavory state, but I was young and thoughtlessly bounced back for round two. It's just like Frank Sinatra used to say, "I feel sorry for people who don't drink. When they wake up in the morning, that's as good as they're going to feel all day." I hadn't insulted anyone, and there was no sexual misconduct, but it was still unmitigated vulgar drunken behavior. What in the hell was I thinking! Apparently, I wasn't yearning to become a statistic? I felt invincible. I was indestructible. Or, was I punishing myself for some act that had never occurred?

On a routine weekend for a demo in a small German village, the location has been long forgotten in the wastelands of my mind; I used extremely poor judgement. As usual, our hosts had treated us well, and the beer flowed, seemingly more in my direction than toward anyone else. The show had drawn to a close, and it was time to head out. The pilots must have had a date and wanted to get home as they were well ahead of us and the helicopter was already running and ready for an immediate departure. I had been otherwise occupied and brought my partial bottle of beer referred to as a "flippy" with me to the helicopter. As I pulled myself up into the right door gunner's position, I was met with a chorus of, "Get rid of that beer!" Well, I was obedient if anything, and followed orders to a "T." The team leader explained that there was to be no beer on an Army helicopter even if the container was empty. At that instant, I was already following the previous order. I was consuming the container in the swiftest most undignified manner possible…I downed it in a hurry!

Next, I concentrated on the second part of the order to get rid of the container. As described by my team members and much to my discredit, I tossed the bottle well away from the aircraft. Up, up, up it went, seemingly in slow motion, tumbling through the air. It appeared to hover as time stood still. Then, with intersecting vectors, glass met the huge whirling blades, followed by the inevitable singular sound of a shattered beer bottle. The glass was instantly turned into a refractive mist, exploding into a cloud of humiliation. "Oops—I mean SHIT! How did that happen? Where did that rotor come from?" Yes, the Army and their pilots take a blade strike very seriously.

If I had been sober, I'm sure that I would have been embarrassed. After shutting down the Huey, both pilots turned to glare at me. Everyone unloaded, and the pilots made a detailed inspection of the blades as if our lives depended on it. Fortunately, no damage was noted, and no transfer orders to Southeast Asia were forthcoming! We promptly departed for Bad Kreuznach in a somewhat somber state. I had already passed out in my seat for the trip home. It's possible to be an honest person and still exercise poor judgment—very poor judgment.

House of the Rising Sun

> "Oh Mother tell your children not to do what I have
> done…"
>
> —By Eric Victor Burton, Eric Burton,
> and Alan Price

I do not excuse my binge drinking, but inadvertently it did seem to be my *raison d'être*. Looking back, I think of it as actually a defense mechanism. The connection between drinking and low self-esteem was very real for me as it is for so many others. The depressive effect of alcohol quietly augmented my preexisting feelings of self-loathing. My conscious effort to withdraw acted synergistically with the drink, and I could temporarily slip away and not have to deal with reality or my tenuous connection to it.

In Special Forces and on the 7th Army Parachute Team, drinking was accepted, and I easily succumbed to peer pressure. I folded like a cheap suit. After all, it was a most social event, and I was desperate for acceptance in the group.

When I was a college student hanging out at the parachute loft, having a few beers was a natural way to unwind and have regular fellowship with other like-minded jumpers. Did my drinking club have a skydiving problem or what? Yes, skydiving and drinking are both pretty risky but acceptable behaviors and are commonly found together. After all, college age is the time in your life for experimentation and pushing the envelope.

After college, my next drinking exposure was with the military, which has a long, deep-seated history, leading back to the Colonies and the Revolutionary War. Add the European culture to the mix, and it all adds up to an easy trap. On the team, we used beer for bonding and as a stress reliever. Binge drinking is common in active duty military personnel and the drinking games we played potentiated the behavior.[62]

There is a difference of philosophy and tradition between the European and American lifestyles. In Europe, the consensus is that when alcohol is not exiled into a corner of society, it is demystified and, therefore, a less alluring vice. In America, you blow out the candles, go to a bar, drink, vomit, and pass out. You laugh the next day when your friends remind you what happened. It is a ritual—but a distinctly American ritual.[63]

---

62 http://www.ncbi.nlm.nih.gov/pubmed/19215846.

63 Europeans Learn Responsible Drinking by Jeff Frantz. http://www2.potsdam.edu/alcohol/YouthIssues/1077563832.html#.U-RoIVYUrwI.

The following quote is from *Psychology Today*:

> Another serious complication of binge drinking is called a memory blackout. Contrary to popular notions, a blackout has nothing to do with the loss of consciousness. Rather, it refers to a period in which a person is awake and can perform complex tasks such as holding a conversation or driving a car but there is no recollection later. A blackout is thus a memory gap. It results from the acute ability of alcohol to prevent a new memory formation in the brain. Consuming a lot of drinks in a short period or binging, particularly on an empty stomach, increases risk. Since a blackout occurs when one is highly intoxicated, it often happens when a person is exhibiting poor judgment. A lot can happen during a blackout. Not knowing what happened can be frightening and potentially dangerous, both medically and legally. The bottom line is that binge drinking is very common and the consequences both costly and harmful. Excessive alcohol use costs society over two hundred billion dollars annually, and 75 percent of these costs are related to binge drinking.[64] The important point is that alcohol dependence involves a "rewiring of the brain's reward circuits" and is associated with defects that require thinking (cognition), emotion, and motivation. Once this rewiring has occurred, it is difficult to reverse and is associated with occupational, social, and medical problems.[65]

---

64 http://www.psychologytoday.com/blog/demystifying-psychiatry/201203/binge-drinking-in-young-adults-and-older-people by Eugene Rubin MD, PhD and Charles Zorumski MD.

65 Ibid.

In the beginning, my drinking started out being "cool." I continued to drink because of peer pressure and, in the end, drank to escape my emotional symptoms of depression and later rejection. I only abstained when work or piloting an aircraft dictated sobriety. Much later, when my current wife Joyce came into my life, I found that I no longer needed alcohol to ease the pain. I felt fulfilled and didn't have to use it as a crutch. It is an asinine habit that I still think about, but my urges are fleeting and quickly pass. I challenged myself to a one-year hiatus from June 6, 2014, to June 6, 2015, and I can say that I have successfully earned my one year chip without difficulties. Many of my friends during that year tried to tempt me with all kinds of failed ploys, but I held steadfast in my conviction.

CHAPTER 23
I learned About Skydiving From That

An old high school classmate, Larry Gee, had flown home from college for an early holiday and offered to take me up in his tiny rented Cessna 150. It was Saturday, November 4, 1972, and I "jumped at the chance," of course pun intended! I had just returned home from the Army, and my initial civilian skydive would be at the Central City Airport. Overall, it was pretty uneventful with a 20-second delay from 5,400 feet, and I was alone. Of course, the real trick was getting my bulky parachute rig past the control column and safely out the door of the tight cockpit that had a narrow bench seat. I was happy to see and interact with Larry under those momentous conditions. It was an odd connection, to say the least, with Gee as the pilot and me the skydiver/pilot. He always wore a smile, was friendly, and was an excellent student. Having grown up on a farm, he wasn't afraid of hard work. Larry was big, a lot taller than me, and we had played high school sports together.

Three days later, on Tuesday, November 7, he was to fly back to the South Dakota School of Mines in Rapid City where he was finishing his degree. That evening, as dark clouds continued to gather, we discovered tragedy had struck. It had been a widely overcast Midwestern day when Larry departed Central City. In Nebraska, the terrain rises as you head northwest. Gee wasn't licensed to fly into the clouds (IFR), so he stayed below them. Eventually, it caught up with him in the Sandhills. He was flying under and around low-lying clouds (scud running) and flew into the side of a grassy basin during cruise flight. He died instantly. It was a tragic case of controlled flight into rising terrain.

My father and his partner in our airplane, Dr. Ken Treptow, were part of the search team that found Larry's body. It was a very gloomy day following my welcome home skydive. I didn't have my logbook with me at the time, so I never did get his signature for that jump. It would have been comforting to be able to look at it now and then. The

Lutheran Church in Central City was overflowing for his funeral. It makes me melancholy to this very day to think about it. Larry was a good man, had a gentle soul, and I still miss him all these years later.

Home from Europe in the winter of 1972-1973, I was still accustomed to jumping and working around helicopters and large military aircraft. Although I had piloted small civilian planes and my father even owned one, I checked my brains at the door, almost literally, when it came to propeller discipline and positional awareness.

I was jumping on North 48th Street at Arrow Field in Lincoln. It was the first flight of the day and a cold start for the Cessna 185. I was the last one in and therefore the person sitting next to the updated in-flight door that hinged upward under the wing when opened. Marv Helman primed and cranked the big Cessna engine several times and then he primed it again until it backfired. The 185 caught fire. Flames licked the side of the airplane and instantly shot fear into everyone.

As soon as I saw what was happening to the 185, I jumped out of the right-hand door and in two steps was addressing the source of the flames. It had only ignited excess fuel in the very large exhaust pipe projecting well out of the right side of the cowling. Protocol for an engine fire is to continue cranking, and the inferno is sucked back into the engine when it starts. However, I was fixated on the flames, and while standing in the arc of the propeller, I thrust my well-protected right forearm against the roaring orifice. It was extinguished instantly. To ensure that flames did not reappear, I unwittingly held my arm in place an instant longer. I was very focused because of my cold weather start experience, and I did not recognize my lethal position. My head was directly in the arc of the deadly propeller.

I surveyed the situation for only a fleeting second. Then, when I felt assured of the safety of the jumpers and the aircraft, I started to step back to signal Marv that I had it under control. At the same instant, I felt the rush of the large and lethal 86-inch long blade pass close enough to my face to know that I was, in fact, still alive. Then, with a surge and a puff of black exhaust, the engine roared to life. The gasoline/air mixture, at last, had been ignited in just the correct proportion for continuous combustion. I felt that my "Guardian Angel" had moved me aside at the very last moment or, at least, had her hand on the aircraft ignition. Nothing less than a force field protected me from the deadly blade. Never before had anything that life threatening ever come that surgically close to me—well, maybe.

My heart was racing as I started to breathe again, and I was so very thankful that my head was still on my shoulders. Unable to see me from the pilot's seat in the plane, Marv had no idea what had just happened. We made the jump but my heart was not in it that day. I performed a couple of dozen skydives that spring and jumpmastered several students that included static lines. Back in Central City during May, I jumpmastered both my friend Dan Hord and my brother Loren with my dad at the helm. It was good to be home!

I recalled another fire that had occurred during a winter cold start when I was with my dad years ago in Central City. The cold start for aircraft engines is a problem in three respects: First, the air-cooled engine is constructed from dissimilar metals that contract and expand at different rates when cold; therefore, binding and causing excessive friction on startup. The engine should be preheated as designed to function. Second, the cold oil is viscous and does not lubricate well at low temperatures. Third, when the battery is cold it simply does not have the cranking power for a regular start. It should also have an electric blanket to warm the battery properly to produce optimal power.

My dad and I had the plane out of hangar number seven and, after multiple attempts to start the cold engine, the carburetor flooded. Eventually, the 172 backfired and ignited the raw gasoline that sat inside the cowl waiting for a spark unlike the fuel-injected 185. Without a word, I sprang into action as soon as I saw the flames coming out of the engine compartment. I leaped out of the right door and started scooping up snow with my bare hands. I used the old style large oil access door on my side of the cowling to jam snow into the engine compartment as fast as I could. In less than a minute, the flames turned into white plumes of steam. I had saved the aircraft and possibly the entire building from a tragic fire. Dad ran around the hangar to phone the fire department, and they were already on the way. That day in Lincoln with the 185 was a reminder, and my actions were triggered by the same old reflexes.

While it was good to be home, I was also experiencing a profound contrast in my life. Leaving the 7th Army Parachute Team created a great void in my life. I was no longer the center of attention in front of the cheering masses; I was just a small town farm boy again. I no longer felt revered and beloved for my skills and applauded for my exploits. I yearned for the exotic travel and discovery of new and enchanting lands. I missed dining with royalty, the pomp and ceremony of the Army, and the security of the military uniform. There was no audience; there was no cheering. I seemed to have a total lack of "essential purpose" in my life.

The long-distance relationship with Melea added to my lack of direction. Melea had moved back to Ellensburg, Washington, for college in September. One month later, I was released from the Army and returned to Nebraska. Over Christmas break, I paid for Melea's plane ticket to come to Nebraska and meet my parents. Dad and I flew the Cessna 182 to Eppley Field in Omaha to pick her up in our airplane at the VIP gate. She was flawlessly beautiful in her jacket with a large fur collar and wearing some very sexy tight new blue jeans. I found the perfect diamond, and we became engaged. Accepting that ring was her commitment to stand by me.

Now I was making the biggest jump possible for a young man. I was also the happiest person on the planet. Everything seemed so perfect to me, but maybe she wasn't so impressed with my one bedroom single-wide trailer home at Riverside Park. I labored from 8:00 a.m. to 11:00 p.m. to make all of this work. Finally, she had to return to school, and I was sick—lovesick! Melea was all I could or even wanted to think about, and I called or wrote faithfully. She was a busy college student now, living away from home with critical studies and all the usual extracurricular activities.

After her visit, I was once again unable to think clearly, and I felt very alone. I was depressed, and I had to deal with it. The exciting life that I had lived was forever gone; it had evaporated into the same thin air that I loved to play in. Now, my days were occupied with a hammer in the morning and a bedpan in the evening. In addition to the emptiness that I was feeling, I yearned for time with Melea. I missed her deeply. She was my counterbalance to all other daily external stresses. I knew that with her by my side, I could overcome anything!

My circumstances brought to mind the lyrics of the 1969 Johnny and June Carter Cash song:

> If I were a carpenter,
> And you were a lady
> Would you marry me anyway?
> Would you have my baby?

Meanwhile, I was struggling financially. I was serious about carpentry as an honorable profession and was being groomed for a carpenter apprenticeship by Johnny Sanderson. He was the same homebuilder that I had worked with the year before entering the military. Carpentry was the only thing keeping me in Central City. My chosen field in a depressed economy would only pay me to work from 8:00 a.m. until noon as a finish carpenter at $3.25 per hour. From 3:00 p.m. to 11:00 p.m., I worked as an orderly in the local hospital at $3.50 per hour to help make ends meet. I still loved the hospital job (going back to my training as a medic in Special Forces), its challenges and the people that worked there. Although I was an orderly, I was asked to catheterize all male patients and anything else that the nurses thought I was suited to do. I was in demand for my expert care such as applying lotion and giving massages at bedtime.

Later that winter, I moved to Lincoln so that I could make better money. I worked with my brother Jerry in construction as a laborer for Geo. Cook Construction Company on the new Lincoln Airport Terminal. Now, making $6.25 an hour, I felt that I could afford a fiancé. Soon, I was taken on as an apprentice by the Ironworkers; that bumped me up to $6.40 an hour. The new job was where I learned to "snap tie" rebar and walk the red iron of structural steel.

Anxious to see Melea again, I sent her money for a car. She agreed to drive out to Nebraska over spring break so we could spend some quality time together. I thought about her coming visit to the point of obsession. I was counting the days and so looking forward to spending time with her. There were many things that I wanted to show Melea and share with her. I wanted her to understand my roots and see and experience the country where I was born and raised. I wanted to make a life with Melea and meet all of her expectations.

On a dreary Sunday evening in late February of 1973, I called Melea from the kitchen phone on South 10th Street. I needed to hear her voice, to check in, catch up, and to tell her how much I loved her and asked how things were going with school. However, I was shocked when a man with a thick German accent answered the phone. His decisive words cut like a dagger straight to my heart. "Yes, she is here, but she does not want to talk to you. She is finished with you!" I was stunned and caught off guard. The words felt irrevocable. Once they were out, they could never be taken back. The knife began to twist slowly in my chest, and I felt like part of my life was leaving my body. I asked to speak to Melea, but she wouldn't come to the phone. She couldn't even speak the words that now seemed so vitriolic. Should I say goodbye or just hang up the phone? I was in total shock and disbelief. Suddenly, I felt so small and utterly demoralized, like nothing in the world mattered anymore.

Melea was not ready to settle down with a farm boy from Nebraska, and college had evidently helped to change her mind about what we could have been. I felt like I had been beguiled! As reality sank in, I was utterly devastated, and fell to my knees and started to cry without reservation. My life was over. I couldn't get those words, "She is finished with you," out of my head! They tore through my brain like a chainsaw, ripping, cutting, and destroying everything within the nagging sound of that voice. The tears ran like rain until there was nothing left. I cried that night and into the next day.

Why? Why had this happened to me? What did I do that was so very wrong? I was a mental and a physical wreck! I couldn't do anything except think about missing her for the rest of my life. We could have had it all! I felt so sorry for myself, helpless and without any possible recourse. Why had I not seen this coming? Was I so blind and stupid? I felt ashamed. How could I be losing the only thing in this world that mattered to me? It was the perfect storm, and I stood naked with nowhere to run from the tempest. I could have managed better if she had died. Then I would have been able to say goodbye in person.

Instead, I was suffering a silent requiem for my lost lover, my soulmate, my very reason for optimism. I had lost all hope for the future.

Spring break was just around the corner. However, the real break occurred in my heart and mind when I discovered that Melea no longer had feelings for me. The very fabric of my soul had been torn apart. I wanted to be alone and started to drink heavily. I looked for answers at the bottom of a bottle with a reefer chaser. Drinking was no longer for recreation; now I pursued it for lethal escapism. What did it matter if I lost my body now? I had already lost my soul. I honestly didn't care about my life, and I fell into a deep depression. She was the only woman that I would give up everything for, and she took it all from me.

For a very long time after that, I used sex, drugs, and alcohol to ignite my "pity party." It was a genuinely sad and Sisyphean solution to my problem. I didn't feel one bit misogynistic. I didn't feel anger; I didn't feel anything at all. I was in the grip of deep depression and felt her love slipping farther away with time. I wanted to give up, and I did give up. I was a solitary man listlessly wandering alone in the wilderness. I thought about what D. H. Lawrence once said, "I never saw a wild thing sorry for itself," but even that was no solace.

I couldn't believe the intense pain of rejection, and I knew it was about to change the rest of my life. Would I choose to come out of my "funk" or let it hopelessly take me to the deepest, darkest levels of melancholy and beyond? I hadn't seriously considered suicide, but it was very close to the surface. It wouldn't have taken much to push me over the edge. Reckless behavior didn't seem so impetuous to me. Somehow I felt that I deserved the pain and suffering. It seemed to suit me.

I had spent my childhood as a loner and soon fell into my old ways of isolation and dark depression. I did not hate Melea; I still loved and cared about her deeply. I knew she was gone as a person, but the idea of her was still close to me and very real. How could I possibly despise anyone who had been so important and so instrumental in my happiness? Without explanation, I felt that the very purpose for living was unexpectedly gone forever. We had never had a fight, let alone angry words or a disagreement. How could I possibly go on? I felt very self-destructive.

The idea that I would only live to be thirty renewed itself. So I foolishly thought that if I only had seven more years, the pain would not last any longer than that. I continued to use drugs and alcohol to dampen my sorrow and hollow ambitions. Sex seemed more like a morose and pathologic diversion. There was no way I would ever want to trust someone with my heart or seriously pursue an adult relationship again. I was finished with plans for the future. I only cared about living for the present. There…I said it! Moments came and moments passed, and at least, I still had my skydiving diversion.

I wanted to embrace skydiving again with gusto, but it was a mistake. The fire had died, and the ashes turned cold. I knew that I was still strung out over Melea and found it hard to focus. My heart was stoic, and my head was no longer in it. Cheryl Crow said it best, "The First Cut Is the Deepest." My enthusiasm for jumping was diminished since my inner being had been irrevocably broken, destroyed, and cast out along with my soul. My greatest two loves had been interlaced and losing one was diminishing the other. Nothing in my life felt right.

However, in time, my love of skydiving would eventually pull me back to sanity. My skydiving family took me back unconditionally. The logbook entry indicates that there were seven of us crammed into the Cessna 185 on May 27, 1973. I happened to be the first one in and the last one out. I remember positioning myself 90 degrees to the long axis of the fuselage in the very rear. Cramped, knees to chest, I sat on my gear. That was my configuration for the duration of the flight. Stacked like cordwood, I distinctly remember thinking that I didn't care that I would not be able to get out in the event of an accident. I was still dipping into depression and self-pity.

We (LSPC) were attending a jump meet in Fulton, Missouri. It was a two-hour flight and the "Short Man" was flying the club 185. I don't know how we thought we were all going to fit in there along with our gear and take off safely! We departed Lincoln to the north on most of the very long commercial runway in the grossly overloaded tail dragger. The climb-out was pensive, and I believe that we were only able to gain altitude as we burned off fuel. I guess that I was taking Shorty for granted at that point. He had a multitude of aviation skills that I did not fully appreciate, but I think that even he was pushing the envelope that day. Each one of us in that aircraft had a personal relationship with Shorty, and all of our lives were in his hands. He was the go-to guy with almost any situation for us. As far as skydiving went, he was the final authority.

Fulton, Missouri. Back Row: Left to Right, Randy Lippincott, Don Dingman, Claude Wilson; Front Row: Left to Right, Carol Lytle, Richard Brehm, Cliff Dobson, Shorty Janousek. Photographer unknown.

I did not do well in individual or team accuracy at the Fulton Meet. My heart and head were not in the competitive spirit. It simply no longer mattered to me, and I was just going through the motions in my pathetic state. But skydiving was still the brightest thing in my life, and my dark times were fewer.

I was still able to appreciate a beautiful day in Nebraska. On June 3, 1973, I had completed jump number 999, and I wanted to make number 1,000 notable and personal. In the small rural community of Fairview where I grew up, everyone gathered at the Fairview

Methodist Church on Sunday. So it was going to be my little surprise to land in the Fairview Church parking lot just when services were letting out. To gain their attention, we made a couple of low-level passes, and once the congregation had gathered, I jumped from 2,500 feet. The performance made the local paper, and I had some new admirers. I was jumping my red and black Cloud, and the exploit came off without a hitch. The landing was on the mark and tiptoe to boot! My little community congregation loved me, and that was a most welcome feeling!

Randy Lippincott under a Cloud parachute trailing smoke. Photographer unknown.

Following the demo at Fairview, I applied for and received my Gold Wings. They were number 617. That meant that only 616 people in the U.S.A. (or worldwide USPA members and who had applied) had earned and been awarded Gold Wings for 1,000 total sport jumps before me. It was a lofty ambition, and I was exceptionally proud of this substantial accomplishment. I felt temporarily distracted by the achievement. When I had first started in the sport, I could only see 100 jumps as a primary gauge of progress. My work on the 7th APT was a dream come true, and now 1,000 jumps and Gold Wings was a real milestone. It gave me pause to think that this singular, unique thing was only achieved through my single-minded and occasional reckless pursuit. I had arrived. I had found that one thing that I could excel at and embrace with fervor. The journey had been long but what a great ride! It was everything that I thought it would be!

The annual Der Loaf'n Stein "Drink-up Throw-up" was held on June 17, 1973, where I made a single demo jump on my Cloud. I didn't make a notation of the exact location in Lincoln where the drop took place, but I didn't hang around for the drink-related festivities. It was hard for me to be openly social and engaging.

Soon afterward, I recorded in my logbook that I jumped from Bob Brown's Aeronca Champ in Central City. The Champ had tandem seating with one seat behind the other. I didn't care that Bob only had a student pilot's license; after all, I wasn't going to land with him. My position in the Champ for this little stunt was in the very cramped back seat. The plan was to slow somewhat, shove the door open, roll out missing the strut and the main landing gear, and then go right into freefall. Now the cardinal rule was still to guard the ripcord handles to avoid any accidental deployment. That type of mishap would pull the small aircraft in half thus killing both of us. When I felt that we had arrived at the exit point, I gingerly rotated in my seat, stuck my butt out of the right-hand door, and then classically rolled out backward from the tiny aircraft similar to a scuba diver entering the water. It happened all in one motion and was simply not an issue.

I attended other demos around Nebraska in Chappell, Red Cloud, and Eagle before heading to Tahlequah, Oklahoma, and the National Parachuting Championships.

Some of my most memorable skydives were at home in Central City with my father as the pilot. On occasion, we would take a passenger along, who would observe my exit from the safety of the backseat. I think I loved that more than anything! It was the exhibitionist in me. In my research for this book, I had reason to speak with Dr. Ken Treptow by phone. He was my father's partner in the airplane, and before we hung up, he mentioned the thrill of watching me exit and how quickly I disappeared from his sight. Forty-five years later, I could still hear the excitement in his voice. It was a lasting memory for both of us.

CHAPTER 24
Tahlequah

My jumping continued when I returned from Europe, but my attendance at the 1973 National Parachuting Championships in Tahlequah was halfhearted. On the drive from Lincoln to Oklahoma, I stopped at the unpretentious Dwight D. Eisenhower Presidential Library in Abilene, Kansas. Then I continued overnight in the Peugeot to my destination of the national meet and arrived mid-morning.

The mood was somber when I reached registration. Paul Keith Thacker had just become a fatality during a practice jump that morning. He suffered the classic reserve/main entanglement. I could hardly believe it! His father, Gene Paul Thacker, the principal founder of skydiving at Raeford was critiquing Paul Keith with the telemeters on a style jump directly over the runway. His very accomplished son had unbelievably never rehearsed a cutaway and frankly did not execute the appropriate maneuver when it became necessary. Once he deployed the reserve into his already malfunctioned main canopy, the fate of Paul Keith was sealed. I was grateful to have been spared the trauma of watching him bounce on that tragic day. Gene Thacker's boy was a seasoned up and coming star in the skydiving world and had the best coach available. How could something like this happen? How had his training gone so wrong? His tragic death made me feel exceptionally vulnerable, incredibly sorrowful, and did not help with my depression but rather fed into my ongoing sadness.

At Me Too

Someone is looking,
at me too
someone is saying,
he is sleeping,
he knows nothing…
let him sleep on.

—Samuel Beckett

I was jumping a brand new square canopy (my red and black Cloud) at the parachuting tournament, but realistically I had little competitive confidence in it. I completed all ten rounds of the competition but only scored two dead centers with my new parachute. It was about what I had expected both from the parachute and my personal performance. The mojo was gone, but I nevertheless enjoyed the experience and camaraderie; I even made some new friends on the national stage. Signatures in my logbook included big names and legends: Steve Snyder D-5, Ray Duffy D-148, Bill Ottley D-298, Russ Gunby C-350, Dan Poynter D-454, Norm Heaton D-565, and the real pioneer Lew Sanborn D-1, I-2, SCS 355—all from that meet. I also met Jack Adkins D-3589 from Salt Lake City. I had never been to Utah, but I was interested in the opportunity to skydive in the mountains, and he gave me a standing invitation. Ultimately, he was my connection there and my reason for heading West in the spring of 1974.

Unfortunately, in the early fall of 1973, I ruptured a lumbar disc at work and underwent back surgery on September 13. I was hospitalized for 30 days and was consuming an extraordinary amount of morphine. I did not remember most of my stay and had no recall of the people who visited me while I was at the medical center.

I thought my active lifestyle was history. As far as I was concerned, I was officially a cripple. Now all of my negativity and depression were justified. All of this went along nicely with already being mentally disassociated. I was in severe chronic pain, unable to get around normally, and I could no longer pursue my usual way of life. Now, along with alcohol and weed, I could add narcotics to fuel my depression. Activities of daily living, including sleep, were extremely troublesome. I became even more reclusive and was in a pitiful and apathetic state. I didn't even know if I was going to be able to skydive again, especially in my mind-altered state. It was a frightening thing for me to question my ability to fall through the air.

Fortunately, after enough time and determination following my painful ordeal, I was able to resume my first love. It was the shot I needed for my mental health to begin to recover. Somehow, I knew that it was critical for me to get back into the air. Without this distraction, I would have continued to wallow in self-pity and my loathsome ways. I jumpmastered a student on that first tenuous skydive back at Arrow Field in Lincoln with the club. Surrounded by the people that I loved, I was still only able to make one jump that day. My next outing was at a competition in Herrington, Kansas, toward the end of October. My second jump was a dead center with a total of three at the meet, but it was an inconsistent effort. My skydiving skills had withered on the vine, and my head was still not in the game. I was just going through the motions.

Our family Thanksgiving that year was held in Hastings, Nebraska, at Dr. Dale and Wauneta Nitzel's house. Dr. Nitzel talked a physician friend of his into flying for me at the local airfield. I made two demo jumps from 5,400 feet on the Hastings tarmac. The jump aircraft was a Cessna Cardinal 177 RG that made the show possible for the family in attendance. The Cardinal was an easy jump platform with the door on. There was no wheel (retractable gear) or strut to contend with upon exit. I believe that it was the first time that any of them had ever seen a square canopy in action. The altitude was high enough to make it enjoyable for me and close enough for everyone to clearly see me exiting the aircraft. There was a very light wind, so I never considered the hazardous "stepping out of my harness" trick. I never attempted that very impressive but dangerous maneuver with my square canopy. Interestingly, the new style harnesses today have step-in leg loops, thus making it impossible to unclip from them while under the inflated canopy.

I made a few jumps on the farm, but my primary activity was in Lincoln with the club. The only real excitement was when I broke the left steering line on my Cloud, which meant that I could only make right-handed turns and that I was unable to flare except using my rear risers for the landing. Therefore, I needed to plan to run exceptionally fast upon landing or pick out a soft impact zone in case I needed to do a PLF. It turned out to be a nonevent.

CHAPTER 25
Happy Valley

Even though I was jumping again, my mind was still focused on self-pity, and I continued to feel depressed and lonely. I returned to my studies at the University of Nebraska in January 1974 on the GI bill; however, without any direction, it simply was no good. I was unable to focus on my studies. All academic motivation was clouded, and my heart was not into education, let alone self-improvement. I packed up and headed to Salt Lake City after college that summer. Jack Adkins had invited me to jump on his DZ in Utah. It just seemed like a good idea, and I needed the chance for a new start. Jack's drop zone was a place called Cedar Valley and was about forty miles south of downtown Salt Lake City. It was going to be a bright new beginning.

Selfishly, I asked Leni Skaar if she would accompany me on my quest for adventure. I met her when she was a 25-year-old cocktail waitress at an upscale bar on "O" Street in Lincoln, and she had prior experience at the print shop as a binder in the Nebraska State Capitol. When we approached her parents, Art and Dorothy, their response was, "Do you think she will be too much trouble for you?" I did not know enough to recognize a red flag when it was in my face. I am colorblind after all! My folks were flat out against the adventure, but I still took Leni with me. It was painful to go against my parents, but my mind and body were in turmoil.

All I could think about was her long blond hair, infectious smile, and that tiny waist. We found a clean but small basement apartment behind Blue Cross Blue Shield on Elm Avenue in Salt Lake City. We were both staying busy with our jobs. Utah was a great place to learn to ski downhill, hike in the mountains, camp, and enjoy all the culture available in a large city. I found that the more active I was, the more physical I could be. That summer, I acquired my real estate license, but that did not work out for me. I didn't have the personality to be a good salesman, and my boss was a real people user. I sold a total of one house that season after I had put in many long and painful hours. I even painted the office building for my boss to help make ends meet.

In the fall of 1974, I started working as a scrub tech in the operating room at the new and very modern St. Mark's Hospital in Salt Lake City. I commuted five miles one-way on my new yellow Schwinn 10-speed bike. Leni worked downtown at the State Capitol Building in the print shop. I loved being back in surgery working with some great people, and I learned a lot. Roberta Holstrom, R.N., the OR supervisor, gave me the break that I needed. To apply to the Utah Physician Assistant (PA) Program, I had to be working in the medical field, and the PA Program only accepted applications once a year. Roberta gave me the on-the-job training that I needed to be a viable employee. After my orientation was complete, I took the National OR Tech exam and started work as a full-time Certified OR Technician.

In addition to my regular workday, I was assigned Emergency Call on Monday nights for the duration of my employment. Cathy Larsen was the nurse who shared that evening call with me. She was beautiful, fun, a delight to work with, and everyone loved her. Cathy was married with children, and our relationship was strictly platonic. She was a professional, and I always admired her from afar. While "on call," I had no idea what specialty the surgical emergency would be in or how urgent the matter would be. Whatever the area of medicine or surgery, I seemed to enjoy orthopedics the most because you could objectively quantitate the problem and fix it mechanically. Most of the work was done with a saw, hammer, chisel, drill, and screwdriver. In my desire to help, I believed that orthopedics was my niche.

My first jumps in Salt Lake City during 1974 were at the Sandy airport. There was a single north/south runway right in the middle of the Salt Lake City suburb. My logbook entries indicated Alta, Utah. Bill Dause ran the drop zone operations, and the location was very convenient. Today, Bill holds the record for the most accumulated freefall time with over 420 hours and 30,000 plus jumps.[66] Leni and I earned a cool $50 waxing N1800E; the Twin Beech jump plane at the Sandy airport. Soon after that, the field was sold and subdivided.

---

66 http://en.wikipedia.org/wiki/Parachuting.

I believe that my first demo in Salt Lake was at the Hogle Zoo. A local stereo store, Circle of Sound, sponsored us. It was a relationship that worked well for several years. I have a photo of me landing in the parking lot jumping my Church Window PC, but Larry Bagley has it recorded in his logbook that I landed "out." Maybe I wasn't supposed to touch down in handicapped parking without the appropriate placard!

Airport Number 2 in Salt Lake City during 1974 is where I used my GI Bill to complete the remaining hours and take the check ride for my private pilot's license. I was no longer a student pilot and could now take passengers with me. Leni decided to try her hand at flying and started taking flight instruction at the same place. I was so proud of her, and it was something that we could share.

I enjoyed the contrast of flying in the mountains of Utah to that of the prairie Midwest. The variation between the Wasatch Front and the West Desert was beautiful, and I loved the Utah mountains and the expansive Great Salt Flats. There was much to learn about weather, winds, exploring, and the wisdom of mountain flying. Later, I used the GI Bill for the "pilot" Physician Assistant Program called MEDEX (defined as a **med**ical **ex**tender). I had neither the time nor the money to jump during my very demanding medical studies.

Robin Cox was instrumental in making my professional medical career possible. After the Army, Robin graduated from the North Dakota PA Program. Later he moved to Salt Lake City where he worked at the Hypertension Clinic in addition to the teaching staff, at MEDEX. Serendipitously, as part of the cadre, he greatly influenced my acceptance into the program. Out of 1,200 applicants, 45 were invited to the Selection Conference in 1975, and I was one of five alternates. I was only called to attend the day before the assembly. My admission into the program was entirely due to Robin's active, positive influence on the rest of the staff. There were 17 students in class VI, and 15 of us graduated. Once selected, it was a tuition free "Pilot Program." As a student, I drew on my GI bill for the duration. In 1975, benefits had jumped from $220 to $270 per month, just enough to pay my rent and have breakfast at IHOP! I felt like I was incredibly lucky and was proud of all my efforts.

That summer I enjoyed a special visit from my past when the Golden Knights came to Sugarhouse Park to perform very close to where Leni and I lived. The Golden Knights are the original Army Parachute Team with 54 members from Fort Bragg, North Carolina. I served on the "little brother" demonstration team in Europe with 16 jumpers. My old 7th APT roommate Pat VanBibber was the first face that I recognized. It was great fun being on the spectator end of the show, but I was a little jealous and nostalgic. Bibber and I had a lot of catching up to do. I still think about our time together and miss him to this day.

Randy Lippincott, Leni Skaar, Sgt. Pat VanBibber Golden Knight, Sugarhouse Park, Salt Lake City, Utah. Photographer unknown.

Jump Pilot

At that point, the aircraft that I was most familiar with and already cleared to fly was the Cessna 182 Skylane. It was a standard jump platform and an all around good utility high wing airplane. In fact, it was the same type of aircraft that I made my first jump from and pretty much the model for the industry during that period. My aviation career was young, and I was anxious to log more time, so I volunteered to pilot the 182 at Cedar Valley and haul jumpers. I only had a private ticket, so I wasn't paid, but I could get some free jumps and build flight time for my efforts.

That short experience taught me a lot about aviation. Depending on the prevailing winds, I could easily take advantage of orographic lifting (the wind striking the mountain is uplifted to push it over the top). I would have to be on the upwind side and very close to the rocky face to take advantage of the free lifting force and ride the wave of the strong updraft. It was a very fast and cheap way to gain altitude with the jumpers on board. The maneuver was not that risky, and the wave was typically a steady flow, but you did have to pay attention when flying so close to the hazardous rocks. There was no room for error and no second chances.

It was good to know and understand meteorology and how it affected the airplane on long cross-country trips in rugged terrain. Historically, the most critical situation for mountainous flight is while crossing an alpine ridgeline. If traversed at a 90-degree angle into a strong headwind and down current, the wind could easily force the aircraft lower and cause it to crash into the mountain. However, if the pilot crossed at a 45-degree angle, he had an opportunity to turn away safely when surprised by a downdraft.

I began thinking of ways to break up my routine when the up and down flights were no longer challenging. I couldn't dive the aircraft in a race to the ground with the jumpers because that would "shock cool" the engine, and that was not prudent. After the last skydivers were safely away from the jump plane, I would try a few barrel rolls to make it more stimulating while I lost altitude. I could fly the airplane straight and level for only so long. Now, a perfect roll is a thing of beauty, and I usually demonstrated a flawless single G (one times my body weight or gravitational constant) during the maneuver.

If per chance my game was off or I was in a hurry, the positive G would turn negative, and I could fall out of the barrel roll. The resultant negative G-force would allow any junk on the floor to float. Typically held in place by gravity, dirt would come off the floor and get in my face, which was disconcerting. What I did not appreciate at the time was that the fluid in the battery was also affected by the negative Gs. Battery acid spilled inside the fuselage was a bad thing and brought my short career as a jump pilot to a screeching halt in no uncertain terms! I only had a total of ten hours logged flying jumpers at Cedar Valley off the little dirt runway.

Around that same time, the Twin Beech pilot hit a car but missed killing the driver. My personal feelings were tempered when I heard about the not-so-super "Buzz Story" which was all hearsay, of course, because I did not physically witness it. Apparently, after dropping a load of jumpers out of a Twin Beech, the pilot, who went by the name of Buzz, flew over the DZ parking lot at a high rate of speed and right on the deck. A "buzz job" is a celebratory tradition, and gained notoriety in the movie *Top Gun.* It is not necessarily considered marginal behavior, but it is usually carried out over the central runway complex, and people should not be at risk. That day the airplane's propeller made significant contact with the top of a parked car. It was notable enough to make it look like a sliced tomato. At the very minimum, any aircraft would require a complete engine teardown, inspection of the crankshaft, and a new expensive propeller—a very pricey proposition for a mere few seconds of celebration!

I'm sure that it cost more to rebuild the engine and replace the car than removing a little acid corrosion from a battery spill. Allegedly, the damaged car was purchased on the spot and quietly buried at an undisclosed location nearby in the remote desert under cover of darkness. It almost sounded like a Mafia-style execution and secret wilderness burial with the help of an illicit backhoe. I'm sure the car is still well hidden and all that's left today is a small rusty depression in the barren sand and an automobile title that was never transferred.

However, when discovered by a future archaeologist, I'm certain the VIN numbers will still be identifiable.

Therefore, if the incident was reported to the FAA, there was categorically no physical evidence of any mischief, just a routinely overhauled airplane engine, new propeller, and a phantom car. Nothing to see here folks! Fortunately, no one was injured, or worse, killed, by the otherwise routine buzz job. It's messy and much harder to get rid of a body without someone asking questions. It reminded me of the classic biplane chase scene in *North by Northwest* with Cary Grant where he had to dive onto the dirt road to avoid being mowed down by the strafing aircraft.

CHAPTER 26
The Saga of D.B. Cooper

The most fascinating and well-known legend in U.S. skydiving history is the saga of D.B. Cooper. It is an epic story with a life of its own that will not quietly fade away. Some people claim that the infamous D.B. Cooper may have had ties to Cedar Valley, Utah, where I later started jumping in 1974. However, on November 24, 1971, I was living in West Germany when a man calling himself Dan Cooper, who was later erroneously identified as D.B. Cooper hijacked a passenger plane from Portland, Oregon, to Seattle, Washington. He released the passengers at the Seattle-Tacoma International Airport in exchange for $200,000, four parachutes, and asked to be flown to Mexico.

The plane departed to Mexico City at Cooper's direction with a skeleton crew. As the jet neared Oregon, he jumped from the lowered rear stairs into the middle of a violent storm. No one knows what happened to him after that. Investigators doubted that he survived the nighttime jump in the freezing rain. He was only wearing a business suit and certainly was not dressed or equipped for wilderness survival. In 1978, a placard containing instructions for lowering the aft stairs of a 727 was found by a deer hunter near a logging road about 13 miles East of Castle Rock, Washington, which was well within the flight path of Northwest flight 305.[67] Nearly nine years after the hijacking, a bundle of money matching the recorded serial numbers was discovered by a boy playing on a Columbia River beach. The parachutes provided to the skyjacker came from an Issaquah Skydive Center, which had recently been purchased from Earl Cossey. The one Cooper used was a military-issue NB6 nylon parachute with a conical canopy;[68] it was never recovered.

---

67 Himmelsbach & Worcester 1986, p. 108.

68 *Huffington Post*, Earl Cossey, "DB Cooper Parachute Packer, ID'd As Homicide Victim," June 21, 2014.

While D.B. Cooper may not have had any direct connection in Utah, the following is from the book *Happy Valley* by Phillip Naugle.[69] Naugle makes a strong case that Larry Patterson was Cooper and later used Richard McCoy to divert attention away from himself. In the book, Naugle concludes from his focused private investigative work that a subsequent skyjacking by Richard Floyd McCoy Jr., a close friend of Larry Patterson's, was in fact directly related to the Cooper chronicle. McCoy's heist was transparently a copycat job in every detail, but this time for a cool $500,000.

It is Naugle's belief that McCoy and Patterson, a pilot, skydiver, member of the Sheriff's Department, National Guardsman, and electronics expert, worked together to pull off the original D.B. Cooper heist. Larry owned and operated the Cedar Valley Skydiving Center along with my friend Jack Adkins. Patterson also had an aircraft (the same one I had flown jumpers in) at his disposal to quickly move about the country in a covert manner. He was a member of the local SWAT Team and the Utah National Guard. Larry was an accomplished skydiver with a background in night jumps. According to Naugle's analysis, he was an expert in all the areas that were necessary for Cooper's jump.

The year following the D.B. Cooper heist, there were 31 hijackings committed in U.S. airspace, 19 of them for the specific purpose of extracting money. In 15 of the extortion cases, the hijackers also demanded parachutes.[70] Larry allegedly helped plan the second hijacking but this time used McCoy as the main character. All of this, five months following the D.B. Cooper incident, was to deflect attention away from Patterson because of Cooper's folkloric popularity. The copycat heist was supposedly planned to terminate D.B., the myth, the legend, and the man for all time.

This time Patterson physically supplied the parachute used by McCoy in the second heist. It was the same rumor that I recalled,

---

69 *Happy Valley*, Phillip and Cheryl Naugle page 113-119, Authorhouse, Bloomington, Indiana.

70 Gladwell, Malcolm. *The New Yorker* (October 1, 2001): "Safety in the Skies." New Yorker Archive.

at the time, when I was actively jumping at Cedar Valley. Strictly a novelty, I never gave it a second thought. According to Naugle, Patterson planned to eliminate McCoy. At a predetermined location in Utah, he allegedly was going to make the fatality look like an accident. If McCoy died in the act with the evidence on him, then Richard must have been D. B. Cooper. All the while he used the same modus operandi right down to the wording of the original Cooper hijack note. Together, all of that would surely prove that McCoy was, in reality, D. B. Cooper all along and silence any possible debate. It would leave Patterson forever in the clear.

Richard McCoy, Jr., a former Army Green Beret, hijacked a United Airlines 727-100 on April 7, 1972, after it departed from Denver, Colorado.[71] He diverted it to San Francisco where he let passengers off and took on fuel. Then, heading southeast, McCoy bailed out somewhere over Cedar Valley with the $500,000 in ransom money. He landed safely but was arrested at home two days later.[72] McCoy had completely missed the planned DZ where Patterson was supposed to be waiting, and fortunately, Richard avoided assassination. McCoy was convicted of the hijacking, but he begged to be incarcerated outside the state of Utah, which was granted. He gave no explanation for the request but admitted that he did know who the real D.B. Cooper was. McCoy was killed in Virginia Beach during a gun battle with 20 FBI agents following a suspicious prison escape in 1974. He was serving a 45-year sentence.[73] [74] All the while, he continued to deny that he was D.B. Cooper.[75]

---

71 *Skyjacker – The Richard McCoy Jr. Story* (March 2, 2011). ParachutistOnLine.com.

72 Richard Floyd McCoy, Jr. – aircraft hijacking. - FBI.gov.

73 Krajicek, David. *The D.B. Cooper Story: The Copycats.* Crime Library.

74 Funk, Marianne (February 21, 1992). "McCoy's Widow Admits Helping in '72 Hijacking." *Deseret News* Archive.

75 *Happy Valley,* Phillip and Cheryl Naugle page 113-119, Authorhouse, Bloomington, Indiana.

In a strange twist of fate, recently the man who packed and supplied the parachutes used by skyjacker D.B. Cooper (71-year-old Earl Cossey) was found bludgeoned to death at home.[76] "The King County Medical Examiner's Office said that Cossey died April 23, (2013) of blunt force trauma to the head in the Seattle suburb of Woodinville. 'We have no information that leads us to believe that this case has any relation to the Cooper case,' King County Sheriff's Sergeant Cindi West reported in an email."[77]

Recently, the FBI has thrown in the towel on the D.B. Cooper case: "During the course of the 45-year Northwest hijacking (NORJAK) investigation, the FBI exhaustively reviewed all credible leads, coordinated between multiple field offices to conduct searches, collected all available evidence, and interviewed all identified witnesses," the statement says. "Over the years, the FBI has applied numerous new and innovative investigative techniques, as well as examined countless items at the FBI Laboratory. Evidence obtained during the investigation will now be preserved for historical purposes at FBI Headquarters in Washington, D.C.," the statement adds.[78] A new revelation, and critical in ruling out false leads, is the DNA isolated from the necktie discarded by D.B. Cooper from the original hijacking.

The experts announced on July 12, 2016, that the FBI had redirected resources allocated to the D.B. Cooper case to focus on other investigative priorities. They surmised that D.B. Cooper was not an expert skydiver, like Larry Patterson because: 1) he chose a dummy reserve parachute—a seasoned skydiver would have known better; 2) the hijacker jumped in severe weather in poorly suited clothing—someone with military training would have known that hypothermia

---

76 http://www.huffingtonpost.com/2013/04/30/earl-cossey-db-cooper-par_n_3188745.html.

77 Ibid.

78 "The D.B. Cooper Case May Never Be Solved," *The Washington Post*, by Peter Holly, http://www.msn.com/en-us/news/crime/the-db-cooper-case-has-baffled-the-fbi-for-45-years-now-it-may-never-be-solved/ar-BBugIcH

was his greatest threat; 3) exiting over remote, rugged, forested terrain guaranteed a tree landing and decreased his chances of survival—a professional would have planned a sound escape route along with a plan "B"; and 4) D.B. picked a non-steerable parachute—a qualified jumper would have used a modified canopy to ensure his survivability.

The D.B. Cooper case remains the only unsolved air piracy in American aviation history.[79] [80] And so continues the tale and mystery of D.B. Cooper in near mythical Keyser Söze-style. In retelling this story, I was reminded of a quote from an old black and white John Wayne movie, *The Man Who Shot Liberty Valance* from 1962: "When the legend becomes fact, print the legend." In this case, the man has become an enigma.

---

79 Gray, Geoffrey (October 21, 2007). "Unmasking D.B. Cooper". *New York Magazine*. ISSN 0028-7369.

80 Pasternak, Douglas (July 24, 2000). "Skyjacker at Large". *U.S. News & World Report* VOL 129, ISSU 4; 72-73. ISSN 0041-5537.

CHAPTER 27
The Caterpillar Club

In World War II, the Irvin Parachute Company awarded lapel pins to aviators and soldiers whose lives were saved by using their emergency parachutes. It was called a Caterpillar Pin in reference to the silkworm since the early parachutes were made of silk. There were different types of pins in both gold and silver, some with jeweled eyes. Red meant bailing out over enemy territory and green supposedly for bailing out over friendly territory.[81] Anyone who documented their aeronautic crisis and applied to the company received the pin, a certificate, and a membership card in the Caterpillar Club. At the end of 1945, there were 34,000 official members. Little did I know but soon I was going to be in a position to make club application. The group's motto is, "Life depends on a silken thread."[82]

Little Silk Worm

Little silk worm—so very small,
You saved me from an awful fall.
Tho you're such an ugly thing,
I owe my life to your man made wing.

—a poem found in Leland Potter's
WWII POW journal

I piloted a rented Cessna 182 and flew from Salt Lake City to Challis, Idaho, for a Ten-Man Speed Star Competition. This trip was my most northern mountainous cross-country flight at the time, and it was very exciting. It was almost a two and half-hour journey, and

---

[81] The Caterpillar Club, Njaco 09-07-2011 10:57 PM, http://www.ww2aircraft.net/forum/aviation/caterpillar-club-30234.html.

[82] Caterpillar Club, http://en.wikipedia.org/wiki/Caterpillar_Club.

I was happy to have Terry (Lobo) Loboschefsky along as my copilot and navigator. The well-attended Relative Work Meet had a smooth start. We were jumping a Beech 18, and the overall conditions were favorable. The team was competing in a large valley deep in the very tall peaks of central Idaho along the Salmon River.

The first day of the contest was routine. I even had time to do some local flight-seeing that first evening in the 182, although late in the day the weather turned marginal. Central Idaho was impressively rugged, and I didn't want the poor weather to box me in one of those narrow canyons, as that would spell disaster! Challis was just south of the famous Lewis and Clark Trail, west of Custer Road, and north of the highest point in Idaho; Borah Peak was 12,662 feet in elevation. The small village on the Salmon River was nestled within the Salmon-Challis National Forest, which covered over 4.3 million acres in East Central Idaho. Included within the boundaries of the national forest is 1.3 million acres of the Frank Church-River of No Return Wilderness Area. It is the largest contiguous such area in the Continental United States. All of this was surrounded by the Bitterroot and Sawtooth National Forest and nearby mountains with names like Corkscrew, Bald, Blue Mountain, and Lone Pine Peak. Wow! Talk about your concoction of alphabet soup; the names were all so spectacular.

Our young, inexperienced jump pilot seemed adept enough the second day until we unintentionally "provoked him." The skydiving meet was a contest for Ten-Man Speed Stars, so there were ten jumpers in the back of the twin-engine aircraft and a single pilot up front. The takeoff and climb to altitude for our second jump of the day was uneventful. During jump run, the ground crew unexpectedly popped red smoke because they had no radio communication with the pilot. The smoke was to signal us that the wind on the ground was too high to land safely under a sports parachute. We made an extended orbit, racetrack-style, at altitude and again started our jump run.

Not surprisingly, the winds remained excessively high, and again smoke was thrown as a signal to warn us of the extremely windy and hazardous conditions. Once more, we directed the pilot to continue to orbit, and that it was unsafe to jump. On the third pass, the same scenario was repeated. Apparently irritated with us or maybe a bit hung over, slightly hypoxic, low on fuel, or possibly on the outs with his girlfriend; he made an uncharacteristically abrupt hard banking left turn to vent his frustration. The maneuver was possibly a lame attempt to punish or scare us in some strange and confused way.

Still at 10,000 feet (more than 15,000 feet MSL for breathing consideration), surprisingly, and without warning, the twin-engine aircraft entered a deadly flat spin. Now a flat spin, by definition, is unrecoverable. If most of the weight of the jumpers is in the back of the airplane…"any loss of control may prove to be uncorrectable except by using…a spin-recovery parachute installed in the tail section,[83] or by jettisoning specially-installed ballast at the rear of the aircraft."[84] There just happened to be ten people in the back, all from the "Ballast" family, that were about to self-jettison most expeditiously!

The Twin Beech is a good jump platform; however, as configured on a jump run with most of the jumpers crowded in the rear section of the plane ready to exit, the center of gravity was considerably out of limits in the extremely thin air. The configuration was the classic scenario for an aviation catastrophe, and the pilot should have been keenly aware of the operational restrictions of the aircraft and followed a standard "jump configuration" protocol. If this accident had taken place at a lower altitude or over nearby tall mountains, I would not be writing about this little adventure.

Rolayne Mattsson was the base person and already situated in the breezy open doorway. Once the violent spin started, people—particularly in the tail section—were instantly pinned in place by the wicked centripetal forces that were generated. The classic "crack the whip," it was nearly impossible to make any deliberate movement without straining. Nobody had to be told what to do, and no one was hysterical. We didn't intuitively understand what had just happened, but we did know that the airplane was in real trouble and that we were inside of it. No one panicked, but rather we worked frantically to help each other out of the crippled aircraft. Everyone had the same

---

[83] "Parachute in Tail of Plane Pulls Ship Out of a Spin" *Popular Mechanics,* January 1936.

[84] http://en.wikipedia.org/wiki/Spin_(aerodynamics).

objective, and that was to help move the person in front of them out the door; the fate of everyone on that aircraft was literally through that portal!

With a couple of shoves, Rolayne was the first out, and others sporadically followed, painfully one at a time. It was the proverbial emergency bailout and all I wanted to see was "assholes and elbows." I was in the very front of the airplane struggling to move to the back as the seconds dragged on. I can vividly recall the high anxiety I was feeling. Everyone worked feverishly as our real world destiny swayed in the balance. My struggle was uphill, against a monumental amount of unwelcome physics, and my personal situation was ultimately perilous. We were wildly rotating in a counterclockwise fashion, and everyone knew we were in dire straits. I can't say that I could keep track of time, altitude, or rotations because it was all in a slow motion blur.

I was anxiously focused on the door and making it out into the slipstream before impact. I knew that I had to take my turn, unlike James Bond, who would already have been in complete control of the situation. I had no idea what our vertical rate was although the wrist altimeter on my right arm was virtually in front of my face. All I had to do was focus on the task and concentrate on the dial. It was scary! I was about to earn my Caterpillar Pin just as long as we weren't descending uncontrollably over a nearby mountaintop. That would complicate things. Then, only perpetual darkness was ahead of me.

Larry Bagley was positioned to be number ten out of the door right behind me, and I knew that he had diverted his attention to the cockpit. Forfeiting any possibility of a bailout, Larry committed his efforts to the flight controls. Uninvited, he quickly maneuvered into the right seat of the flight-deck. Bagley was a seasoned pilot and thought it best to put his skills to work recovering from the spin while the remaining jumpers exited to normalize the center of gravity. Unloading the tail would ultimately make it possible to retake control of the plane. While I slowly approached the back door in the number nine position, I sensed the centripetal forces start to lessen somewhat, and the cabin steepen. First Bagley had to lower the nose and stop the rotations; before he could pull out of the dive. This inkling of reassurance did not impede my advancement nor divert my attention.

I knew that my life depended on making it over that threshold, and I was fixated on that singular task.

Honestly, it was the "fog of war." I still had absolutely no idea what our altitude was above the local mountainous terrain. Time had been obscured, and I truly had tunnel vision. I glanced at my altimeter out of habit, but nothing registered. I remember distinctly believing that I was experiencing my last few brief moments just before the inevitable very final impact. Game over! There would be no reset button to hit… no do-over. From where I stood, I could easily see the end of my time.

As I eventually exited the aircraft, I made sure that I had been thrown clear of the swirling tail section and immediately deployed my canopy. I did it all spontaneously without knowing my position, exact altitude, or terrain proximity. The bailout was as if I only had an impossible 200 vertical feet to deploy my canopy. After all, it was an emergency exit! It might just as well have been in complete darkness over "enemy territory."

At that point, I finally exhaled, looked down, and then checked my altimeter. I was just under 7,000 feet above the ground and looking at a beautiful square "go anywhere" canopy. All around me was high mountainous and foreboding terrain. It had taken 3,000 feet of a spinning nightmare for nine of us to exit the disabled aircraft. Fortunately, we were still over the valley that we had been jumping in and not that far from Challis and our DZ. I checked the sky for the other jumpers and counted eight canopies all spread out well above me and swiftly drifting downwind.

I watched the Beechcraft slowly spin away from me in a most detached fashion. I was confident that Larry was going to survive the hazardous event. My ram-air parachute was the only one on the load that had the capability to land safely back on the airfield near the packing area. Everyone else had round canopies and were at the mercy of the winds aloft. They were strewn about the countryside, landing in an entirely different area but all fortunately out of harm's way. The aircraft made a pass over the DZ, and Larry jumped to complete the once-in-a-lifetime hazardous feat. I'm not sure if we were charged for that flying circus act, but it didn't count against us in the competition.

I was anxious to review the bailout with Lobo and celebrate our good fortune.

That night, it was Shitty Smitty from Idaho City who kept us all entertained around the keg. We needed more of a distraction than just alcohol to relax the nerves and forget about the close call of the day. It was all behind us, and I don't believe the pilot stuck around to buy any of us drinks either. In the final analysis, we won the competition with four jumps, not including the bailout and, thankfully, the flight home in my rental was nothing like the one I had just experienced. Following that impromptu lesson, I vowed to learn spins and spin recovery. I also thought about moving up to the base position so I could be the one in the door and have the best chance to determine my fate when flying with a young, untested pilot.

The following letter that I received from my old roommate, Sam Alston from the 7th APT, is along the same lines and illustrates how an aft CG can change your life. My good friend Mike Wasley transferred to the Army Parachute Team after I left Europe; ironically, he lost his life over Silk Hope, North Carolina.[85] Here is the remarkable story of his last skydive.

40th Anniversary of Golden Knights C-47 Crash

Dear Randy, March 8, 2013

I waited to send this information to you until later today on this Anniversary of the most needless crash and loss of lives of those fine young men. Several months after the crash, Sherm (Hawkeye) Hawkins came to the 8th Infantry Division in Bad Kreuznach from the APT (Golden Knights). I think you had rotated back home by then. We went skydiving one weekend with Bill and Kay Jones, a bunch of other 7th

85 http://www3.gendisasters.com/north-carolina/18535/silk-hope-nc-golden-knights-transport-plane-crash-mar-1973.

Army Parachute Team members, and Hawkeye. On Saturday night, we had a great bonfire and beer at the DZ, perhaps Schweinfurt?

After a couple of beers, Hawkeye began relating the inside details that only the team guys would know. None of the newspaper clippings or the Golden Knights website tell any of this.

It appeared that years ago the Team C-47 had been used for really heavy cargo, and a monster 1 inch thick steel plate was placed inside the cargo door. There was no record of such in the logbooks, no STC issued, nothing. No way for anyone to know what was under the carpet. It weighed several thousand pounds. That plane was so horribly aft CG; it took the very skilled pilots that they had to get used to flying it to successfully control it. The pilots always had the trim control in the cockpit run all the way forward; otherwise, they could never get the tail up to take off. They always assumed that the trim indicator was out of adjustment.

Old Sherm digressed into some really tearful telling of the accident, and nobody interrupted him in any way. It seems that it was a cold, foggy morning, and they began to take on a heavy load of ice in the clouds. At some point, the pilots told the crew chief to go to the back and tell the guys to get out now, that it did not look good as they were getting stall indications, etc.

Of course, all the Team guys were lollygagging around when the crew chief told them to bail out. They all ran to the back of the plane where most of their kit bags were which did not help the pilots fly an already aft center of gravity aircraft. Mike Wasley was the only one to get his rig out of the bag just as the plane stalled and rolled over into a spin.

I never knew if the guys were ejected before the spin, were thrown out, or if the fuselage came apart and slung them out because the descriptions were that a number of the bodies were scattered over a large area. Mike had no time to buckle on his gear properly and so he went out with one arm through his harness. He pulled his ripcord with the other hand and, of course, it immediately was ripped off of his arm upon opening. The Para-Commander opened perfectly and landed in a tree some distance from the crash site.

Picture this. Here was our Mike Wasley, tremendously experienced jumper, with complete positional awareness in freefall, with no parachute. Mike consciously elected to try to make a tree landing to increase his odds of survival. He tracked over to the largest tree near him and rolled over on his back right before impact, so he did not have to see it coming.

The body shucked off all the limbs on one side of the tree, traveled across the ground a distance of 20 feet or so and went up a small sapling and there he was. None of the Team members wanted Mike's wife Judy to have to see him, but her Japanese culture made her insist that she view the undisturbed body. Mike was unscathed on his front side as all the damage was on the back of his body. It was as though he was just asleep. After Judy saw him, Sherm said, "It was amazing at how calm and composed she was." Her faith gave her strength that is on another level than we are conscious of in our day to day activities. It was love incarnate. Peace and grace unknown to the common mortal flooded the scene, and Judy was able to part with the physical being she loved so dearly.

As they evaluated the wreckage, he said that it was unreal to go through the personal effects in the kit bags. Every single item was compressed or deformed in the direction of the impact, including cans of shaving cream, etc.

Hawkeye talked well into the evening, and I am sure that there were many other details that I have forgotten during the last 40 years. I did find that smiling dude, Charlie Hall, in Charleston, S.C. I will copy him on this. That is one good fellow jumper that has not changed one little bit in 40 years!

Let me know if you ever track down Pat Van Bibber.
Best regards,

Sam Alston
Blue Skies in memory of those Teammates!

When I recently met with Judy and her son Kenneth for the first time in 43 years, she explained to me that Mike had a clear vision of what was going to happen that fateful day. Because of the acute awareness of his coming demise, he reviewed all of the necessary papers the week before his departure. Mike explained that the house would be paid off, the amount of life insurance that he had, and what exactly was covered in his will. Mike was confident that his family was going to be taken care of in his absence. Judy also went on to tell me about other premonitions that Mike had accurately described well in advance of consequential events. I had no idea; it was all so tragically uncanny. Mike Wasley was only 25 years old.

CHAPTER 28

A Black Cloud Over My Head

We all know about Murphy's Law that if something could go wrong, it would. I was wearing my black piggyback rig, black Pioneer jumpsuit, and jumping my black and red Cloud. It was a routine skydive from 7,500 feet, at Cedar Valley, Utah, on jump number 1,219. We broke off the four-way at a comfortable 3,500 feet, and I had fully deployed my canopy by 2,200 feet AGL. When I looked up, all I saw was a bushel-sized spinning ball of black fabric at the end of my suspension lines. It was rotating at roughly 200 RPM! I had been trained to handle such a situation, and there was no hesitation or question about my automatic response. I had slowed to 100 mph and was just barely falling in a vertical orientation. With both hands, I reached up, simultaneously popped the Capewell covers, and without looking, yanked the cables forward unceremoniously. I had just jettisoned my malfunctioned canopy, lines, and risers.

All of that must take place before activating the reserve parachute to avoid entanglement (see Tahlequah Chapter fatality). Instantly, I accelerated back into the familiar freefall. It was like two jumps in one! Next, I directed my attention to the reserve ripcord handle and activated it as if it were on a static line connected to my main canopy. By then, I was in the semi-vertical position and recognized the old well-known, near-spontaneous, sizable jolt (12 Gs) of the reserve opening shock. The familiarity came with the same canopy I used on all those traumatic cutaway jumps that I made on the 7th Army Parachute Team. Immediately, I was rewarded with a fully deployed 24-foot white reserve parachute! The black Cloud over my head was gone, and all I could see now were blue skies. So far so good. My main ripcord was in my right hand, and my reserve ripcord was in the left. Quickly, I identified my malfunctioned main parachute as it fell to Earth past me, and I followed it under my steerable reserve for retrieval and proper packing. It was all very straightforward, even though it was going to require a little walking on my part.

The reefing system was an issue with the early ram-air parachutes. The heavy lines were either burning the top of the canopy or snagging the fabric between the lines and rings. One snag interrupting the routine sequencing of the canopy deployment would lead to a malfunction. The reefing system was used to slow the opening progression and make the "G" forces tolerable. A stout line attached to the pilot chute passed through a series of one-inch steel rings. The greater the force applied by the pilot chute, the tighter the rings were pulled together. As the parachute inflated accordion-style, it would finally overcome the drag applied to the rings, slowing the overall process.

This time, however, some fabric was inadvertently caught up in the reefing lines causing the problem. I could have "played with it," trying to get it to inflate until the cows came home. It was locked up tighter'n a drum, so there was only one thing to do—cut away, go back into freefall, and deploy my reserve parachute. It was just that unambiguous.

Today's "square" parachutes no longer use a top canopy reefing system. The modern-day parachute uses a "slider" to delay the opening process. The simple cloth device controls a canopy's inflation by progressively sliding down the suspension lines against the relative wind during deployment. Four separate groups of suspension lines slip through grommets positioned in each corner of a rectangular piece of fabric or slider. Initially, the slider is up against the canopy, causing the most restriction; during the inflation process, it is forced downward against the wind. During deployment, the main canopy cells grab more air, which slows the jumper's descent until it fully inflates. Therefore, the relative wind against the slider is gradually overcome, and it is pushed all the way down near the jumper and against the risers. At that point, it is no longer a factor as the canopy should be completely inflated and generating forward motion.

No matter how long you have been jumping or how experienced you are, each jump has the same potential consequences as the first. Some jumpers make the error of trying to remedy the malfunction and lose track of their altitude. In doing so, they waste valuable height that later results in panic and additional poor decision-making. If they fail to cut away but instead just deploy the reserve parachute, it results in an inevitable reserve/main parachute entanglement and an irreversible critical double malfunction. At that point, both canopies are ineffective and are unable to slow the skydiver for a safe landing.

Remarkably, the primary cause of fatalities today is impacting with "terra firma" under a functioning fully deployed canopy. Principally, this is because everyone is using small high-performance ram-air parachutes, which mean speeds can be excessive. Now, calculated wing loading and personal experience with your canopy is everything. Small parachutes today are unforgiving. It can be straightforward pilot error—virtually a runaway ego combined with poor judgment. Or it can be a mistake in split-second timing and an inability to control your high-speed parachute in a safe manner at low altitude. Push the envelope enough, and it will push back in a "fast and furious" manner.

Second in frequency is midair canopy collision and entanglement due in part to a large number of people in the air at the same time. Fatal equipment malfunctions are third. Gear has become much more sophisticated, streamlined, lighter, and safer overall. Skydiving paraphernalia has become more foolproof, efficient, and technically advanced. This state-of-the-art function cuts both ways. Swooping can be fun, entertaining, and also be used for competition; however, increased velocity near the ground exponentially heightens the risk of bodily injury. The following is a safety report recently taken from the USPA:

The sport of Skydiving continues to improve its safety record. In 2015, USPA recorded twenty-one fatal skydiving accidents in the U.S. out of roughly four point two million jumps…among the lowest rate in the sport's history! Tandem skydiving has an even better safety record with less than 0.002 student fatalities per thousand tandem jumps over the past decade. According to the National Safety Council, a person is much more likely to be killed getting struck by lightning or stung by a bee!

> In the 1970s, the sport averaged 42.5 skydiving fatalities per year. Since then, the average has dropped each decade. Estimating about four point two

million jumps in 2015, that's one fatality per 200,532 skydives.[86]

In medicine, there is a word for the complications that are caused by doctors; it is called iatrogenic or physician-induced. The term used when the skydiver screws up is called death.

86 http://www.uspa.org/AboutSkydiving/SkydivingSafety/tabid/526/Default.aspx.

CHAPTER 29
After Midnight

The spartan and dusty single-story ordinary cement block building at Cedar Valley was guarded by a solitary mercury vapor yard light. The main room had a desk against one wall, dusty windows that looked out on the dirt runway, and some old discarded sofas and chairs that had seen their better days. In the corner, a few mattresses were stacked for overnight guests to use with sleeping bags. The parking lot behind the "clubhouse" was bordered with discarded horizontally placed wooden telephone poles. The surrounding desert was punctuated with a few sagebrush, but there was not a tree in sight. An adjacent building housed the jump plane and next to that was the elevated large red gas tank used to fuel the aircraft.

Last in the SCR series for me was the NSCR or the Night Start Crest personal challenge. I'm not sure who masterminded the jump that night, but each of us was committed. We all had similar automotive red light fixtures attached to our helmets with duct tape and carried fresh batteries for the event. We had daylight practice for the night formation jump as early as June 8th. After a steak dinner at Porter's Restaurant in Lehi on August 13th, everyone took a nap and then positioned themselves for the upcoming jump.

About midnight, someone's alarm went off and out came the coffee to energize us. As you can imagine, it took a while to organize eight skydivers, lighting volunteers to illuminate the dirt runway, and a pilot in the middle of the night. We had to dress, assemble all the gear, safety check it, repeat the dirt dives (practice on the ground) and then load the airplane. It was a very dark night with no moon or clouds whatsoever; the wind was calm, and the sky was wonderfully clear. We were in the desert far away from any city lights. I could easily make out the Milky Way from horizon to horizon in Cedar Valley; the stars twinkled brightly in anticipation. Larry Bagley was on the load along with Barry Depola, Jack Guthrie, Karen Colette, Rolayne Mattsson, Jack Adkins, Larry Patterson, and me.

In the absence of light, dark prevails.
—*Hellboy* 2004

Car headlights along the remote dirt runway were used for lighting to take off and land the Twin Beech in the isolated desert. The single mercury vapor yard light at the DZ was our only visual reference for miles around in the otherwise dark and featureless landscape. We used this lone light to gauge our exit and guided toward it under our canopies to make it back to the DZ. The climb to our exit altitude of 9,500 feet AGL, equipment and helmet-light checks leading up to the jump-run were all uneventful. During the dark flight, people napped or mentally reviewed the parachute drop and were universally mesmerized by the drone of the throaty twin radial engines and the perfect night air forced through the open door. Excitement grew, and when it was time to exit, everyone had adequate night vision and exited smoothly on cue from the airborne silver tube.

The unnatural night freefall penetrating the infinite darkness was both surrealistic and demanding. Because we were inexperienced, no one wore a light colored jumpsuit to make body identification easier in the dark. Read that, to avoid midair collisions. The group had never even rehearsed smaller night RW formations in preparation for the midnight eight-way star effort. Real stars were the only ambient light to help with orientation. We didn't have illuminated altimeters or automatic opening devices on our reserves for safety. No one had any real organizational training about possible spatial disorientation in the complete darkness that could easily end in a fatal midair collision. It would only take one person to cause a deadly chain reaction. There was no visual horizon for positional awareness as the sky seamlessly blended with the Earth below. The homogeneous black orb that completely encircled me distorted time and space. Without a skyline, the lack of visual cues could give the perception of a false horizon. Once established in the brain, the erroneous impression could easily lead to vertigo and loss of control.

If I relaxed and maintained a perfect arch, gravity, and the relative wind would automatically keep me oriented. We had not exposed ourselves to hypoxia and a subsequent marked loss of night vision since we were only at 9,500 feet AGL for a very short period. Once in freefall, it was akin to returning to the womb—dark, lonely, foreign but strangely welcoming and serene—a supremely unnatural act. However, it was easy to visualize the position of each little red light in the black August sky. Everyone had a good awareness of the other jumpers and precisely executed their planned assignments. The jumpers looked like fireflies all working toward a common goal and final reunion with the "Queen." Previous daytime practice helped with muscle memory. It was easy to catch the base, move in horizontally, and then the star came together beautifully. Everyone seemed to be individually focused on their task and our collective goal. We held it for the requisite period to count toward the official Night Star Crest Patch.

Night: when the world spins us into its shadow so we can take the next day by surprise.[87]

Much more important than building the star was the timely break-off and separation. The maneuver was to ensure that no one ran into or over anyone else. There could be no question of assignment or performance at this point. Lives were at stake, and everyone took it very seriously. All of the jumpers were safely in the saddle by 2,000 feet. I could see little red glowworms all around me and hear multiple happy cheers of celebration and hollering that pierced the darkness. Yahoo, we did it! It was 2 a.m. in Cedar Valley, Utah, and way past my bedtime! I was awarded the Bob Buquor Night Star Crest (NSCR) number 373. Jerry Bird SCR 11 signed my logbook dated August 14, 1974.

I remember that my father always told me that nothing good ever happens after midnight. That night turned out to be bittersweet for me. It was a successful jump but the beginning of the end of my relationship with Leni. As I was off skydiving, I believe she was "skin-diving" with someone else. Following that weekend, she started coming home late after work. The change in routine was something

---

87 Allure of the Seas, aft staircase, port side, level 11.

that she had never done before in the year and a half that we had been together. We apparently had grown apart, and I was preoccupied with my studies in the PA program.

As it turned out, Leni left me for some guy she worked with at the State Capitol. I guess he was the hole puncher in the Document Binding Department! It was not a pleasant break-up. No one likes to be deceived. My favorite song soon became "Twilight Zone" by Golden Earring. By then, I was a full-time student in the consuming Physician Assistant Program, and I didn't have the time or energy for an unfaithful partner. Soon after that, I resumed the string of relationships that was part of my self-loathing. I started a search to fill the void and heal the still raw wounds created in me through Melea's departure years earlier.

Ironically it was about that time that Lobo and I left skydiving together to learn how to rock climb. All of this went along with cross-country skiing, ice climbing, and eventually, ski mountaineering. I loved Utah in many ways and most involved activities outdoors. The West Desert was a big draw for me. It was the thrilling hunt for arrowheads and the need to "pop some caps" for target practice. I started reloading ammunition and did a lot of fun shooting in the desert. Near Redford's Sundance Resort was an authentic mountain man rendezvous that inspired me to build a .50 caliber Hawkins rifle exactly like the one Jeremiah Johnson carried in the movie *Jeremiah Johnson*. I even used it to hunt big game. It wouldn't be long for me to add scuba diving and sailing to my other out of doors adventures.

After graduation, my first position as a PA was in Spanish Fork, Utah. It was an excellent experience in family practice, but soon I wanted more and applied to the Post Graduate Surgical Residency Program at Montefiore in the Bronx, New York. I continued to climb while in New York City, but returned to Salt Lake City after graduation to complete my BS at the University of Utah.

Colonel James (Jim) W. Webster Jr. MD

It was December 1980, and I had just completed my General Surgical Residency in the Bronx. Because the PA School that I attended was only a certificate program, I wanted to use the remaining two years left on my G.I. Bill to earn my Bachelors Degree in Health Science. My new position in Radiology Research at the University of Utah Medical Center qualified me for an employee discount at the university. The job allowed me the flexibility to attend class full time, and I was assigned a medical student assistant, Stewart Landau.

To maintain my clinical exposure, I joined the Digital Replantation team at St. Mark's with Dr. John Ream. I also signed up with the 19th Special Forces Group on Sunnyside Avenue in Salt Lake City as a warrant officer. My commanding officer and supervising physician was Colonel James W. Webster Jr., M.D. He was my mentor and was grooming me to work with him in cardiothoracic surgery in Salt Lake City. We had many things in common and soon his family and wife Gwen accepted me into their home. His large personal office was lined with beautiful tall wooden cabinets filled with rifles and shotguns. He even had a shooting range in his basement! We worked together in the clinical setting in conjunction with military and the academic fields. We used our annual two-week commitment in the National Guard to participate in Operation Brim Frost for two consecutive years. I returned to Alaska to attend the Northern Warfare Training Center (NWTC) in Delta Junction, for a Winter Survival Course. These were very exciting times and were filled with personal growth. I felt that I had found my niche and had a splendid friend and ally in Jim.

Colonel Webster made a Friday night military jump at the Cedar Valley DZ. Ironically, I was not on jump status, so I was not with the colonel that night. Our group veterinarian, Officer Jackson (who went by the name of Stonewall) was with him hiking back to Camp Williams where he was to teach a Closed Chest Trauma Course the following day. About midway on the dark rural 12-mile hike, Colonel Webster was walking against traffic on the edge of the blacktop in his camouflage fatigues. The country road was hilly and families had picked up loved ones from the DZ and were on their way home. As a car from behind Dr. Webster crested the hill, it was passed by a pickup loaded with young men headed into town. There was no warning when Jim was struck from behind by the truck. Dr. Jackson's attempt at resuscitation was futile. The colonel, my counselor, buddy, future boss, and good friend was gone in an instant! I was devastated.

As a pallbearer, my position at his military funeral was painful, and I could not have taken it any harder if he had been a devoted member of my family. My love for Jim and everything that he represented had been taken from me overnight. Grief filled my waking hours after that, and my enthusiasm for the 19th Group faded. I completed my Bachelor of Science degree and, inspired by Dr. Webster's love of Alaska, I procured a PA job in Fairbanks. I lived and worked there for nearly eleven years. My application to the National Guard in Alaska for the High Altitude Rescue Team (HART) was rejected. Shortly after that, I hung up my Green Beret and dropped my military affiliation. I was destined not to jump while in Alaska.

During my schooling in Salt Lake City, I had rekindled an old relationship. It had been six years since our first meeting at St. Mark's Hospital in 1974 when I returned from New York, I discovered that Cathy was single. We quickly developed a relationship. It is said that time heals all wounds, and years had passed since that Sunday afternoon in the tall grass with Melea. I considered that my heart could take another stab at maturity and the ultimate responsibility of becoming a family man. I had waited until I was 33 years old to marry and thought that I had found my life partner in Cathy.

After I had completed my Bachelor of Science Degree, we moved to Alaska and were wedded in the fall of 1983. The condition was that I stop skydiving when we married, and I did quit. As it turned out, there was no jumping in Fairbanks. My first-year distraction there was focused on climbing Mt. McKinley at 20,320 feet, and I reached the summit on May 25, 1984.

Cathy had two beautiful children, and I felt that we could function as a family. But over time, I was like a third wheel, and the child-rearing decisions did not seem to include me. I focused on long work days in Alaska but subconsciously I was resentful and did not feel accepted as part of the family unit. Cathy and I had a superficially good relationship and family life in Alaska for the entire time, but the separation from the rest of her biologic family became too stressful for her. She moved to Phoenix where her son and grandchild were living. Ultimately, I too found a job in Arizona and moved away from my beloved Alaska. As it turned out, my job in Phoenix was high stress and physically demanding. I had a rush hour commute, and I was not tolerating the anxiety of the "rat race!" My lower back was terribly bothersome with chronic pain shooting down both legs. Resting up on the weekend in preparation for another work week was the focus of my free hours. I became depressed with my hopeless situation. I had absolutely no recreational releases and soon I grew resentful. Later we separated. It was hard on both of us, and I regret that I was the one who had initiated an affair out of frustration.

CHAPTER 30

What Goes Up Must Go Down

After leaving Alaska, I worked at the Scottsdale Mayo Clinic in Orthopedic Surgery from 1993 to 2009. During part of that time, I was employed in hand surgery and most of it was with Kay Jackson as the primary nurse. I had no idea that she was sick. I only knew that she took vacation time with her family. Kay did not bring her personal life to work unless it was constructive or fun and she had pictures to prove it. Her work and attitude did not suffer, and she never let on that she was dying. In 2004, Kay Jackson took time off for palliative surgery and chemotherapy but ultimately lost her battle with ovarian cancer in 2009 following a stay in intensive care. It was the same year I lost my Dad.

Kay was not only enthusiastic and lighthearted to be around, but she was filled with grace as well. Kay was a delight to work with and intuitively understood Dale Carnegie's principles on *How to Win Friends and Influence People*: don't criticize, condemn, or complain, give honest, sincere appreciation, be a good listener, and make the other person feel important. And while you're at it, smile at everyone too! During that period, we spent a lot of time together in close proximity. Over that span, she was subjected to many of my personal real life adventure stories.

Of course, some of the more exciting themes included skydiving and scuba diving. I made it sound fascinating, and Kay took Tim McGraw's song, "Live Like You Were Dying" to heart. She was interested in what I had to say and asked me a few fundamental questions but nothing to make me suspicious of her motivation. I just thought that Kay was a superb listener. The next thing I knew, she had done her homework and talked almost her entire family into skydiving. From out of the blue, Kay took her extended family to Eloy, Arizona, for tandem jumps. Her husband, Dennis, stayed on the ground to document the seminal event.

I had no idea what she had planned until she returned to work with the photographic evidence. She loved the jump and was so excited to share her story with anyone who would listen. You could tell by the pictures of the skydive that she was having the time of her life! I enjoyed the fact that she took my stories to heart and was able to check that box on her personal "bucket list." She had placed it in the number one position and gave it her full attention. It paid off handsomely for her, and I was proud to have been a small part of that fantastic adventure.

Kay Jackson making a tandem jump circa 2007,
photo courtesy of Kay Jackson.

It was exciting for me to think that I had any influence over another person by just sharing my stories. Unintentionally, I began to talk more about my scuba diving adventures and how I believed that it was an exceptional progression for a skydiver. I explained that it was a natural transition from thin air into the extreme density of the subterranean world. It was very consistent with my life of extremes. I told her that I could so vividly recall the wonderfully unique feeling that very first time I put my head under the surface in my first open water dive. It was, after all, 150 feet of crystal clear visibility in the Grand Cayman Islands. In fact, it was breathtaking. I explained to her that it was the same overwhelming excitement that I felt on my first jump and that it was simply amazing!

Yes, you guessed it, that was the next adventure to cross off of her official bucket list. Again, the whole family followed her to Mexico for their Open Water Certification after completing the pool work locally. Whenever I recall those days, it makes me feel sad and happy at the same time—to have known and worked with such a delightful, gracious lady but to recognize that I can no longer share any new stories with her. I am proud that I was the one to have led her down a path that exposed her to such eye-opening and enjoyable experiences that she may otherwise have never known. I am blessed and honored to have called nurse Kay Jackson my friend.

Unconsciously, the next nurse that I influenced was my grandmother. Nancy Lippincott received a gift certificate from her co-workers for a tandem jump on her 80th birthday. She worked full-time at Banner Baywood Hospital in Mesa, Arizona, as an R.N. in the recovery room. Yes, Nancy still took call and worked the regular swing shift. All of my emails from her were time stamped at 3:00 a.m. when she got home from work and was unwinding!

I call Nancy my grandmother, but she is actually my step-grandmother. She was 34 years younger than my grandfather, Harvey, who has since passed away. Nancy lives across town, and I have to schedule a weekend with her months in advance because she not only works full time but also does a lot of volunteer work. She is very civic-minded, and there is no grass growing under her feet!

In 1972, Nancy visited me in Europe while I was on the 7th Army Parachute Team and has listened to my freefall stories and exploits for most of my life. I guess some of it rubbed off because when she called me about her gift, it wasn't whether it was a good idea or would be safe, but rather, "When can you go with me?" It was a perfect day in Eloy, and she went through her class first thing on a Saturday morning in March 2015. There was a five mile an hour breeze out of the east with clear blue skies. Nancy was like a giddy school girl and her tandem instructor Bob knew all the right things to say.

Nancy Lippincott making a tandem jump,
photo courtesy of Nancy Lippincott.

She was thrilled that I was going up with her and was loving every second of it. We jumped from 14,000 feet and, as you can see from the photograph, she was having the time of her life! The exit, freefall, opening, and landing were all nearly perfect. I was so proud of her, and her infectious response to skydiving caused a chain reaction.

Other members of my family have also experienced the thrill of skydiving. On June 12, 2015, my wife Joyce and her granddaughter, Zoe Berk both made flawless tandem jumps landing within a minute of each other. They both loved it and had great experiences with Skydive Arizona. Soon the whole family will be involved.

Joyce Berk-Lippincott and Granddaughter Zoe Berk after their tandem jumps, photo by Randy Lippincott.

I am particularly proud of my wife because her decision to jump was entirely on her own and without any input from me. My enthusiasm for jumping can go on for days, but I have to be asked about it first. I have never tried to convince anyone that skydiving should be on their personal bucket list. Uniformly, the women all mentioned that "I never had a sensation of falling." And then I try to explain it to them. They were already traveling at nearly 100 mph when they exited the aircraft so the primary input for that sensation, the biological response to acceleration, was bypassed. Also, visual cues that aid in the feeling at 14,000 feet are gone as there are no stationary objects nearby for comparison.

CHAPTER 31
The Last Word

I wanted to feel free to write my personal account of my storied adventures, occasional successes, frequent failures as well as the "uncomfortable" truths of my past. Some are fun, others terrifying, many are just plain embarrassing. To force myself to write this story is to remember who I was then and how I arrived at where I am now. It was a bit surprising and disconcerting once I started to put all the pieces of the puzzle together and only then could I grasp the bigger picture. The brain is a most selective organ, and skydiving is only a sidebar in my drama, a topic to focus on and explore the real me. Yes, we all have some painful honesty to address and, if you've hung in there for the duration, you know some of mine. Many of these stories reveal how my memory and the truth collide. Hopefully, you will be kind but, the much larger issue of course is, was I, in fact, truthful to myself? I was taught in Sunday School to love my enemy, but as an adult, I learned from Tai Chi to love the enemy inside of me as well. Peace is not just the absence of conflict, now I see it as the acceptance of conflict.

I stopped skydiving because my "practice wife" insisted upon it. But to research and write this book, I decided to start jumping again. My feeling was that I could not just rely on my memory, that I would have to reactivate the old neurons! Yes, I had to see if I could still "ride the wild pony." I had never really been "thrown," so I harbored no fears or had any real issues.

Randy Lippincott on his checkout jump after nearly 40 years. Photo Skydive Arizona.

My life of risk has been voluntary due in part to situations and my desire to engage in those opportunities at a young age. For me, real extremes, include mental stress, physical stamina, exposure of all types including excessive speed, sleep deprivation and, unfortunately, inebriation. Actual extremes for others can take many different forms. It is up to the individual to choose a discipline and commit the mind and body to achieving excellence. My Father was not a fearful man and never taught me to fear anything; but rather to just to do it! I recall his words to me, "Choose your battles wisely and if you must fight, do it to win!" Along those same lines, skydiving and Special Forces were the springboards for all of these exciting diversions. Whether it was HALO, precision jumping, shooting, technical rock climbing, ice climbing, mountaineering, SCUBA, sailing, kayaking, or surviving in the wilderness, there was always a challenge around the next corner.

When I was a child, I marveled at the giant Midwestern thunderstorms. To watch them build, turn black, pour sheets of rain out of the bottom, and golf ball sized hail out of the top was a wonder for me. Then to witness the fearsome cell march across the prairie, using lightning bolts for legs was an unforgettable and remarkable sight. Afterward came the overwhelming indelible smell of ozone and nitrogen left behind by the transformative rain In the Winter, it was the unrestricted howling wind and wicked blowing snow that could drift as high as a telephone pole on the Nebraska plain. The well consolidated endless cold white drifts in our shelterbelt begged to be tunneled into by a young boy.

In retrospect, it was all training for me at an early age in preparation to climb the formidable summit of Mt. McKinley at 20,320 feet. At that altitude, I experienced the extreme wind chill of 94° Fahrenheit below zero. I also survived severe oxygen deprivation with only 42% of usually available oxygen in the high stress, high workload environment. Later, it was the self-imposed wilderness travel in the mountains above 10,000 feet during overwhelming serious blizzard conditions in the Wind Rivers. It included the very aesthetic but dangerous ice climbing and vertical limits of frozen waterfalls. No Winter storm would be complete without an avalanche or two; the perilous hazard of being buried alive and not knowing my fate was an eye opener! It's one thing to penetrate the elements but entirely another for nature to unilaterally consume you.

I have also willingly experienced the extremes of the desert with high heat, severe dehydration, exposure to heat stroke, and sepsis. The stress of breathing underwater (SCUBA) in a small cave with the unknowns as the gloomy jagged walls continued to narrow, hoping it would open enough for me to turn around and be able to escape back to the life-saving surface along with my tank. The extreme adrenaline rush of skydiving at night, along with many other people, thrown in as potential deadly variables. And, of course, a lightning strike is always the great equalizer. These are all real tests of self-control and mental toughness. It is the ability not to panic when everything around you demands it!

For all of you viewing this from the moral high-ground, I must explain my motivation. Now, as some of my ancestors will also read this, I must prove that I do have some personal redeeming values. According to Socrates, "The unexamined life is not worth living." Well in this narrative I have attempted to do just that in a somewhat candid fashion. I have mentioned the great mentors that have helped mold my life, and I indeed have been fortunate to have had their associations. Besides, my family has been my foundation and a positive influence on me. The discipline of medicine and surgery has taught me about life and the people in it. In writing about my personal adventures, I have openly confessed my most human qualities. All of this has helped me satisfy, the "self-examination" part of the Socrates edict. In reflection, I believe that it has been cathartic and a most positive thing for me….

> "Try not to become a man of success but
> rather try to become a man of value."
> —Albert Einstein

"The good news is that it is never too late to start examining our life more thoroughly and to reap the rewards. We all have blind spots. Sometimes when I review a chronic problem in my life, I have that unsettling feeling that I must be missing something, but I can't quite see what it is. We try to evaluate ourselves, but none of us can see our own back side, our shadow. That's why Socrates' method of self-examination included an essential element that became known as 'Socratic' dialogue. Chatting with a close friend, a spouse, a skilled psychotherapist or spiritual adviser helps reveal those blind spots we cannot see by ourselves. Socrates believed that the purpose of human life was personal and spiritual growth. We are unable to grow toward a greater understanding of our true nature unless we take the time to examine and reflect upon our life. As another philosopher, Santayana, observed, 'He who does not remember the past is condemned to repeat it.' To analyze our life helps reveal patterns of behavior. Deeper contemplation yields an understanding of the subconscious programming; it is the powerful mental software that runs our life. Unless we become aware of these patterns, much of our life is unconscious repetition. Our society discourages self-awareness with a weekly cycle of working and consuming that keeps us too busy to slow down for self-reflection. For the consumer, capitalism's game plan prefers an unaware and vaguely dissatisfied populace that tries to fill the emptiness inside with shiny new products. It's a radical act to stop and contemplate your life. But, according to Socrates, it's the only game that really matters."[88]

> "If anyone can refute me – show me I'm making a mistake or looking at things from the wrong perspective – I'll gladly change. It's the truth I'm after, and the truth never harmed anyone. What harms us is to persist in self-deceit and ignorance."
>
> —Marcus Aurelius in Meditations

I fulfilled my small part in self-examination when I decided to pursue my story about my extraordinary and unique talent. My gift was honed in the air as I welcomed freefall. I loved jumping from the start and was extremely fortunate to have been selected to the 7th Army Parachute Team. I cherished my time in Europe, and that's where I fell deeply in love with a beautiful woman. The fact that it did not end in a lifelong relationship is immaterial. As described in Tennyson's 1850 poem, "Tis better to have loved and lost than never to have loved at all." Melea, after all my mental anguish, had been my favorite mistake.

Lastly, through the Grace of God and a little patience on my part, I am married to an amazing woman. Joyce is a most positive influence in my life and supportive in more ways than I can count. She has made all that I have done in my retirement a possibility. Joyce is a perfect match for me, and I love her more than I have shown or can adequately express. I hope that she knows just how much I care for her. Thank you, Sweetheart, for all that you do for me every waking hour. I know that I am a better man because of you. Unbelievably it was through rock climbing that we met. I had joined her rock gym before it opened, her son facilitated our introduction, and we hit it off. Following an "over the top" day-long introductory flight over Meteor Crater, the Navajo open-pit coal mines, Monument Valley, Lake Powell, Rainbow Bridge, the Grand Canyon, back to

---

88 Conscious Earth - Personal and Planetary. http://www.consciousearth.us/socrates-unexamined-life.html.

the San Francisco Peaks, and Sedona; we started to date. Together we discovered that we shared many of the same interests including Country Music. After a long courtship, I proposed in our library, and we were married in the rock gym precisely where we first met.

My Mother, Rosalie Lippincott gave me life and guided my hand to this page. She has significantly influenced and helped form me into who I am through her prolific writing. Mother has quietly been the example that I have tried to follow throughout adulthood.

Inez Frazell, my loving Grandmother, entertained me well into her 90's with many different well-practiced stories. As a child, I was mesmerized and held under her captivating spell every time I listened to them. Even though I had heard the tales many times and knew the endings, I was still transfixed by her melodic voice. Each parable was expertly parlayed and had a moral to it. One of the fables came straight from Prohibition. It was called Little Blossom. The story was all about the devil in alcohol and it left an impression on me as a child that does persist to this day although my actions have been paradoxical in nature. I still can perfectly "hear" the inflection and polished cadenced in her speech. She fluidly played each character as she changed her affect along with her body language during the captivating monolog. It was far better than any commercial-laden TV program or movie, and her tale was so very personal. Each time I was riveted to the story like it was the very first time that I had heard the heartbreaking fable.

My story is about skydiving, adventures, loves, close calls, losses, and near misses. But it is also much more than that. It is about a generation. It is about the Baby Boomers that rebelled in the 60's with free love and pot. The rest of their lives were molded by the tragic Vietnam War in one way or another. My book is about people who did not want to live their lives in quiet desperation but rather explore and push the envelope. The Boomers worked hard but, we played hard too. They took responsibility, raised families, paid their taxes, and became productive American citizens. It is about the people who grew up in the shadow of the "Greatest Generation," and learned patriotism by example and I am one of those patriots.

Today, I reflect back to the emotional ending of the movie *Saving Private Ryan*. When the now elder James Ryan returned to the gravesite of Captain Miller (who gave his life to save the young Private Ryan) and asked his wife the question, "Tell me I have led a good life?" Today I ask my wife, Joyce, "Tell me I have led a good life. Tell me I'm a good man?" I am only human, and if I have helped, saved, or positively influenced one person then I am happy, I am satisfied, and I am indeed fulfilled.

All I have ever asked for is what is fundamentally articulated in the Declaration of Independence. "We hold these truths to be self-evident, that all men are created equal, that they are endowed by their Creator with certain unalienable Rights, that among these are Life, Liberty, and the pursuit of Happiness."

When I look at the man in the mirror, I can say that I did my best. It's not that I stumbled, but rather it's that I got back up. I tried to honor my Father and my Mother, served my country, and worked toward the best education that I could afford. I have lived a daredevil life at times, but I was never malicious toward anyone. My only regret is that I did not spend additional quality time with my Father and more closely share the very adventures he made possible.

APPENDIX

Licenses and Personal Awards

USPA member since 1969
Parachute Club of America, A-License 2054
United States Parachute Association, B-License 7520
United States Parachute Association, C-License 6474
United States Parachute Association, D-License 2973
Gold Wings #617, (for the first 1,000 freefalls) June 3, 1973
Jumpmaster Rating, September 15, 1970
Instructor Rating, December 15, 1971
FAA/Senior Parachute Rigger #2146510, seal symbol GA6 - December 21, 1971
Bob Buquor Star Crest Memorials:
SCR 1151, December 28, 1971 Agarn, Switzerland
SCS 415, July 19, 1972 Hoppstadten, West Germany
NSCR 373, August 14, 1974 Cedar Valley, Utah - 2 a.m.
Navigator (Cross-Country Patch) #74, March 1972 Aviano, Italy, for landing on a 10-meter target after piloting an open canopy from under 10,000 feet (exit altitude), and traveled a minimum distance of ten miles to the target.

Aviation Benchmarks

Student Pilot License May 19, 1966
First Solo June 14, 1966
Private Pilot License June 20, 1974
Commercial Pilot License 1989
Instrument Pilot Rating 1989
ATP (Airline Transport Pilot) 1991
Wright Brothers Master Pilot Award June 14th, 2016 (for 50 continuous years of accident-free aviation)

7th APT Members During My Tenure

*Captain Gordon (Mike) McPherson
Command Sergeant Major Harold B. Stanley
*First Sergeant Don Strickland
Sam Alston
*Steve Bienert
*Cal Callaghan
†John Cutts
Jeff Devon - arrived on the team one week before me
Hershel Fisher
Bruce Groff
*David Layne
*Guy Leverett
Randy Lippincott
Ray Lowe
Moe Mohundro
Tim Monsees
Terry Patterson - Company Clerk
Michael J. Povlsen
Rob Robinson
*Pat (Rip) VanBibber
*Ronnie Walker
*†Mike Wasley
†Bill Waters
*†Dan Williams
*Pete Zadick

*7th APT team members who also served on the Golden Knights, the United States Army Parachute Team.
Steve Bienert, Bruce Groff, Ray Lowe, and Don Strickland had rotated before I left the Team.
†John Cutts, Mike Wasley, Bill Waters, and Dan Williams, are all deceased.

Aircraft Types from which I Have Jumped

This alphabetical list of aircraft from which I have jumped is taken from the pages of my logbook. It is not in chronological order but rather by the manufacturer. When appropriate, I have added a particular memory. The span is from a 1937 fabric covered twin-engine biplane (De Havilland Rapide), to the formidable military C-141 Starlifter, jet type aircraft with blast deflectors in front of both rear side-doors.

I have the most jumps and my highest skydive out of the UH-1H Huey, but my first jumps were from the old reliable Cessna 182, and some of them were piloted by my father over our farm with a grass runway. The most historic was the C-47, the same pedigree as those used on D-Day in Europe to launch the World War II invasion of Germany. I was introduced to HALO in this rugged bird by the 10th Special Forces Group in Bad Tölz, West Germany.

The fear factor was the highest (pun intended) in the Twin Beech 18 during a deadly flat spin while over Challis, Idaho. It was a genuine emergency bailout from a disabled aircraft spinning out of control. A hairy close second was landing in a C-119 Flying Boxcar during a hailstorm in Paris, France and surviving low-level wind shear. From an auditory standpoint, it was off the charts! The traditional macho and most aesthetic jump for me was tailgating the classic military C-130 Hercules. It would peg my fun meter every time, no matter the altitude.

My skill level negated any apprehensions I had while jumping the Italian Piaggio 166 pusher turboprop. The left-hand door was in front of the wing and the unforgiving propeller blades extended below the wing. I could look directly at the front of the propeller upon exit. Now from experience I knew that my velocity was as fast the aircraft's when I exited, so if I could not jump back intentionally and contact the prop when on the ground, it was also impossible to do while in the air.

Combined List of Civilian and Military Aircraft

Aeronca Champ - smallest two-person aircraft - tandem seating
Beech 18 - flat spin Challis, Idaho
Britten-Norm Islander - twin-engine - West Germany
Cessna 150 - also two-person aircraft - side by side seating, Cessna Bird Dog 170, Cessna Skyhawk 172, Cessna Cardinal 177, Cessna Skywagon 180, Cessna Skylane 182, Cessna Skywagon 185, Cessna Businessliner 195, Cessna Stationair 206
Dornier Do-27 - West Germany
DC-3 - Demo Jumps
C-47 Skytrain - HALO jumps, C-119 Flying Boxcar - Paris hail storm, C-123 Provider - Camp Mackall jump, the loudest aircraft that I have ever jumped
C-130 Hercules - my first tailgate jump, C-141 Starlifter - jet blast deflectors used in front of the rear side doors
UH-1B, UH-1D Iroquois, UH-1H Huey - altitude record and service ceiling: 19,400 feet
CH-21 Shawnee, CH-34 Choctaw, CH-47 Chinook - classic front door and tailgate jumps
Howard DGA-15
Lockheed Model 18 Lodestar - Toole, Utah
Piaggio 166 pusher turboprop - Italy jump #666 - most bizarre turboprop, my exit was in front of the propeller blades
Pilatus Porter - Switzerland, first eight-man star record, base of the Matterhorn
Piper Super Cub - 2 person aircraft - tandem seating, Piper/PA22 Tri-Pacer, Piper/PA28 Cherokee, Piper/PA32 Cherokee Six
De Havilland Rapide twin-engine biplane 1937 model - Bad Lippspringer, West Germany - oldest fabric covered aircraft
Twin Otter - Fontainebleau, France

USPA History

Much has happened to USPA since its humble beginnings when ex-military parachutist Joe Crane incorporated a loose-knit group of barnstormers into the National Parachute-Riggers, Inc. on July 10, 1946. First, working from his home basement on Long Island, New York, Crane later gained the help of other dedicated thrill-seeking pioneers like Jacques Istel and Lew Sanborn to grow the organization from just a couple of hundred parachuting enthusiasts to more than 34,000 members. Changing its name in 1957 to the Parachute Club of America, it finally became the United States Parachute Association in 1967.

Early pioneering efforts in writing safety procedures and license requirements gave the organization its due recognition. First, they convinced the National Aeronautic Association (NAA) to issue sporting licenses similar to those it issued to pilots. Then, on their behalf, the NAA recommended that the Fédération Aéronautique Internationale (FAI) include a Parachute Category in their Organization. The stature gained by its relationship with the NAA allows USPA to represent all U.S. skydivers, before not only local, state, and federal government bodies, but also at all international skydiving events and meetings worldwide.

By creating certificates of proficiency, instructor and jumpmaster ratings, and instruction course curriculum, USPA continues to lead the world in safety and sport promotion standards. Its unique ability to promote skydiving through the hosting of national and world competition events guarantees its place in the aviation community on par with every airport and airspace user. Every component of the skydiving community—DZ owners, pilots, manufacturers, equippers, riggers, and individual skydivers—depend on USPA for its leadership as they enjoy one of the most thrilling sports known to man.[89]

[89] *History of the USPA*, reprinted with the permission of the USPA.

In Memory Of and in Chronological Order

H.R. (Dick) Lippincott 86

My beloved father not only gave his permission for me to pursue skydiving but also was a primary facilitator. As my principal pilot for jumping when I started, Dad supplied the aircraft, the runway, and the DZ. It became a family affair. He made my early flight instruction possible and encouraged my pursuit of all things aviation. To this day, I feel his love any time that I am in the air or even thinking about taking to the skies. His military service history inspired my actions leading to the opportunities afforded me on the 7th Army Parachute Team. My motto for him will always be "nulli secundam." T. S. Elliott sumed up my father's legacy that lives on in my family, "A man is not dead until he is forgotten."

Carl Sisskind 84

I wish to acknowledge my very first aerial influence. Carl was a private pilot, TV personality, and a relative by marriage who gave me my first exposure to the world of flight. He ignited the aviation spark in me when he gave me my first plane ride at the tender age of five; I never saw him again. But those two hours spent together in 1955 left an indelible impression on me. Carl passed away in 2013 in San Diego, California.

Marion (Shorty) L. Janousek 55 D-273

A skydiving pioneer and adventurer in all categories of air transport. Shorty was a principle organizer of the Lincoln Sport Parachute Club, worked hard at building the Club, the loft to support the club, and made aircraft available to club members for skydiving. Shorty succumbed to heart disease following an extended cold-water scuba dive in 1992. His favorite saying would spring forth following a sojourn in the air with a parachute, balloon, or ultralight, "and now you know why the birds sing!" He had a gentle heart but was single-minded in his pursuit of speed and the feeling of the wind in his face.

George Kenton (Ken) Sisler 29 D-157

Medal of Honor recipient. He and Shorty Janousek were the founders and early trailblazers for this antigravity sport. Ken and Shorty formally launched the Lincoln Sport Parachute Club in 1959 and made it a safe organization that has stood the test of time, remaining active to this day in Weeping Water, Nebraska. Ken was tragically killed in an ambush on a Special Forces mission in Vietnam during February 1967. Ken was more than just a thrill seeker; he was an American Hero and set the bar high for all who followed.

Stephen (Steve) C. Steckmyer 59

My first skydiving buddy. We jumped at the farm from my father's Cessna 172 and then later the Cessna 182, along with his father's Tri-Pacer. At first, all jumps were made with the aircraft door on. I even jumpmastered him while hanging from the airplane doorsill. I gave head signals on jump run to Steve that he, in turn, passed on to the pilot. Steckmyer challenged my early jumpmastering and helped me focus on honing my skills. Steve succumbed to a sudden massive heart attack in the Fall of 2010. He had hiked to the top of a local hill that he had done countless times to paraglide, sat down to rest, and quietly expired. There was nowhere in the world that he would have rather been than outside in pursuit of celebrating the freedom of flight!

Gene Paul Thacker 81 D-167

He influenced me directly through my introduction to the Green Beret Sports Parachute Club, the Raeford Drop Zone, and his commitment to the United States Parachute Association. In addition to his lifelong involvement in sports parachuting, he lived a full and exciting life and promoted early skydiving. Gene received the USPA Lifetime Achievement Award in 2004, "for over 40 years of contributions to USPA and the sport of skydiving, particularly in the Style and Accuracy community as an athlete, coach, leader, inspiration, volunteer, conscience, and catalyst." His son, Paul Keith Thacker, lost his life on a practice style jump at the 1973 National Parachuting Championships while Gene watched.

Michael (Mike) D. Wasley 25 D-2921

Mike took me under his wing and welcomed me into the very elite fraternity of the 7th Army Parachute Team in West Germany. He was a kind soul, hard worker, my best friend, and he loved to jump. His wife Judy made me feel like part of the family, fed me, and was a gracious hostess. Mike transferred to the Golden Knights at Fort Bragg and at 25 was fatally injured in the 1973 crash, ironically over Silk Hope, North Carolina. It was to be Mike's first demo with the Golden Knights in an ill-fated C-47 that was transporting the team in ice laden clouds.

John D. Cutts 53 D-3420, A-2571, SCR-1268, SCS-268

John was an extremely good-natured handsome fellow. He loved having fun and was as carefree as anyone I knew. When I first met John, I could not resist asking him about the long, clean scar that vertically traversed the entire left side of his face. He explained to me that it was from one of his 17 different motor vehicle accidents. I commandeered his Harley Davidson for transportation while I lived in West Germany. It was because of John that I met the first woman that I fell head-over-heels in love with. John was tragically killed in a midair accident while helicopter crop-dusting in Heflin, Alabama, on September 16, 1999. He was only 53 years old.

Robert (Robin) Cox 60

Robin was my Special Forces class leader and later my salvation and ticket for getting into the very selective Salt Lake City Physician Assistant pilot program (MEDEX). He was instrumental in making my professional medical career possible. Robin was a North Dakota PA School graduate and had moved to Salt Lake City where he worked at the Hypertension Clinic in addition to a position on the teaching staff at MEDEX. Serendipitously, as part of the medical staff, he was instrumental in my admission to the program. Out of 1,200 applicants, 45 were invited to the selection conference. I was one of five alternates. The day before the conference, they called to ask me to attend. For the 17 students in my class, there was no tuition once selected because it was a "pilot program." Robin later joined the National Park Service and succumbed from unknown causes.

Colonel James (Jim) W. Webster Jr. MD 49

He was my beloved mentor in the 19th Special Forces on East Sunnyside Ave. in Salt Lake City. He was dedicated to the Army, ran marathons, was an expert marksman, and loved the out-of-doors. Jim welcomed me into his family where I felt at home. We made our first trips to Alaska together for the Brimfrost Winter War Games. Jim was grooming me to work with him in cardiothoracic surgery. He lost his life following a military night jump at Cedar Valley in 1982. The Colonel was on a 12-mile hike back to Camp Williams for a Closed Chest Trauma lecture the next day when he was fatally injured by a pickup truck on the shoulder of the highway. I still miss him dearly.

GLOSSARY

Adiabatic Lapse Rate - under normal atmospheric conditions the average rate of change that results in a temperature decrease of 3.5°F/1,000 feet of altitude.

A-License - basic license that signifies that a skydiver has advanced beyond the student phase. They can jumpmaster themselves, perform basic freefall jumps, water jumps, participate in certain competitions, and pack their main parachute.

AAD - automatic opening device. See also: Automatic Activation Device.

Accelerated Freefall (AFF) - student training is facilitated by instructors holding onto the pupil's harness throughout freefall.

AGL - altitude above ground level. It changes with the local barometric pressure and is very important to skydivers. See also: **MSL.**

AIT - Advanced Individual Training. Secondary training after Basic Training in the Army.

Altimeter - a device that measures height above the surface (altitude). For skydivers, it is typically above the intended skydiver's landing area.

Apogee - the highest point in the arc of a missile or thrown object.

ATC - Air traffic control or referred to as Center.

Automatic Activation Device (AAD) - self-contained mechanical or electro-mechanical device that is attached to the interior of the reserve parachute container, which automatically initiates deployment of the reserve parachute at a pre-set altitude, time, percentage of terminal velocity, or combination thereof.

B-4 Container - old-style military surplus parachute system. See also: **Container.**

B-License - second level USPA license. People holding a USPA B-License are authorized to participate in the USPA Collegiate 4-way Formation Skydiving Event, perform night jumps, and when qualified, can apply for a USPA Coach rating.

Base - 1: When building a freefall or canopy formation, the initial target individual or group of people to which the others fly toward. 2: Base (leg): The portion of the three-legged landing pattern where the jumper flies perpendicular to the wind, downwind of the landing area before turning for final approach into the wind and toward the target.

Belly Flyer - all Relative Work started as the face-to-earth stable position, now freeflying takes it to a higher level.

Bivouac - a military encampment, to sleep out in the open without a tent.

Bounce - a reference to a skydiver impacting the ground following a parachute malfunction.

Bracketing - a term used in artillery to fire one shot long and another short of the target to identify the exact area to be shelled.

Bundeswehr - the German Army.

C-License - third level license holder may apply for the USPA AFF, IAD, Static Line Instructor ratings, ride as a passenger on USPA Tandem Instructor training and rating renewal jumps, participate in intermediate altitude jumps, open field, level 1 exhibition jumps.

Canopy Release - a device that allows immediate separation of the parachute canopy and risers from the harness. Used to separate from a malfunctioned parachute. Replaced the old Capewell.

Capewell - early mechanical parachute release devices used to connect the parachute riser with the harness. Designed in a single shot, shot and a half, and double shot configurations.

Caterpillar Club - lapel pins, cards, and certificates were awarded to soldiers who could document that they saved their lives using their emergency parachutes.

CDT - Central Daylight Time is five hours behind Coordinated Universal Time (UTC). Central Daylight Saving Time is used in the Midwest.

CG - Center of gravity, usually measured on the long axis. It is the point of reference for the entire weight of the aircraft or where it may be balanced while not in flight.

Cigarette Roll - a descriptive type of parachute malfunction with a completely collapsed canopy. See also: **Mae West**.

Comeuppance - punishment or fate that someone deserves.

Container - a portion of the parachute system that closes around and houses the folded parachute canopy and deployment device until activated. The old sports style is a military B-4 container.

Coordinated Universal Time (UTC) - See also: **GMT**, or **Zulu time**.

Coup or Counting Coup - pronounced kōō, a tradition of the Plains Indians. Warriors gained power by acts of bravery in the face of the enemy, i.e., touching the enemy without killing them. This behavior was cumulative and brought honor to the combatant.

Cow Pies - droppings from cattle in a semi-liquid form result in the size and shape of a pie. When dried out, it can be burned as fuel or used as a Frisbee.

Cutaway - a procedure where the jumper releases the main parachute before activating the reserve parachute. Used in the event of a main parachute malfunction to prevent an entanglement with the deploying reserve or another jumper's canopy. Also used in case the wind causes the canopy to drag a jumper after landing.

D-License - the fourth and highest level or license issued by USPA. D-license holders may participate in all national competitions, apply when qualified for all USPA instructional and proficiency ratings, and engage in high altitude jumps.

Delta - freefall position with legs fully extended and arms at the side for horizontal movement across the ground. See also: **Tracking**.

Demo - also called an Exhibition jump. It may be a jump at a location other than an existing DZ, done principally for the benefit of spectators.

Deployment - after activation, extraction of the parachute from the container and full extension of the risers, lines, and canopy before inflation.

Dirt dives - jump practice that includes the exit, entry, and final formation while on the ground.

DME - usually collocated with another navigational aid (the VOR), **D**istance **M**easuring **E**quipment used in aircraft for quantitating speed and distance to a fix.

Drogue - a trailing drag device used to retard the movement of an object through the air, in skydiving to regulate the fall rate and orientation of tandem skydivers.

Drop Zone (DZ) - 1) Skydiving establishment or intended parachute-landing area. 2) Any pre-determined area upon which parachutists land, making an intentional parachute jump.

Emergency Parachute - a parachute designed for emergency use. Typically, it is the parachute a pilot wears.

Euclidean-Based Information - founded on mathematics and geometry.

Exhibition Jump (Demo) - also called a demonstration jump. It may be a jump at a location other than an existing DZ, done principally for the benefit of spectators.

FAA - the Federal Aviation Administration.

Fichét - stiff wire marker used by a judge in Competition to indicate the first point of contact.

Flake - the physical act of separating individual panels within a parachute in preparation for the packing process.

Flare - 1) Under canopy: To convert the downward speed of a parachute momentarily into lift. 2) In freefall: To decelerate vertical speed before approaching a formation horizontally.

FNG - Fricking New Guy in military slang.

Formation Skydiving - 1) Aerial maneuvers by two or more freefalling skydivers with each other usually to form geometric formations. 2) Competition discipline of flat-flying. See also: **RW** or **Relative Work.**

Founder - gorging on sweet feed can cause a nutritional imbalance in a horse causing it to lose the physiological attachment of the hoof, a fatal condition.

Fragging - during the Vietnam era, the use of a hand grenade was an anonymous way to kill someone with "friendly fire," or the assassination of a soldier in his own unit.

Freefall - the portion of a parachute jump between aircraft exit and parachute deployment.

FUBAR - **F**ouled **U**p **B**eyond **A**ll **R**ecognition in military slang.

G or G-Force - one times the body weight or gravitational constant. It may be a positive or negative force.

Gauche - lacking any social grace, pronounced "gōSH."

Glory - a small circular halo below the skydiver. The sunlight refracted around the falling body of the skydiver casts a shadow in the cloud with a dazzling rainbow ring around it called a "glory." It is an optical phenomenon that resembles an iconic saint's halo around the shadow of the observer.

GMT - **G**reenwich **M**ean **T**ime, Coordinated Universal Time (UTC), Zulu time (military), all are an indication of 0° longitude, a standard fixed time for world reference.

HAHO - parachutes are opened at high altitude to avoid any noise detection from the ground. From the opening point, jumpers will navigate many miles under the open canopy. **H**igh **A**ltitude **H**igh **O**pening jumps are used for strategic military purposes usually at night.

HALO - **H**igh **A**ltitude **L**ow **O**pening jumps are conducted for clandestine insertions. Usually, small teams of special ops soldiers freefall from 30,000 feet and land together for a specific mission.

Harness - the nylon webbing of a parachute system that surrounds and retains a jumper.

Hydrologic Cycle - continuous water movement from water to vapor, next to condensation, and then back to liquid.

Hypoxia - a pathological condition in which the brain lacks adequate oxygen to function normally.

Instructor Examiner (I/E) - the highest level of the Instructional Rating Program. The USPA I/E has all of the privileges of a USPA Safety & Training Advisor.

Jump Altitude - The actual altitude of an aircraft above the ground when a skydiver exits. See Also: **AGL**.

Jumpmaster - 1) A senior jumper or instructional rating holder who coordinates boarding and exit order, jump flight procedures, spotting, and emergency operations with the pilot. 2) Before 2002, a USPA instructional rating for supervising student jumps.

Jump Run - the flight of the aircraft before exit generally on a predetermined path.

Keyser Söze - A character from the movie *The Usual Suspects*, he had a near mythic and a vengeful reputation. Held hostage by a Hungarian gang he killed his own family just to demonstrate his resolve. Following that, he disappeared underground and remained elusive.

Knights Templar - Christian Knights considered to be some of the most skilled fighting units of the Crusades. They wore distinctive white mantles with a large red cross.

Low Pull - parachute activation anywhere below 2,500 feet AGL. See also: **Smoke It**.

Luftwaffe - the World War II German Air Force.

Mae West - this type of malfunction comes from a suspension line over the middle of a round canopy forming two smaller bubbles that look like a brassiere. See also: **Cigarette Roll**.

Malfunction - the complete or partial failure of a parachute canopy to accomplish proper opening, descent, or flight characteristics.

Master Rigger - the higher of two certification levels for FAA riggers. May perform more complex repair tasks and approved alterations. See also: **Senior Rigger**.

Métier - being accomplished at an occupation or activity.

Metronome - the ability to maintain a low pulse rate (a calm and calculating focus) in the presence of extreme stress or combat. Exceptional Special Forces/Black Ops demeanor.

Microburst - a column of cold air emitted from a thunderstorm falls to the ground and then sudden extremely strong wind rapidly spreads outward in all directions.

Mid-Air Collision - in skydiving this can be vertical when someone opens below you or horizontal if someone runs into you while tracking.

Military Static Line - jumps are commonly performed at 1,250 feet AGL, and no freefall is involved. Civilian static line jumps are from 2,800-3,500 feet AGL.

Misogyny - the hatred of women.

MOS - Military Occupational Service. Your job in the army, usually designated by a three letter/number combination. For example, today, a Combat Medic is 18 Delta.

MSL - Mean sea level. Altitude measured from above sea level that changes with barometric pressure. See also: **AGL**.

NCOIC - Noncommissioned Officer in Charge.

Night Jump - a skydive made from one hour after official sunset to one hour before official sunrise. The FAA requires appropriate equipment specified in FAR 105.

Nulli Secundam - Latin for second to none.

OD - Olive drab, standard camouflage military green.

Opening Point - an area of reference on the ground over which the skydiver opens the parachute. See also: **Spot**.

Opening Shock - the decelerating force exerted on the load as the parachute deploys and inflates. It is caused by the abrupt resistance of the canopy resulting in positive G forces.

Orographic Lifting - as wind strikes the face of a mountain it is uplifted to go over the top. Rising air cools at 3.5 degrees Fahrenheit per 1,000 feet (Adiabatic Lapse Rate varies).

Pack - to fold and close a parachute system in preparation for jumping.

Parachute - a fabric device that slows the descent of a falling object. It's derived from the French words "para," to shield, and "chute," to fall. It literally means "to shield from a fall."

Para Commander (PC) - American made highly maneuverable round sport parachute design.

Piggyback Rig - original style sports container system with the bulky reserve parachute positioned above the main container on the jumpers back.

Pilot Chute - a small parachute used to initiate deployment of a main or reserve parachute.

PLF - parachute landing fall. The jumper distributes the force of the impact in an orderly and sequential manner over the entire lateral aspects of the body.

Porosity - the ratio of open area to closed area in a fabric. Graded as high, low, or zero. Tightly woven and treated material has a lower porosity than loosely woven material.

Praetorian - a special force of skilled troops serving as the personal guard of Roman emperors.

Psyops - psychological warfare.

Raison d'être - the most important reason for being or purpose for something or somebody's existence.

Ram-Air Parachute - a parachute canopy consisting of an upper and lower surface that is inflated by forced air entering through specially designed openings in the front of the canopy to form a gliding airfoil.

Reserve Parachute - worn for emergency use to be activated upon failure of the main parachute or in any other emergency where the use of the main parachute is impractical.

Revenant - a person who has supposedly returned from the dead.

Rig - 1) the complete parachute system used for skydiving. 2) the act of maintaining, repairing, or modifying a parachute system.

Rigger - a Certificated Parachute Technician. See also: **Master Rigger** and **Senior Rigger**.

Ripcord - an assembly usually constructed with a metal cable that, when pulled, releases tension on the container and activates the opening sequence on a parachute system.

R&R - rest and relaxation.

RW - relative work or maneuvering in free fall with other jumpers to create predetermined formations. See also: **Formation Skydiving**.

Scud Running - flying under and around low-lying clouds. Usually a dangerous activity.

Senior Rigger - the initial certification level for FAA riggers that allows its holder to pack and maintain a parachute system and perform simple repairs. See also: **Master Rigger**.

SF Q-Course - the Qualification Course to begin Special Forces training circa 1970.

Sisyphean - describes a task that can never be completed.

Skyfall - James Bond's Skyfall was the name of his Scottish home. It was a remote, austere country estate. For me, it is more of an attitude or a state-of-mind.

Smoke It - intentional or unintentional dangerous very low opening well under 2,500 feet AGL.

SNAFU - Situation Normally All Fouled Up.

Spot - a general area upwind from the desired landing site from which an open canopy at 2,500 feet could easily drift onto the target with minimal input from the jumper.

Spotting - selecting the correct ground reference point over which to leave the aircraft and directing the pilot on jump run to that point.

St. Elmo's Fire - a luminous plasma is created by a coronal discharge from a prominent object (like the nose of an airplane) within a strong electrical field in the atmosphere (such as those generated by thunderstorms).

Stability - property of a body to regain its equilibrium if disturbed; it tends to return to the original configuration. In skydiving, positive control of body position during freefall.

Stable Freefall Position - a position attained by a freefalling skydiver in which only controlled, planned movements are made.

STC - Supplemental Type Certificate, FAA-approved modification or repair to existing certified aeronautical equipment. As it adds to the existing type certificate, it is deemed "supplemental."

Sublimate - ice transitions directly to water vapor, skipping the liquid phase of water.

Swooping - high-speed canopy piloting near the surface (ground or water); an act that is spectator-friendly.

Syrette - a small disposable device for injecting liquid through a fixed needle. Similar to a syringe except that it is a preloaded closed flexible tube (similar to a small tube of toothpaste) instead of a rigid tube and piston.

Tandem Jump - any skydive made using a tandem parachute system with a student attached to a licensed skydiver.

Telemeter - tripod mounted binoculars with angled eyepieces for viewing airborne objects.

Terminal Velocity - the equilibrium speed that a freefalling body can attain against the resistance of the air. The greatest speed at which a body falls through the atmosphere.

The Man Who Rode The Thunder - the book about Lieutenant Colonel Rankin, who is the only known person to experience freefall and a forty minute parachute deployment inside an active thunderstorm and lived to tell about it.

Three-Ring Release - the system is based on three interlocking rings on each riser held in place by a small loop that is retained by a stiff plastic cable. Pulling one handle releases both main risers (and, therefore, the parachute) simultaneously.

Time Dilation - in physics, time travel is closely linked to Einstein's theory of relativity which dictates that as speed increases, time slows; i.e., an inverse relationship.

Tracking - also known as a Delta, a freefall with legs fully extended and arms at the side for horizontal movement. See also: **Delta**.

United States Parachute Association (USPA) - a not-for-profit, voluntary membership association of skydivers whose purpose is promoting and representing skydiving.

Valsalva Maneuver - a maneuver in which one tries to exhale with the windpipe closed and tighten or strain against flexed abdominal muscles. With the nose pinched closed, the effort is made to normalize the middle-ear pressure through the eustachian tube.

Veni, Vidi, Vici - Latin for I came, I saw, I conquered.

VOR - **V**ery High-frequency **O**mnidirectional **R**adio beacon, a navigational aid for aviators.

WDI - wind drift indicator. A brightly colored weighted crepe paper streamer ten inches wide by 20 feet long. Descends at the same rate as a man under an open canopy, 1,000 feet/ minute.

WHUFFO - an insensitive term for a non-skydiver. "Whuffo you jump out of airplanes?"

Zero Porosity - fabric that does not allow any air to pass through it.

Zulu - military time, an indication of 0° longitude (Greenwich England), a standard fixed time for world reference same as **GMT** and **UTC**.

USPA Terminology used in Glossary[90]

90 Reprinted with the permission of the USPA, May 2014.